Cliviger Gorge

To Todmc

Rock Face

Sheepdog Trials Course

Church

Ram Inn

Track to Thieveley

Clough

Waterfall

From Burnley

Broc

D1391651

GAEL'S REALM
THE LAND SHE WANDERED

The topography of the land has been slightly
disorientated to protect certain species of the wildlife.

- Eric Halsall

GAEL
Sheepdog of the hills

GAEL
Sheepdog of the hills

Eric Halsall

Patrick Stephens, Wellingborough

Dedication

To Rita, Peris and Bob, whose love of Gael was as great as mine, and for Simon, who also loved Gael, in the hope that these writings may foster his initial interest in wild creatures—and the interest of all the youngsters to whom I have been privileged to introduce the living countryside.

Frontispiece *Gael at two years old.*

© Eric Halsall 1985

First published 1985

British Library Cataloguing in Publication Data

Halsall, Eric
    Gael: sheepdog of the hills.
    1. Sheep dogs—Great Britain
    I. Title
    636.7'3   SF428.6

    ISBN 0-85059-676-9

Patrick Stephens Limited is part of the Thorsons Publishing Group.

Text photoset in 11 on 12 Plantin by MJL Typesetting, Hitchin, Herts.
Printed in Great Britain on 115 gsm Fineblade coated cartridge, and bound, by Butler & Tanner Limited, Frome, Somerset, for the publishers, Patrick Stephens Limited, Denington Estate, Wellingborough, Northants, NN8 2QD, England.

Contents

Preface		6
Illustration credits		9
Chapter 1	**Carefree adventure**	10
Chapter 2	**Growing up**	22
Chapter 3	**Pond puzzles**	33
Chapter 4	**Sheepwise**	45
Chapter 5	**Inhospitable night**	56
Chapter 6	**Strange friendship**	64
Chapter 7	**Respectful neighbours**	75
Chapter 8	**Not wanted**	85
Chapter 9	**To the rescue**	93
Chapter 10	**Lapwing anxieties**	102
Chapter 11	**Decoy acts**	115
Chapter 12	**False impressions**	124
Chapter 13	**Making hay**	132
Chapter 14	**Life is perplexing**	141
Chapter 15	**Good friends**	152
Chapter 16	**New neighbours**	162
Chapter 17	**Timely intervention**	170
Chapter 18	**Merry Christmas**	176
Chapter 19	**Colourful superstition**	185
Chapter 20	**Blood runs hot**	192
Chapter 21	**Miner activity**	202
Chapter 22	**Storm shelter**	210
Chapter 23	**Glad companion**	217

Preface

During many years of wandering the North Country I have come to know a number of collies named Gael. Two of them, mother and daughter, were particular favourites.

Thomson McKnight's clever Gael from Canonbie in the Scottish Borders was, in my opinion, the greatest sheep-bitch that ever lived, a legend in her time after competitively winning the greatest accolade in the sheepdog trials world — the supreme championship of the International Sheep Dog Society — in 1967.

She herded Blackface ewes and Friesian milk cows at Glencartholm on the banks of the River Esk in Dumfries-shire, and she enjoyed the shy company of roe deer, and the bold criticism of a bright-eyed robin in day-to-day work on the farm. On the sheepdog trials fields of Britain she won the supreme championship — the blue riband of the heather — and represented Scotland seven times in international competition.

When she died peacefully on a dull September day in 1968, after 11 years of loyal service to her master, she was buried amid snowdrops in the garden by the grey stone house she had made famous throughout the farming world.

The other Gael for which I had great affection was the Scottish Gael's daughter. A trim little, smooth-coated, black bitch, she watched over Swaledale ewes, on the slopes of Whernside across from Kilnsey Crag in Wharfedale, for Michael Perrings. She was determined, and intelligent in the ordering of sheep and the understanding of their whims, and kind and gentle in carrying out her duties. She had a good, but short, life.

She had been ill to the extent of missing her lambing duties in the spring of 1971, yet she had the courage to compete in the vilest of weather conditions against 127 collies, from England, Scotland and Wales, to win the coveted Fylde trials championship in April, faulted in her work by a mere half-point.

It was her grand finale, for although she was able to return to the lambing fields, it was a brief stay. She died later in the year before she was five years old and, buried on the hillside where she had spent her working life, her irrespressible spirit roams with the fresh winds which blow across Conistone Moor.

Both Gaels were gentle in nature, clever in their country craft, strong in their integrity and completely loyal to the people whose lives they shared.

Gael, the little collie of this story, was named after either — or both — of these two great sheepdogs. Of Shetland descent, she had all the inbred wisdom and sheep-sense of the little collies of the Islands and, living in the Pennine hills of the Lancashire–Yorkshire borderland, it was inevitable that sheep would figure largely in her life.

Gael showed an affinity with sheep at the first meeting — a tiny puppy trembling with suppressed excitement as inbred traits coursed the shepherding instinct through her veins. Sheep were to become her constant companions on the hill, yet this is the diary of her adventures with the wilder neighbours with whom she came to have equal communion.

Gael was the last of three collies which readers of the 'Country Notes' articles in the *Burnley Express* — from which these stories are derived — came to know. All of them — Rhaq, the best pal I ever had; Meg, the most devoted companion; and Gael, the most lovable of collies — were faithful friends, loyal in their comradeship, and totally committed to my wishes. I never ceased to wonder at their integrity and intelligence.

Gael had such nice ways. She was quiet in her manner, broad-minded about the faults of others, and respectful of her neighbours in the countryside. Yet, her enquiring mind and independence of spirit led her into many adventures which I was privileged to share — from a distance.

'From a distance' is the pertinent comment, indeed it was often from a

Gael had come to me at seven weeks old.

binocular distance, for whilst animal trusts animal — or at least knows its intentions — wild creatures, without exception, do not trust we humans. Nor do I blame them, for we are a nasty lot, for the most part bent on the destruction of others, if necessary, for our own selfish gains.

Gael helped me to overcome many of the inhibitions of the wild creatures, for, coming to know her, they came to accept me — as long as I kept my distance. With Gael's superb senses of smell and hearing, her skills of stalking and wind interpretation, I entered a privileged world. As long as I kept quiet, and had the patience to wait upon the whims of the wildfolk, and as long as I treated all with courtesy and respect, I became accepted.

I sat and watched — and recorded — and these notes were born. Often they are interpretations of observations in the ways of the wild, with the insight of knowledge gleaned over 50 years of careful field activity. I believe them to be correct — whilst not for one minute discrediting the views of others. Would that I could become a dog, a badger, a fox, a kestrel, or some similar creature for a day — with the ability to record my experiences!

Turning a host of articles, observations and notes into a book such as this entails time, and the goodwill of others. So, thank you to my wife, Rita, to my sister and brother-in-law, Persis and Bob, for their encouragement and for tolerating some extrovert activities — and to Gael for her company. Thank you to the farmers on whose land I have wandered, most of whom became personal friends; for the youthful adventures with SJG, which laid the foundations of it all; to Phil Drabble for the many wildlife discussions we have had, mainly to my benefit; and to Norman Turner with whom I have regularly talked 'wildlife' on BBC Radio.

I greatly appreciate the encouragement of my professional colleagues, in particular Keith Hall, the editor of the *Burnley Express*, and the staff of that paper, whose enthusiasm down the years has fostered a weekly 'Country Notes' feature. I acknowledge the diligence of the editor of this book, Carole Drummond, for her interest and work on the manuscript.

Photographs in such a book as this are paramount, so thank you to Robert Howe and Herbert Holgate for their expertise with a camera, and to Keith Snowden for care in printing my own photographs.

The sketches are taken from my field-book notes and jottings, and are intended to convey information and salient facts, and by no stretch of imagination do they purport to be works of art.

Eric Halsall
Cliviger, August 1984

Illustration credits

Sincere acknowledgement for the use of photographs is made to the *Burnley Express* on pages 27 and 57; *Farmers Guardian,* 159 bottom; Herbert Holgate, 22, 27, 81, 82, 106, 107, 122, 135 and 145; and Robert Howe, 13, 16, 18, 40, 42, 68, 76, 77, 88, 90, 91, 95, 96, 98, 99, 100, 111, 119, 121, 125, 138, 148, 150, 173, 177, 180, 181, 192, 193, 195 and 205; all other photographs, and all sketches, are by the author.

Chapter 1

Carefree adventure

Gael is born to roam the hills of the Pennine sheep country where she learns her woodcraft through play, and receives some timely lessons in the ways of the wild.

Rain-wet and mud-spattered, Gael, the little collie puppy, lay quietly in the shelter beneath the rock shelf. Her earth-stained forepaws were crossed over each other, and she was motionless for the first time that morning, her almond eyes watching Motator, a pied-wagtail who only had one leg, as he balanced and bobbed his long black and white tail on a stone on the bank of the stream.

The stream hurried past Gael's shelter, narrow brown water rushing and bubbling away from the high hills. Cascading in white falls over rock, swirling in clear transparent pools before leaping onward, the hill stream sang a throaty stone-song on its way to the River Calder in the valley. Across the stream, the side of the clough rose steeply, wet ground held by the roots of silver-birch, rowan and sycamore trees, and covered by a carpet of brown grasses, green mosses and the golden skeletons of dead bracken plants. Oak trees clung to their withered raiment of summer. Above Gael's shelter, the bank was even steeper, grey gritstone faces interspersed with bracken-covered earth, and gripped by old alder trees. Beyond the twisted hawthorn trees, which formed the sparse hedges on both sides of the clough, stretched tired green pastures grazed by sheep, extending upwards to the rougher, unclaimed moorland where the curlews bred in spring.

Typical of the East Lancashire Pennines, the woodland clough — Rack Clough — offered shelter to Grey, the fox, Jan, the badger, Pyat, the magpie, Trogo, the tiny brown-feathered wren, and a host of other wild creatures. In the few stunted, full-leaved, shiny holly trees, blackbirds and thrushes found refuge from the cold rain and wind.

Upstream from where Gael rested, the stream took its biggest fall over the stepped rocks, splashing and cascading, and throwing spray over an extensive growth of mosses. In these mosses the dippers built their nest each year. The January afternoon was grey with rain drizzle, and the wind-bent trees dripped water from leafless branches. Gael stood and shook the raindrops from her coat, frightening away Motator, who called 'tschizzick' and flew up into an alder tree to watch her.

She was so youthful, three months old and not long weaned, but she had

Points of a Collie·Dog

`Right dog - You must like it - It must like you
Companion for hours on end.

Box Head - Brain box
Level top. Blunt nose

Rough or Smooth Coat
Colour. not white

Back - Firm e strong
Slight slope to withers
Very flexible spine
- for quick movement

Ears - well set on corners.
Prick or flop.

Coat. Top Lubricant
Under warmth
Weatherproof

Head e Shoulders
Set on to look
Proud

Withers

Round. clear. bright
Eyes - dark. placid
Wise. keen. alert
Forward vision.
Eye of Control.

Nostrils - wide and
open. Good
air passage.
Black.

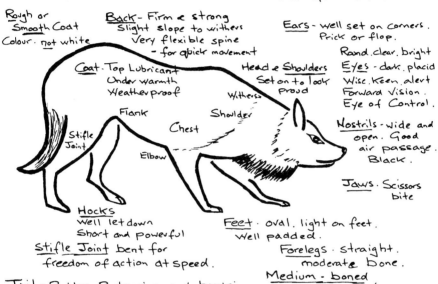

Flank

Chest

Shoulder

Stifle Joint

Elbow

Jaws. Scissors
bite

Hocks
Well let down
Short and powerful
Stifle Joint bent for
freedom of action at speed.

Feet. oval. light on feet.
Well padded.
Forelegs. straight.
moderate bone.
Medium - boned
- Stamina. Vigour.

Tail - Rudder. Balancing and braking
Well set·on. Good sweep.
Feathered. Carried low with
Upward swirl tip.

Movement - Perfect balance
and co·ordination for effortless
ease. Crouching and creeping
attitude typical.

Balanced and Compact form

Nature and Temperament
Good and Placid

Likes Work

Yardstick. is ability
to work stock.

Gael
- her
mark

already found the woodland to be an exciting place. Fear was still unknown to her, and she adventured with carefree heart, for there were brown furry rabbits to run after, tiny squeaking mice to nose in the grasses, and Krark, the heron, to chase into the air. Krark had been annoyed when she had nearly nipped his long green toes before he tucked up his feet in his slow ponderous take-off from the bank of the stream.

Gael was full of mischief and out for fun, and always on the look-out for a playmate. She still had memories of her own sister and three brothers with whom she had played not so long ago. Her rest under the rock was brief, and she rose to sniff the strange musky scent of voles which came from holes at the back of the cave-like rock overhang.

Wisdom in the ways of these small creatures and the other residents of the woodland would come as she grew in experience. As yet she was learning, and her stature was of alert curiosity. Her head angled, first on one side, then on the other, as she listened to the many noises around her — the wistful notes of a robin, the harsh 'pawk' of a crow and the quizzical voice of the pied-wagtail. Her nose, held high, wrinkled continuously as she tasted and sorted the scents of the damp air.

Gael was a beautiful puppy. Her lean body, soft in puppy fur, was vital with energy. She had the sable* colouring of a sunlit fox and a dark russet stripe, the colour of a kingfisher's breast, running along her spine. Her chest was snow-white, as was each paw of her slender legs. She had a thin white blaze on her face running down from between her flop ears to the start of her black nose and, true to sheepdog character, a white tip to her tail.

She had come to me at seven weeks old to roam the sheep lands of the Lancashire-Yorkshire borderland. Within sight of Pendle Hill (the Witches Hill of Lancashire legend), this hard land of bleak stormswept moorland was cut by deep cloughs of bog and trees, with brown waters tumbling to green lowland pastures, and she quickly found an affinity with her wild environment. She was to become a close and much-loved companion.

Of aristocratic line in her breeding, she quickly came to know the ways of sheep and the doings of her wild neighbours on the hill. She became known throughout the area, and was to appear on televised programmes about the countryside. On one occasion she commanded her own dressing-room at Wood Lane Television Centre during a *Blue Peter* programme.

In Gael's cave-like shelter in Rack Clough a spider scurried over the pale green heart-shaped leaves of wood-sorrel which grew from the damp earth, and she watched it dodge from sight under a brown leaf. Following the action, she nosed the dead leaf but the spider had gone. Returning to the back of the cave to taste the vole scent again, her questing nose broke the pattern of a spider's web. Sneezing at the tickle on her nose, she drew back and pawed the sticky strands away from her face.

---

* Although 'sable' means 'black' in heraldry, when applied to the colour of an animal's coat it means a brown colour which can be anything from pale golden-yellow to deep russet.

She watched the raindrops lacing across the grey opening of the cave. The rock was wet and moss-grown with green lichened patterns, and water dripped persistently to the brown earth. This constant plop of water noise intrigued her. She stalked it, belly-crawling to where the drops bounced back from the ground, and she pounced with puppy ferocity to mouth them.

From his perch on the alder, Motator, the wagtail, watched this performance and called 'tschizzick' to her. Gael noted every voice she heard, for they all came to mean something by interpretation.

The rain started to fall more heavily between the tall trees, and Pyat, the magpie, flew down to the river bank. Gael yapped a welcome and the black and white crow immediately flew away grumbling. Gael only wanted to play.

She mouthed a stone from the riverside, and bit at it with her sharp puppy teeth before tossing it away in order to scamper after a sycamore leaf which the wind stirred across the grass. The dead leaf was wet and blew into the low branches of a small silver-birch tree. Snarling in mock anger, Gael leaped at it, shaking it in a worry, and tearing it into shreds.

A little puzzled at her puppy frolics, a blue-tit, warmly dressed in a tight

A blue-tit tilted its head to watch Gael.

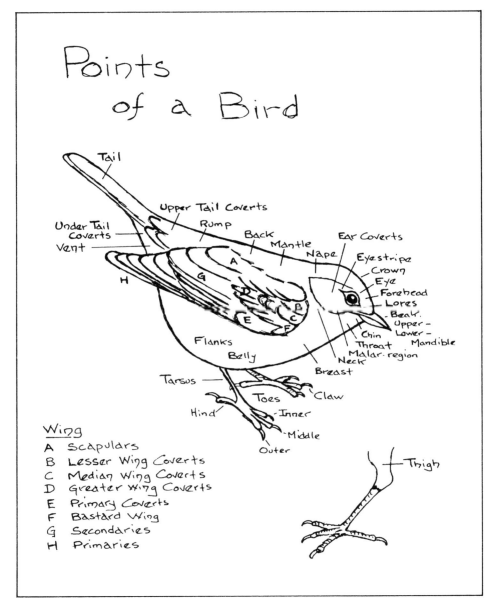

Points

of a Bird

Tail

Upper Tail Coverts

Under Tail
Coverts
Vent

Rump

Back
Mantle
Nape

Ear Coverts

Eyestripe
Crown
Eye
Forehead
Lores
Beak
Upper –
Lower –
Mandible
Chin
Throat
Malar region
Neck

Flanks

Belly

Breast

Tarsus

Toes
Hind
Inner
Middle
Outer

Claw

Thigh

Wing
A Scapulars
B Lesser Wing Coverts
C Median Wing Coverts
D Greater Wing Coverts
E Primary Coverts
F Bastard Wing
G Secondaries
H Primaries

feathering of yellow, green, blue and white, angled its head, the better to watch her from one black eye. Gael scattered the leaf-shreds and looked up as the blue-tit called 'tsee-tsee-tsee-tsit' to her. The bird was joined by two others of its tribe, and they swung in the branches to search for insects, often clinging upside down to break open a tiny swelling bud.

Gael watched them. She was fascinated by the acrobatics of the tits. Her tail wagged, her nose wrinkled as she took their scent, and her head inclined in rapt attention. Up and down the tree, with their sharp, pointed beaks probing into every dry cranny where insects might be hiding, the blue-tits were a lively trio. Gay and industrious, these tiny jewelled birds talked to each other as they searched. They searched the barky cracks of an oak tree for spiders, flitted through alder twigs hung with purple catkins, and flew across to the lichen-covered trunk of a sycamore.

Gael galloped off through the wet, brown fronds of last year's bracken, stopping by a sawn-off tree stump to sniff at the soiling of Grey, the young dog fox, who had passed that way earlier in the day. Kek, the sparrow-hawk, launched himself from a perch on a sycamore branch at the head of the clough and flew swiftly between the trees. He saw Gael nosing the fox's mark, and his keen eye watched the sinuous movement as Hob, the stoat, darted into the cover of a bramble patch. The sparrow-hawk tilted his barred tail feathers and darted away.

Gael scampered on towards the brambles. She found a rabbit tunnel under the prickly stems and, exploring it, sucked the scent of stoat, a strong distasteful smell of musk which she did not know. Faced with an angry, chakkering creature, an animal half her size and of a colour similar to her own, she hesitated.

Hob was fearless and unafraid of the puppy. He chattered his defiance, stretching his height on short legs, his black-tipped tail slowly flicking from side to side, his eyes blazing with fury at Gael's interruption of his hunting. Bloodthirsty by nature, sharp-toothed, and sinuously fast in movement, he spat his contempt at the dog.

Gael inched backwards, prepared to retreat before this spitting, bad-smelling, creature. Sensing her indecision, Hob ran at her, jumping for a bite at the side of her neck. Such aggression, such liberty from one she had just met, piqued Gael, for young and inexperienced though she was, she was of a noble and capable bloodline. Snarling her displeasure at such irresponsible treatment, she jumped back whilst twisting her head to evade the stoat's strike.

Hob's teeth raked the fur of her face, but did not reach the skin. With no issue at stake — food was the only issue he fought over — Hob did not pursue his attack. He darted back to the shelter of the brambles and Gael was content to see him go.

Such an issue meant little in her young life and, indeed, in her first test, she had aquitted herself well against such a vicious and merciless creature as Hob. And so she learned that there were hazards in roaming the woodland clough. Skipping along on her spindly legs across the grass, she stalked round the end of a grey gritstone boulder, and suddenly stopped in surprise. There before her, almost within nosing distance, and equally stilled in surprise, sat another furry creature, a tiny field-vole.

Gael squatted on her haunches, and stretched forward her head. The vole, in shock, started to wash its face and whiskers with its two forepaws. Known as Hirtus after his family name, he was scared at meeting the puppy, and reacted in this curious off-hand manner as though refusing to accept her presence. Although not frightened, Gael was equally at a loss. Hirtus was the first field-vole that she had seen, and she watched him in wonderment. She was intrigued by the

When he risked the dangers of running in the open, Hirtus, the field-vole, always kept close to possible cover, and equally was always conscious of danger from above.

russet-furred beauty of the vole as he sat before her, alert and bright-eyed, a greyish-brown, buff-chested, blunt-nosed creature, about four inches in length.

The stoat forgotten, Gael moved forward for closer knowledge of her new acquaintance — and the spell of immobility and trust was broken. Hirtus darted into a black hole in the ground and was gone. Gael was disappointed and surprised. Her new friend had left her as suddenly as he had appeared. She poked her black-tipped nose into the hole, but all she sucked was lingering scent.

There were many such voles living in the open woodland of Rack Clough and Gael had already run their scent lines in the grasses. Clear-eyed, they roamed in the twilight jungle of grass-framed tunnels where they were hidden and sheltered from outside interference. Christened by the scientists *Microtus agrestis hirtus*, to define them from other varieties of voles, the field-voles — or grass-mice or short-tailed voles as they are also known — lived, as Gael was to discover, in a maze of tiny tunnels which they ate through the grass-covered floor of the woodland.

They were of the tribe of *Microtus*, the dominant tribe of plant-eating rodents which comprises around 50 species in total, though they are the only branch of this large family resident on the British mainland. Ever aware and fearful of danger from above, Hirtus and his relations, when building their tunnel runs, always left the upper layer of grass as cover so that they would not be visible to Aluco, the tawny-owl, and to his mate, Tui, who preyed upon them, and each of whom ate over 1,000 voles in a year.

Although Hirtus liked to feed on the clover plants which grew in the open field alongside the woodland, he was bold if he left the extension of tunnels, for Kee, the kestrel, was ever watchful to pounce, and the hawk rarely failed to strike death with his fierce talons. Like the owls, Kee brought terror to the voles with his sudden death-dealing strikes from the air.

The voles were a persecuted tribe and, in addition to the hunting birds, they were sought by Gael's recent adversary Hob, the stoat, and by Ressel, the barbarous weasel, who was small enough to enter the privacy of their tunnels to kill them.

Hirtus had been clever and fortunate in escaping so many enemies, although his above-ground meeting with Gael was a slip which could have been disastrous. At 18 months old he was dominant within his group, one of the lucky ones to survive into his second winter. Few of his tribe saw their second winter.

Hirtus was strong and fit, and well-grown to just over four inches in body length. His tail was less than two inches long, his nose typically blunt, his eyes and hairy ears small, his legs short. His winter coat was dense and a little shaggy in order to keep him warm.

Mainly vegetarian in his feeding, his teeth grew continuously and were crowned at acute angles to crush grass stalks, roots and other coarse green food. To change his diet for a little variation, Hirtus caught whatever insects he could, and he was partial to the sawflies which spent so much of their time just sitting on the plant leaves, and which were so slow to fly away.

He lived in a home built of chewed grasses which was below the thick mat of vegetation at the end of a small burrow in the ground. It was warm and snug,

Ruddock, the robin, was one of the first birds to meet Gael.

deep enough down to miss the chilling cold of all but the hardest frost. Although he did not sleep the winter away in hibernation, he was wise enough to stay curled in its cosiness through really bitter weather. If he became hungry, and it was too cold to venture out, he was surrounded by acceptable food. A few weeks before his meeting with Gael, Hirtus had been so hungry when the frost-spirit had hardened the ground for three nights that he had eaten the grass lining of his home.

Active little animals, the voles roamed the woodland during both daylight and night time and, as long as there was sufficient food for all, they were sociable with their neighbours, although they did not always tolerate strangers from an adjoining community, of which there were many in the surrounding farmlands.

As her experience in Rack Clough grew with her age, Gael discovered that Hirtus lived in a large community in the open woodland on the steeply sloping and bracken-covered east bank of the stream. With the life-span of each vole rarely over 12 months, it was an ever-changing community. But, like all their kind, these voles were a prolific race, breeding when only six weeks old and bearing three or four families of between three and six babies in the season. In this way the number of the colony was kept level and not reduced or wiped out by the ravages of owls, kestrels, stoats, weasels or foxes.

When Hirtus disappeared into the hole by the rock he left Gael wondering just where he had gone. Thinking that he had narrowly escaped from a little fox, the vole was in no mood to leave his sanctuary, and Gael left to seek another playmate.

The clouds passed over the hillside and the rain ceased. Weak sunshine burst into the trees to brighten the land. Ambling along a sheep-trod between the soaking bracken, and looking for the next adventure, Gael met Ruddock, the robin redbreast. Sitting on her haunches in the middle of the muddy track, her snowy-white chest splashed with dirt, she watched, enthralled, as Ruddock, his red throat throbbing, whistled exultant notes from a perch in the thorn bush five feet above her head. The robin sang to the sun, the notes trilling of happiness at the passing of the rainstorm.

All these happenings — the joyful notes of the robin, the stoat's nastiness, the flight of the vole and the acrobatics of the blue-tits — added to Gael's woodcraft knowledge, each a lesson which would mould her character. Because of her sheepdog breed she was naturally intelligent, with an inbred wisdom and capacity to learn. Gael enjoyed the song of the robin, and she could not contain her approval. She opened her mouth and yapped her pleasure.

Much to her surprise, Ruddock did not welcome her vocal encouragement. He stopped singing and, cocking a black eye at the little dog in a most reproving manner, scolded her with his penetrating 'tic-tic-tic' notes. How dare this puppy distract him when he was singing to the sun — and, hopefully, singing a love song to the charming female robin across the stream? Naturally aggressive, and master of his woodland territory, he would have to teach this newcomer to the community to watch her manners if she wished to be accepted by the wildfolk.

So excited did his scolding become that Gael was quietened by the volume of his noise. She turned tail and trotted away up the track, mincing her steps as jauntily as ever. She could see no fault in her actions and if Ruddock wanted to be bad-tempered, she would simply ignore him. Squeezing under the prickly branches of the hedgerow hawthorns at the top of the clough, she disturbed a flock of lapwings which were picking and searching for worms in the grass of the field. The birds rose into the air with flashes of black and white feathering. They stumbled and fell in their slow, throbbing flight, and called 'pee-wit' to each other.

Gael watched them go up over the hill before she crossed the pasture to nose into the gaps in the bottom of the stone boundary wall of the field above the clough. These walls, she was to discover in later days, were the home and retreat of the upland rabbits and of the weasels and stoats which hunted them.

Beneath the wall she found an interesting new toy, a wet furry pellet cast out from the mouth of Kew, the little-owl, whose favourite perch was on the wall top. Gael doubted the pellet at first, then she sniffed it, stretching forward like a pointer dog with left forepaw raised off the ground until she overbalanced. The pellet carried an uncertain scent, but was tasteless when she bit at it. She tossed it in play and broke it apart with her sharp puppy teeth. It comprised of the wing cases of beetles, other insect remains and the tiny delicate skull of a mouse entwined in a mass of dank fur — all the indigestible remains of the little owl's meal.

Perched on the top of the wall, five feet above Gael's head, Kew became a little agitated as he watched the dog, but as she played more and more below his perch, he lost his usual quiet composure and bobbed up and down like a wide-eyed clown, anxious to know more of her antics.

Named in science after Athene, the warrior goddess of great wisdom, he was not afraid, although suspicious, and he called out his country name of 'kiew, kiew' to Gael. The many differing voices she heard in her early days were Gael's primary education in woodcraft. Gael had not seen Kew, and she looked up in surprise at his voice, angling her head and pricking her ears as she sat on her haunches. Here was another strange creature she knew nothing of.

Kew stared back at her, his big yellow-ringed eyes watching the puppy, the edges of his facial discs raised to open his ears. His features were inscrutable and did not mirror the surprise and interest of his feelings. He was a plump-bodied, flat-headed owl, no more than nine inches tall, and he was one of the residents on the hillside. He and his mate, Athen, had made their nest for the past two years in the hollow trunk of the old sycamore tree which grew solitarily in a corner of the high pasture.

Gael strained with excitement and she yapped a bark. Like Ruddock, the robin, Kew did not appreciate this response and he spread his wings and went flying from his perch with soft feather strokes. Again Gael was left wondering why she had been deserted. All she wanted was to be friendly, and she was having no success at all in finding a playmate.

Kew flew to the sycamore tree which was his home. He was the smallest owl in the countryside, scarcely bigger than a thrush, and only half the size of Albo, the barn-owl, or Aluco, the tawny-owl. Unlike them, he hunted the daylight hours as well as the darkness, and he prefered the open countryside to their woodlands and buildings. His ancestors had been brought from Spain in the 19th century to breed and establish their kind in Britain. He was dressed in fine fringed feathers, coloured brown and striped in white for effective camouflage. His round eyes were sensitive enough to follow a moth at dusk, his hooked bill was strong enough to tear apart a vole, and his sharp talons were the deadliest of weapons.

Alone again, Gael was too full of fun and boisterous energy to worry about Kew's departure. She was happy in her own company, and it was not possible to be lonely with so many strangers to meet on her travels. She trotted away across the field — and saved a lapwing's life. Pushing between the rushes by the hill pond, the pond known in the locality as Scholey Pond, her noisy progress frightened the bird into flight, and saved it from becoming the victim of a hunting stoat. The lapwing winged into the air above Gael's head, and, as surprised as the bird at their meeting, she crouched into the rushes, momentarily frightened by the sudden action. Lying there between the tall brown stems of the rushes, she heard the frustrated gibbering of a stoat.

Tigrid, the stoat and the brother of Hob whom Gael had already met, had been stalking the lapwing which, totally engrossed in preening its feathers after bathing in the shallows of the pond, had been unaware of the danger. Gael's intrusion had lost Tigrid a meal.

Fierce in the hunt and a killer by nature, Tigrid, who lived in the tunnel gaps between the stones of the dry walls, was one of the most hated creatures on the hill and was feared by all. From the safety of a gap in the stone wall he snarled and chakkered his rage at Gael before disappearing into the maze of the wall's myriad gaps and passages. (The dry-stone walls which crossed the upland pastures and ran up to the moor were covered highways for the many small creatures of the area, allowing them to move without being seen across the hillside.)

Up on the higher land, the lapwing glided down to the ground to preen its bedraggled feathers in safety. Careful after her earlier experience with the tribe of the stoat, Gael nosed the lingering rankness of musk left by Tigrid. She was alone again until a sudden whistle of wind lifted her ears to the passing of a flock of 30 golden plovers. The birds swept across the hillside, their sharply-pointed wings slicing through the air as they flew at speed in tight formation. The whistling was created by the thrust of their wings through the air, and Gael stood rigid, listening. They were gone before she could blink her eyes, leaving the memory of their liquid 'tu-tu-tlui' notes. Soon they would break up their flock and pair for the breeding season.

Chapter 2

Growing up

Corbie, the black crow, plays the fool in a frozen land; Gael plays a game with the wind, and in saving the lives of baby dippers, makes an enemy of Ressel, the weasel.

Days of mild weather at the end of February brought the curlews back to the hill, and Gael lifted her head to their happy bugling as the birds returned to their summer home. It was the first time that the little collie had heard such wild music and she sat and listened with ears cocked in rapt attention. Every year the curlews came to the Pennine moors to rear their families, after having spent the winter in wandering the bleak mud-flats of the River Ribble's estuary, 30 miles to the west.

They sailed over the hill on hollow wings, opening their long, hooped beaks to

Every year the curlews returned to the Pennine moors to rear their families.

Poised to strike.
He seeks 1 lb. food
    each day.

Patience is a virtue.
Silently waits his chance.

Wings lazily
flapping, spear-
bill couched, legs
trailing - Krark
flies off over
the hill.

Speed. 30 m.p.h.

Blue-grey
    feathering.
Head-crest.
        3 feet tall.

Krark
the heron.
(Ardea cinerea)

Alert in
the rushes
by Scholey
Pond.

He is quick of hearing.

trill their liquid notes over the land they loved. Slowly, they glided down to the moor, touched ground and, with wings poised above their heads in a gesture of greeting, sent a final bubble of music into the wind for Gael's benefit.

Tall and solemn-looking on long grey legs, the curlews wore a plumage of brown-streaked feathers which blended into the herbage background of the moor. They were the largest of the wading birds in the area, and were almost comically distinctive with long, down-curved beaks which grew to seven inches.

The air was fresh, the morning bright, and Melos, the song-thrush, sang spring notes from his perch in a sycamore tree in Rack Clough. Pyat, the magpie, chattered happily and played tricks with the rabbits, breaking off small twigs from the trees and dropping them on to their backs to frighten them. In the warmer, denser woodland in the deeper valley the erect green spears of snowdrops tipped their heads in white array across the soaking leaf-mat.

Three days after the arrival of the curlews, the weather became wintry again and a bitterly cold wind carried flurries of snowflakes and tossed them in a white carpet between the brown rushes of the hillside bogland. The wind whipped at the reeds and whistled over the hollows where skylarks and pipits crouched for warmth with puffed feathers in the snow. The rushing air sleeked Gael's fur tight against her slim body, and parted a knife-edge in the golden hairs. She nosed among the brittle rushes, which tossed their heads in constant ripples to gossip of the wind spirit and stifled all other sound.

Gael's feet broke through the thin ice-covering on the damp ground, and the noise alerted Krark, the heron, who was standing, crouched and miserable, in the rushes. He spread his great wings and flew up over Gael's head, squawking his harsh notes of annoyance — though he was glad for some action — as he lifted into the full force of the cold wind. He couched his spear-bill between his lean shoulders, trailed his long legs and, wings beating in ponderous flight, flew across the moor to drop into the rushes by the side of the pond in which an early spawning frog had laid three clumps of jelly-covered eggs.

Sheltered by the rushes, Gael watched Krark fly from her sight. She listened to the song of a brave skylark. Liquid notes trilled, in defiance of the cold wind, from the throbbing throat of the lark, and spoke of the soft warm summer days to come. Rapidly beating wings carried the crested bird into the air, although its ascent was bent by the wind force. Soon it surrendered to the force and pitched back into the rushes. With brown feathers finely pencilled and marked, the skylark ran quickly between the brown rushes in search of a warm couch.

The only true master of the wind, Kee, the kestrel, hovered against the grey clouds of the sky. Playing the wind over his brown feathers, his eyes, round yellow-rimmed pools of knowledge, watched the lark settle into the base of a rush clump. He saw Gael run through the bogland, treading the frost-hardened cover of damp mosses, splashing through the ice over shallow brown water, and pushing between cold brown rushes. She stalked imaginary goblins in the bogland, and was startled when a pair of mallard ducks shot up from her path. They sped away into the sky, their long necks outstretched as they swept round over her head, before turning towards the distant reservoir.

Kestrel.
Kee.
Above Scholey Pond.
January.

Sheep moved quietly from Gael's approach when she ran across to the shelter of the grey stone wall. Here was the only barrier to the wind's force and, through the gaps in the stonework, it screamed of frustration in Gael's ears. Snow had drifted behind the wall, and Gael played, rolling over and over in the white drift, and nosing and biting at the cold flakes. She ceased her game when she heard an angry cry in the air above her head.

Corbie, the black crow, had flown at Kee, the kestrel, in a display of bad temper. Gael watched the aerial conflict. She saw Kee slip the wind from his pointed wings and fall away through the air to avoid the crow's unwarranted attack. Slicing down the wind, the air screaming in his pinion feathers, Kee levelled out and raced away to hunt the adjoining hillside, leaving Corbie floundering, his heavy flight ability no match for that of the speedy kestrel.

The crow called his frustration, and seeing Gael below, the only visible creature apart from the sheep on the open moor, he planed down for a close inspection. His composure restored, and his black wings cleverly feathering the wind, he glided down to alight on top of the stone wall. At his chosen perch, the highest growing trees of the woodland clough broke the direct force of the wind.

   Puffing out the feathers of his throat, he called a vibrant 'kaak-kaak-kaak' to Gael. Corbie was a wise bird and saw no danger in shouting his presence to a small dog. He would not have called to one of the older collies which shepherded the moor, for they had no time for Corbie and his tribe and scattered them into confusion when they met. Gael he had seen before, and he knew she was yet too

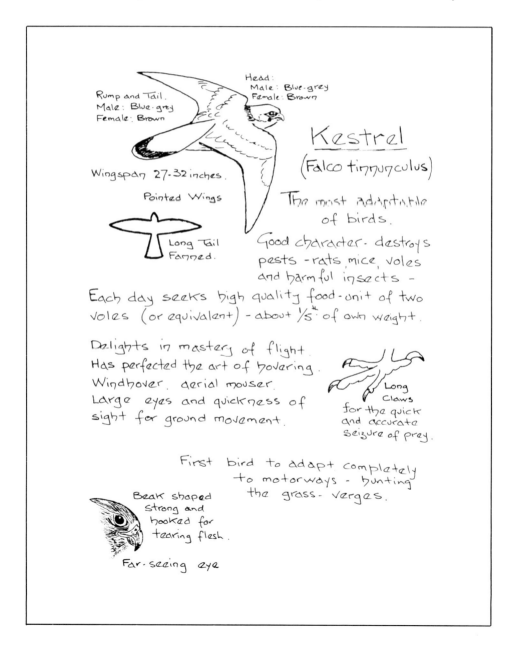

Rump and Tail.
Male: Blue-grey
Female: Brown

Head:
Male: Blue-grey
Female: Brown

Wingspan 27-32 inches.

Pointed Wings

Long Tail
Fanned.

Kestrel

(Falco tinnunculus)

The most adaptable of birds.

Good character - destroys pests - rats, mice, voles and harmful insects -

Each day seeks high quality food - unit of two voles (or equivalent) - about 1/5th of own weight.

Delights in mastery of flight.
Has perfected the art of hovering.
Windhover. aerial mouser.
Large eyes and quickness of sight for ground movement.

Long Claws
for the quick and accurate seizure of prey.

First bird to adapt completely to motorways - hunting the grass-verges.

Beak shaped
Strong and hooked for tearing flesh.

Far-seeing eye

Sleek and bold, the female kestrel was slightly larger than her husband. Feeka knew that mice and young rats often made indiscreet crossings of the farmyard.

young and inexperienced to trouble him. She could well prove an interesting diversion to his boredom and annoyance with the cold weather.

Hearing the crow's call, and intrigued by the big black bird, Gael ran down the wallside until she was standing below Corbie. She sat down and her almond eyes filled with interest. Corbie was pleased. He had a rapt audience and his eyes twinkled, for he could be of a humorous nature when he wished.

He dipped his head in a bow to Gael, lifted his fanned tail, and called three times in quick succession in a gutteral voice. He clowned. He rocked from foot to foot on the grey stone perch, flapped open his wings, and called again. He shook his head from side to side and rapped his strong black beak on the stone.

Corbie was only acting the fool. He was one of the most intelligent creatures on the hill. He was of the long established family of *Corvidae* and had lived in the Pennine locality for three years. He knew all the other residents and their characters, and most important, he had learned how to exploit their weaknesses for his own gain. He was smart and well able to fend for himself, knowing where to find the eggs of ground birds in season, the young of rabbits and other small creatures and, when such delicacies were not available, he could be content to live on insects, worms and vegetable matter he foraged.

For a full two minutes the play-acting continued, Corbie enjoying his role of

Carrion crow.
Corbie.
Rack Clough.
March.

character actor, and Gael watching every move with her sharp, intelligent eyes. A probing sunbeam broke through grey clouds and bathed Corbie in a spotlight of stardom as his performance came to an end. With the light glinting his black feathers with a green and purple sheen, he made a final bow to the collie, puffed his throat again and croaked 'kaak-kaak-kaak'.

Unable to contain her excitement at this strange performance, Gael yapped a reply — and the spell was broken. She had not yet learned that to bark was to startle. Unused to applause, and alarmed — as robin and owl before him — at this reaction from his hitherto silent audience, Corbie screeched reproval, and launched himself into the wind to fly off towards the distant grey rocks of the Cliviger Gorge.

Here, amidst the impregnable fortress of sheer gritstone rocks, weathered and moulded into horizontal ledges and vertical cracks, Corbie and his mate had reared their family in complete safety. High on the rock pinnacles of the Earl's Bower, White Kirk and Waterfall Rock, crow and kestrel found safe nesting sites. They followed the recorded tradition of Harrison Ainsworth's eagles in his story of *The Lancashire Witches.*

Gael watched Corbie leave her, interested in having made such close aquaintance with the talkative bird. Corbie gone, she ran to the woodland clough and played a game with the east wind. She chased the brittle leaves of last winter which the wind plucked from the ground and tossed about in a whirling brown fury. She snapped at them when they danced to the wind's whistling tunes across the grass. She leaped into the air to mouth high-flying leaves, and, caught off-balance by the force of wind, rolled over and over down the steep slope of the clough.

Unhurt and happy in her play, she shook the hairs of her sable coat into place, and continued the hectic chasing game, running sure-footed across the slope in the midst of the swirling leaves. A pair of great-tits, searching for spiders by probing their sharp beaks into the dead wood crevices of a tree trunk, flew up in alarm as she raced by. They perched in the boughs of a silver-birch tree, their bright yellow, black and white feathers tight against the cold, and scolded her with a harsh, resounding 'churr' which voiced their anger at the puppy's thoughtlessness.

Although the snow squalls had ceased, the wind had the touch of winter ice, and blew with force between the high trees of the clough, whipping at the brown grasses, pulling at the dead skeletons of last year's bracken, and tugging at the interwoven sticks of a magpie's old nest in the top of a birch tree. Every loose thing swirled before this bitter onslaught. Gael flopped down to rest, and panted her pleasure with open mouth and lolling tongue at the fun she was having with the wind.

From a perch close up to the windbreak of a sycamore trunk, Pyat, the magpie, sat with hunched shoulders, feeling miserable and bad-tempered with the weather. He looked down with scorn on Gael and, making the effort, opened his beak and cackled derision on her youthful exuberance. Gael peered up at him and drew back her lip in an assumed puppy snarl. She could not appreciate his misery at having to live in the frozen land. Grey rocks glistened with ice in the light, and silver icicles hung where water had dripped the day before.

Gael stalked a blackbird which probed for worms into ground which had been sheltered by the covering of dead bracken and therefore was soft. Close by, the bird's mate perched with feathers fluffed out, making it look like a round ball, in order to conserve its body warmth. By fluffing it was able to hold, between the outer and inner feathers, an insulation of air which was heated by its body temperature. Like a warm blanket, this insulation protected the blackbird from the bitter cold.

Gael pricked her ears to the sudden whistle of a dipper when it flew down the line of the stream in the valley of Rack Clough. It flew to the waterfall where a new nest was being built into the ferns which grew from the rock face. The dippers, round, chunky birds of the water, liked to be early with their family duties and had started to build their nest in the first days of mild promise. They were hardy birds and were able to withstand all the hazards of winter, so that the return of the cold weather did not deter them.

A mistle-thrush gripped the topmost branch of a pitching sycamore tree and sang defiance at the wind. Its loud notes called on spring to hasten and bring warmer days of hope.

Gael ran down to the banks of the stream which flowed in a valley, cut deep by the moorland water. Here the wind lost its bite. The valley echoed the murmur of water music, the splash of tumbling water, the tinkle and bubble of water over obstructing stone, and the drip of water drops from the moss-grown rocks.

Smartly dressed in her waistcoat of clean white feathers under her dark brown overcoat, Zoie, the female dipper, perched by the waterfall in the clough. Cheerfully she called 'zeet-zeet-zeet' and, from her perch on the moss-covered rock, bobbed her head to the cascade of sparkling water drops.

Zoie was one of nature's specialists, designed for life and survival in an unusual environment; a happy, stocky bird which liked to be in constant contact with moving water. She had a sturdy, well-feathered body with short strong wings which carried her on a rapid, weaving flight between the rocks and trees along the stream, or swam her as paddles on her walks below water. (She was able to walk underwater to feed on the larvae of aquatic creatures, with her feet strongly gripping the stones of the stream's bed to resist the pull of the water current.)

She loved her home stretch of the stream, flying through the fall of water over the rocks, basking in the shifting spray, and diving to the bottom of the deep pools. She was two years old and had been born in a nest on the same rock face on which she was now building her own nursery.

A robin added its pleasant song to the dipper's calls. Completely happy with her life, Zoie burst into a sweet, warbling song as, with a flash of his white breast, Zit, her mate, flew upstream to join her on the rock. Song swelled to a frenzy as both birds joined together in a hurried duet, their beaks almost touching as they faced each other, their wings quivering in delight.

The birds had chosen a site for their home in the roots of ferns on a tiny ledge in a rock which was to the side of the main fall of water, and five feet above the base pool. The foundation moss was already in place. It was a spot beloved of dippers, wet with dripping water, and often showered with spray from the waterfall.

Zoie, the smaller bird of the pair of dippers, pulled moss from her perch and flew up to the ledge. She pressed it with her beak into the bowl which she was forming. When completed, the dippers' home would be a ball of moss, round and roofed, and though externally damp, snug and warm for the chicks to be born there. Inside the domed nest would be a cup of grass, lined cosily with dead leaves. Clinging to the moss and fern-covered rock, the completed nest would blend with its surroundings, in perfect camouflage, as protection for the family-to-be.

Bouncing down the rocky side of the gorge like a mountain goat, Gael disturbed the dippers at their work. They called to each other in alarm and flew away downstream, each skimming low over the water and following the course of the narrow valley. Gael listened to their 'zeeting' calls as she watched them flash away on fast, whirring wings.

Then she came down the side of the waterfall, leaping from rocky step to rocky step which made it possible to reach the side of the base pool. The rock was wet and slippery and its laminations were widened by the strength of root formations. In the water splashes it was green with moss and festooned with the brown skeletons of bracken fronds. A tall-growing rowan tree clung halfway up the staircase, its water-thirsting roots probing deep between the layers of rock. Lichens, silver green and grey in colour, clung to dryer boulders.

The mosses stored water on the sloping rock and Gael slid over them, her sharp claws extended for a hold. She had grown very agile in her weeks in the open, and she leaped as lightly as a cat across the rock ledges. She lapped water from the pool at the base of the falls and, shaking the spray from her sable coat, trotted away downstream.

Fifty yards from the waterfall, Zit dived down into the water of a quietly flowing stretch of the stream. He walked on the stream's bed, flicking his wings against the current of the water to stay submerged, probing under the stones and seeking out caddis grubs and beetles. He collected a beakful and bobbed from the water to fly up in a spray of drops to perch on a rock. There he enjoyed his food.

Close by, Zoie gathered moss for her home, and flew back to the ledge by the waterfall. Gael, in one of her favourite rests on the bare earth under a rock overhang by the side of the stream, watched the bird go whirring past towards the

The wall top always gave Gael a vantage point to look for sheep or wild friends.

nest. During that first early spring of her life, Gael came to know Zit and Zoie well, and, after the initial days of introduction, they in turn accepted her. They became unafraid of her presence by the waterfall, though on occasion she spoiled their trust by chasing towards them when they perched on the rocks at the stream's edge. It was only her wish to be playful and friendly, but the birds did not appreciate her boisterous approach.

Nevertheless, Zoie would 'zeet' a welcome and curtsey to her when she visited the nest site. Zit ceased to call an alarm when he met her by the stream. They were cheerful birds and Gael regarded them as her friends. Never quite able to understand how Zoie disappeared into the face of the rock when she entered the nest to brood her four white eggs, Gael was equally baffled when Zit dived below the surface of the water to search for food on the bed of the stream.

One morning of cold bright sunshine in March, Gael heard, for the first time, the cheeping of chicks in the nest by the waterfall. Standing at the top of the rocks, she leaned over, swivelling her ears to listen. So excited did she become at the tiny sounds that she almost lost her footing. She recognised that a change had taken place in the lives of Zit and Zoie when, in the days which followed, she saw how busy they were in bringing food to the new family.

It was during the nursery days of the young dippers that Gael repaid the trust and friendship of their parents. One afternoon she was lying quietly by the waterfall, her nose resting on her white forepaws, her ears turning to the song notes of Ruddock, the robin, when a warning call from Pyat, the magpie, brought her to her feet.

She sensed a movement in the bracken patch by the side of the fall. Immediately alert, she watched to see Ressel, the weasel, slink quietly from cover and start, slowly and carefully, to pick a foothold across the rock face towards the dippers' nest. An agile, sinuous creature, his sharp claws found sufficient hold in the tiny water cracks of the rock.

Gael barked a warning then splashed and floundered through the pool at the base of the rock. She jumped towards Ressel, but could not reach him and she fell back into the water. Unaware of her presence by the stream, so still had she lain, Ressel was taken by complete surprise. He lost his concentration, slipped and fell the five feet to the water below.

In a mêlée of splashing water and flying spray, Gael and Ressel sought, yet evaded, each other. The weasel, not liking the water, swam the short distance to the bank, scrambled into the cover of the bracken, and quickly found refuge under the bared roots of an alder tree.

Gael snapped, and missed the marauder. Her attack was instinctive, partially in excitement and somewhat in play, for though she distrusted Ressel and knew he had meant harm to the baby dippers, she had not yet learned of his true nature. Only in later months did she learn about his vicious and bloodthirsty character. Ressel, for his part, was to remember her as his enemy.

Chapter 3

Pond puzzles

Gael is both puzzled and fascinated by the mass spawning of frogs as the weather enters spring, and brings Chacka, the wheatear, on the long journey from Africa.

The wind lost some of its bite and the temperature rose. Rain showers splashed across the land, soaking the ground until drainage ditches ran full, and the ewes on the hill shook cascades of water from their thick wool and sought shelter under the field-walls. Between the showers a weak sun beamed over the fields and turned the thoughts of all wild creatures to spring-time love.

On a damp night in mid-March when Aluco, the tawny-owl, hunted voles

The cold, still waters of Scholey Pond where the frogs gathered to mate in March.

between the trees of Rack Clough, and Gael lay curled in sleep at home, the frogs started their annual journey to the spawning-pond on Scholey Hill. Those that had not spent the winter in hibernation, in the mud at the bottom of the pond, crawled from many hiding places in the boglands around the area. They awoke from a life-phase which had been almost dormant. Those at the bottom of the pond were sustained by their skin glands which were able to draw oxygen from the water.

Hopping between tall rushes, jumping with strong thrusts of their long hind legs over cropped pasture grass, and wriggling through the tough bent grasses, the multi-hued frogs crossed the hill to their pond. Their homing instinct was sure.

Most of them were males preceding the females which would travel the journey on later nights. Aluco was the first to see them and he called his mate Tui to come and enjoy a change of diet. During the night the two owls fed well as a result of the frogs' migration.

The frogs were the first of the amphibians to breed in the year. Cold-blooded creatures which grew from water-placed eggs, the frogs tolerated the cold more happily than their cousins, the toads and newts. Weather conditions of alternate rain and sunshine of the past weeks had been ideal for them, for they produced a quick growth of algae, the gelatinous mass of green vegetation on which their tadpoles would feed.

Falling back from the edge of a hillside rock when, with an over-bold leap, it did not quite reach the ledge, a frog was snapped up by Taxus, the sow badger who was feeding cubs in her breeding sett in Brockholes Wood at the bottom of the clough.

Hob, the stoat, and Ressel, the weasel, also dined that night on frog meat. Not a great number of the frogs died, and by dawn most had reached the pond in the hollow on the hillside. They were happy with this high pond set on the 800-foot contour line for, although the water temperature was lower than the boggy ponds in the valley, the cover of rank rush growth, and the food available, suited their purpose so that their kind had spawned there for many years.

The scientists call the frogs, which gather at Scholey pond, by the name *Rana temporaria temporaria*, and they are the common frogs of the area. The other two species of frogs living in Britain — the big marsh-frog and the more aquatic edible-frog — are unknown in this locality. *Rana temporaria* is variable in the colouration of its smooth, moist skin, and no two are exactly alike. Colour ranges through grey, yellow, brown, orange and marbled, and is usually dependent on the general background colouration of the surroundings in which the individual lives. The frogs are adept at catching the snails and worms on which they feed. Flicking out their forked tongues, they snatch the prey and draw in their eyeballs to squash the food in their mouth. These large eyes, golden coloured and speckled with brown, have three lids, one almost transparent which protects the eyes under water.

Other than when hunting food, frogs keep their mouths tightly closed, breathing through valve-like nostrils to supplement the respiration through their

The Naming and Classifying of living creatures by codewords - so that all nations may understand - was devised by the Swedish naturalist Karl von Linné (Carolus Linnaeus) 1707-78, and recorded in Latin to be universal.

Each Kind or Species of creature is known under two names - a generic name which defines its relations (written with a capital letter in italics) - and a specific name which identifies it precisely (in italics - no capital letter).

Each Species (in which any male could mate with any female to produce fertile offspring) is grouped in genera (species with strong similarities), genera grouped in families, families in orders, orders in classes, classes in divisions (or phyla), and divisions in Kingdoms (the two main ones being animal and plant Kingdoms).

Main Levels of Classification (with examples).

Creature :-	Gael. Collie. dog.	Frog.	Kestrel	Soft Rush
Kingdom	Animal	Animal	Animal	Plant
Division (Phylum)	Vertebrata	Vertebrata	Vertebrata	Spermatophyta
Class	Mammalia	Amphibia	Aves	Angiosperm
Order	Carnivora	Salientia	Falconiforme	Monocotyledon
Family	Canidae	Ranidae	Falconidae	Juncaceae
Genus	Canis	Rana	Falco	Juncus
Species	Canis familiaris	Rana temporaria	Falco tinnunculus	Juncus effusus
Sub-species	collie	temporaria		

skin. When the females arrived at the pond, they were larger and more stoutly built than the males, and, although only just out of hibernation, were at their maximum weight. They were welcomed by a croaking chorus from the males, by Krark, the heron, who had been drawn to the activity in the pond, and by Gael who was out early that morning on the hill.

Krark, frightened away when Gael arrived on the scene, returned to feast on the frogs once she had gone. Gael, ears cocked in puzzlement by the dull whirr of voices, waded into the shallow water between the rushes to watch the play of the frogs. Krark speared the frogs with his long, pointed beak and greedily gulped them down his throat until his crop was bulging.

After a while, the heron was less successful. The frogs had become more wary, and at the slightest shadow across the water or the slightest disturbance, even from his stealthy tread, they dived under the water. They swam to the cover of the underwater weeds, using powerful strokes of their hind legs, their forelegs held back against their bodies to stream their line. Skulking among the stems of growing weeds and the debris of rotting vegetation in the semi-stagnant pool, the frogs peered through eyes covered by their transparent lids. They were screened from above by the murkiness of water, coloured by their disturbance of the mud at the bottom of the pond.

The frogs had many enemies — more than any other British amphibian — and they were very vulnerable. As well as for Krark, and badgers, owls, stoats and weasels, they provided food for rats, hedgehogs, otters, hawks, gulls and ducks, and Corbie, the crow, was partial to this change in his diet. They were timid and excitable and their only defence was flight.

Unlike the toads who were intelligent enough to blow up their size and stand their ground, the frogs fled below the water or into the cover of the rushes. Neither had they got the acrid-tasting poison glands of the toad in order to make themselves distasteful as food. Their survival as a race depended entirely on their great fertility, and each female frog laid around 2,000 eggs each spring, though the majority of the tadpoles which hatched from the eggs were eaten during their 12 weeks in the pond.

Two days after the females had joined the males at Scholey Pond, Gael lay in the shelter of the rushes by the water's edge. The sun was warm on her back and it was a morning of spring promise. She raised her head and worked her nostrils across the scents of the breeze which rippled lightly from the surface of the pond water. Her ears twitched to the cries of lapwings dancing in black and white courtship flights over the hill. High above her head, a snipe flew in sharp, irregular bursts, mounting up to swoop down towards the ground so that the rush of air through its spread of tail feathers made a persistent bleating noise.

Gael licked the fur of her foreleg where black mud stained her white hair. She had romped in the shallows of the pond, sending the frogs diving for cover and frightening a small party of five twites that had come up the hill that morning. Often known as moorland linnets, the twites held a whispered conversation before flitting across to the rush cover on the far side of the pond. Gael could still hear their quiet nasal voices discussing their return to their breeding ground.

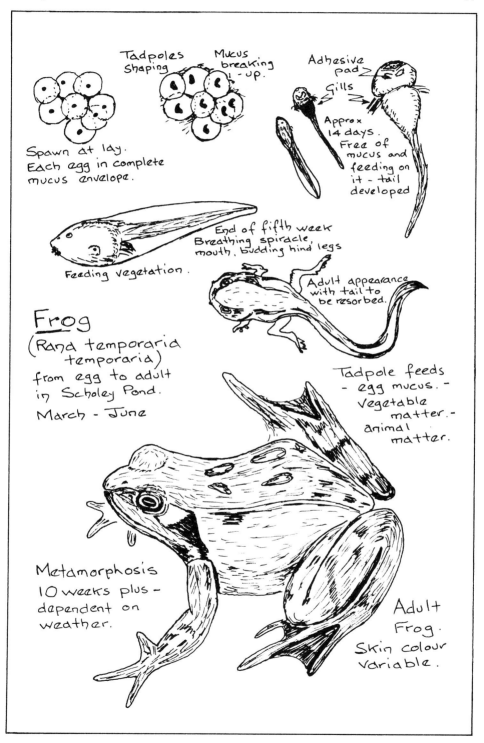

Tadpoles Shaping

Mucus breaking up.

Spawn at lay. Each egg in complete mucus envelope.

Adhesive pad

Gills

Approx 14 days. Free of mucus and feeding on it - tail developed

End of fifth week Breathing spiracle, mouth, budding hind legs

Feeding vegetation.

Adult appearance with tail to be resorbed.

Frog
(Rana temporaria temporaria)
from egg to adult in Scholey Pond.
March - June

Tadpole feeds - egg mucus. - Vegetable matter. - animal matter.

Metamorphosis 10 weeks plus - dependent on weather.

Adult Frog. Skin colour variable.

Every day on the hillside brought new interests to widen her experience of the wild folk.

She was now well-grown and was becoming gazelle-like in stature. Her nose and ears constantly strained for fresh scents and sounds, and her senses had developed to match the wild creatures around her. Her scent was keen, her hearing acute, and she could even equal the speed of Lepus, the brown hare, over a short distance.

The reflection of the sunbeams from her golden coat attracted a tortoiseshell butterfly. It flitted above her body before realising that she was not a source of food. Having survived the rigours of its winter hibernation in the old sheep-shelter on the hill, the butterfly danced a welcome to the sunlight pouring from the blue sky.

Gael lay still, dozing in the warmth, and one by one the frogs swam up from among the underwater vegetation to float on the water's surface. They, like Gael and the other wild creatures, found the new warmth in the sunshine most pleasing.

The quiet movements over the silver water made Gael's eyes open, but she remained still, watching. Heads thrust out of the water, blue-white throats and bulging eyes making them quickly visible when faced, the frogs' sombre, spread-eagled, brown limbs, seen from the rear, blending into obscurity on the dark water. Hovering above the pond, even Kee, the kestrel, with the best eyesight in the countryside, found difficulty in marking them until they moved.

Sunbeams flashing on the water excited the frogs, and the males croaked their pleasure, their vocal sacs swelling on each side of their throats with the effort. The males called to the females. Their mating instincts were aroused and they were anxious to breed.

Gael cocked her ears to the strange noise for, collectively, the frogs' voices sounded like a dull whirring of farm machinery, a quiet wailing sound which increased in ardour. Her senses alert, her head raised to take the scents of the wind on her damp nose, she rose to her feet quietly and unseen, screened by the depth of rushes. Slowly, she pushed between the tall rush clumps, the rustle of wind through the brittle stalks covering what little noise she made. Her feet sank through the shallow pondside water into the black ooze, staining the snow-white hairs of her legs. Crouching with the careful stealth of her breed, stretching her head forward to peer between the last barrier of rushes before the open water, she watched the spawning of the frogs.

There were a hundred frogs in the water and each was seeking a mate. The water heaved and swirled in the turmoil of their urgent quest. Males embraced females in order to fertilise the eggs as they were laid in the water. Accepting her mate, the female laid her eggs — a mass of ova, tiny black pin-heads, some 2,000 in number, streaming in a dense black mass from her body within a period of five seconds.

The male, clasping his partner tightly with the rough nuptial pads on his hands, squirted his sperm over the eggs as they sank under the water. The jelly-like cover of each individual egg absorbed the water, and the whole large spongy mass floated back to the surface. Until the eggs hatched, the gelatinous cover would protect them and control their temperature.

Fascinated by the whole scene, Gael crouched in the shallow water, her light body supported by the soggy mat of rush clumps. She tilted her head to the plopping sounds as frogs dived from the floating vegetation into the water, and she saw the water spout into the air as they went under the surface to swim, thrusting a way with their long hind legs. She listened as some of the male frogs dryly croaked harsher notes above the general wail of voices.

Very soon there was a floating mass of jelly-like spawn in the water and frogs crawled and swam among it, struggled over floating weeds, and reared up in the water to show their light under-bellies. So much commotion was too much for Gael to ignore. She could no longer restrain her eagerness to join in the apparent fun, and she yapped an answer to the croaking chorus. Almost immediately, as she splashed out into the pond, the frogs disappeared, each diving for cover below the water surface.

Gael missed them all. Sinking into the mud, the water lapped almost over her back as she nosed the spawn, flicking her tongue over the jelly-like mass. She did not savour the taste and, floundering from the ooze with her golden beauty smeared in black mud, she returned to the hard bank of the pond.

She shook a muddy spray from her coat then flopped on the grass, a little bewildered at the sudden disappearance of the host of frogs. All that remained on the water was the bulbous mass of spawn, a partially transparent sponge-like clot of jelly containing the thousands of black dots from which the tadpoles would hatch within the fortnight.

For all the solid appearance of the mass, each egg was separate and wrapped in its own cover which was vitally important to the uniform rate of growth of each egg. The gelatinous casing (about eight to ten millimetres in diameter, and comprised almost entirely of water) around each black egg (only two to three millimetres in diameter itself) took in the radiation of the sunshine and maintained the egg at a higher temperature than the surrounding pond water.

The frogs at Scholey Pond laid their eggs in the shallow end so that they received the full benefit of the sun's rays. Gael also enjoyed the sunbeams on her back and, having shaken much of the muddy water from her fur, she rolled over and over on the bankside to dry herself. Not until she had ceased her antics and was dozing quietly in the sun's warmth did the frogs, bobbing up one at a time, return to the water's surface.

These frogs were of the family of *Ranidae*, within the order of *Salientia* of the amphibians, a group of cold-blooded, back-boned creatures which breathe through gills when young and through lungs when adult. In the same order, though of the family of *Bufonidae*, Gael knew the toads — and the newts of the *Caudata* order — which also bred in the pond. They were the common amphibians of the area.

In days gone by amphibians had made perhaps the first step in the progress of vertebrate creatures when they had left the water to become the first back-boned creatures to use their legs ashore and to develop lungs. Since then they had

Related, but with a drier skin than a frog, the toad was more likely to be seen out of the water.

progressed little, and others had developed more rapidly, including the family of *Canidae*, the dogs, to which Gael belonged. Her ancestors, mammals of the order of *Carnivora*, had outstripped the amphibians in mobility and wisdom.

From the eggs which the frogs laid in the pond, tiny gilled tadpoles, bearing no resemblance whatsoever to their parents, would emerge within two weeks. Over a period of 12 weeks of strengthening sun those tadpoles would grow into miniature frogs, feeding on the algae and vegetable matter in the pond before turning to more substantial animal food, and even cannibalising their own kind.

A great number of tadpoles would never reach maturity. Helpless, particularly in the early stages when they could only cling to the leaves of water weeds by what could be termed adhesive suckers, for their mouths are not then formed, the black tadpoles provided food for all the stronger creatures living in and by the pond — the newts and water-beetles in the water, and the mallard ducks and other birds which visited the pond. *Aeshna juncea*, the nymph of the dragon-fly, was the terror of the pond, a 40-millimetre long, plump, dark brown creature with strong nipper-jaws which crushed the tadpoles to death.

The tadpoles which survived would change from fish-like water breathers to air-breathing creatures in around 12 weeks, but their growth was very dependent upon food supply and water temperature.

'Kaak-kaak-kaak,' called Corbie, the crow, to Gael as he flew over the pond; and a skylark, singing a song of joy, climbed towards the black bird through the warm air. Alauda, the male skylark, had won his mate, and his song was for her alone. She listened with love as she explored the bank by the pond in search of a suitable nest home.

Gael dozed, but was alert to all the sounds, her raised ears, their feathery tufts blown by the breeze, moving to identify and place each individual voice. She lifted her head with new interest when a stranger flew across the hillside to perch on the top of the stone wall. It was Chacka, the wheatear, resplendent in his clean-cut feathers of clear grey, buff and white, and bobbing his black-tipped tail in convulsive jerks. He was glad to be home again on the Pennine hill after a journey which had started in tropical Africa.

Seeing Gael, Chacka 'chacked' his welcome notes and bowed and curtsied to her. Chacka had left the lion lands of savanna and scrub by Lake Victoria in central Africa the previous month. He had flown up the Nile Valley to cross the Mediterranean into Italy. Keeping to the shelter of the valleys, he had crossed the Alps into France. When he flew over the waters of the Channel to land on the English coast he had made a journey of around 6,000 miles.

Rested, he made his way northwards to join Gael on the Pennine hillside. Gael leaped to her feet, anxious to make closer acquaintance with the dapper stranger. Her movement frightened Chacka and he flew away, calling 'weet-chack-chack' over the pond so that some of the frogs dived for cover.

Gael ran away to the woodland clough. Nosing into the undergrowth of spiny bramble and dusty bracken, she was surprised when a hare broke cover. With a spurt of ground dirt and bracken powder, the big brown hare leaped past her and fled for the open ground beyond the trees. Big hind pads overlapping its forepaws to grip the slippery grass, it bounded away at speed, its long ears flattened to stream its line.

Gael, starting the chase late to follow the hare, was watched by Feeka, the female kestrel. Feeka was perched on an upright branch. One foot above the other, she clung to the topmost bough of a sycamore on the woodland fringe. She balanced the bough, as it swayed under her weight, by stretching her wings. Her keen, yellow-rimmed eyes followed Gael across a rough patch of grassland which, being the home of many voles, was one of her hunting grounds. She saw a tortoiseshell butterfly go dancing across the grass tops in the warm sunshine.

Gael did not chase for long. She was out-distanced on her slow start, and as Feeka left her perch to flap up into the blue sky, the collie turned aside to follow a low-flying blackbird in a similarly hopeless chase. But all her chasing was in fun. Feeka soared into the air, able to ride with outstretched wings and fanned tail on the heat waves rising from the woodland for the first time that spring. At mid-day the sun was the hottest it had been all year and its beams pierced the intricate tracery of the leafless trees to warm the vegetation on the woodland floor. Gael chased after the blackbird, and when it sought shelter in the green gloom of a

The dashing moustache, cruel beak, and pools of light which mirror the world in minute detail. Feeka, the kestrel.

prickly holly bush, where its nest structure was almost completed, she raced on to the lower end of the clough where the air was warm and still. There was no breeze, and wild daffodils opened their yellow trumpets to the heat of the sun on the bank of the river in the wooded valley of Brockholes into which the stream from Rack Clough ran.

Gael trod deep, clear imprints with her small pads in soft mud before splashing into the cool, clear water. Her coming scared away a white-breasted dipper. It bobbed once to her before whirring away up the clough on short, strong wings. Gael lapped the water, shook a rainbow spray from her coat and, regaining the bank, crossed a yellow carpet of bright celandine flowers on her way to the rabbit warren among the rhododendrons. Five yards away a white-speckled pattern of wood-anemones changed the carpet colour, and beyond, on the drier sandy bank, leafless coltsfoot bloomed with a splash or orange.

Gael rummaged among the green bluebell spears and frightened a wood-pigeon which went wing-flapping up to the branch of a tall elm tree. Gael lifted a forepaw and stretched her nose for scent. Her ears lifted to the buzz of a bee which was foraging among the pink flowers of the elm tree.

Although scent hung sluggishly on the warm air, the noises of the woodland were clear and distinct. Gael settled in the sun's warmth, and listened. A slate-

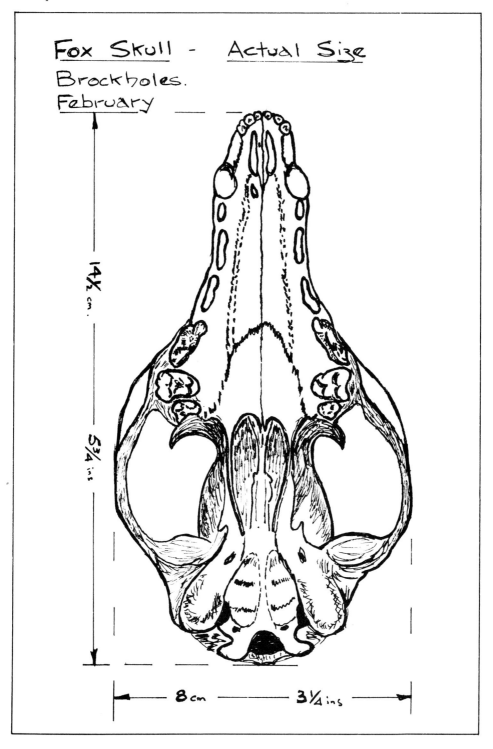

Fox Skull - Actual Size
Brockholes.
February

14½ cm.

5¾ ins

8 cm

3¼ ins

grey dunnock, trimly feathered as ever, sang high-pitched notes from a perch in the hawthorn bush; a cock chaffinch, the sunlight reflecting the brightness of its pink breast, sang a lilting, rollicking song from the nearby beech tree; and Ruddock, the cock robin, perched in full view on a riverside post, added his fine, sweet song while his mate filled a bankside depression with the leaves of her nest foundation.

Cigar-shaped buds were swelling on the twigs of the beech tree from which a starling, throat distended, mimicked the mellow notes of a blackbird; and high in the top of a sycamore, a song-thrush repeated its loud clear notes so that none should miss its message of joy.

Gael sought a plaything. This she often did when the wild creatures were about their own business, and she found many in the course of her wanderings over the farmland. Sticks, the skulls and bones of dead creatures, water-rounded stones which would roll down the bankside, all became her toys. Stone had fascinated her ever since she had been a tiny puppy, and she had lost her puppy-teeth on stone — her favourite piece in the garden rockery was scored with her teeth marks.

The mineral taste pleased her, and she was forever testing the strength of her now mature white teeth on the rocks and pebbles which she came across on her travels. From the riverside she mouthed a piece of gritstone and held it between her forepaws. She bit and chewed at the dark rock, making such a harsh grating sound that Pyat, the magpie, flew down from the sycamore tree to see what he was missing.

The magpie had become accustomed to Gael's regular presence in the woodland and he treated her as one of the residents albeit, like all the others, as one to be exploited if ever the opportunity arose. Perhaps she had found a bone from some dead animal which he had overlooked? He hopped to within two yards of the dog, holding his fine black tail clear of the ground, his eyes glinting with mischief. He was sprightly and confident.

Pyat's confidence disappeared quickly when Gael left the stone and ran towards him. Wings flailing for a grip on the air, his arrogance went as he retreated in scattered confusion. He clutched the lowest branch of the sycamore tree, almost over-balancing in his unseemly haste, and poured out his usual flow of bad language. Gael watched him go, her ears cocked to his angry voice. She yapped, and wagged her tail. Her mouth opened and she gave the magpie a superior doggy smile.

Chapter 4

Sheepwise

Gael meets Tup Lamb, and in accomplishing her first practical test of shepherding, learns something of the maternal instinct of sheep when she has to outwit a ewe to save another lamb from a gruesome fate.

The first lambs were born on the high pastures in the first days of April when the hill was the most inhospitable place in the world. After three weeks of warm promising sunshine, the rains fell continuously for days and the wind turned cold. Ewes sheltered under the protection of the grey stone walls to bear their lambs and they shielded their newborn with their own bodies. Water poured from dark skies to soak the wool of the sheep, flood vole tunnels, puddle the

Gael goes round the hill-hoggs on Scholey Hill grazings.

Above *A hour old—a Lonk lamb is a sturdy youngster born in the shelter of the stone wall.*

Below *The first lambs were born on the high pastures in the early days of April. Looking over the town of Burnley—and the distant outline of Pendle Hill.*

hollow places, and turn the stream in Rack Clough into a leaping white torrent.

Gael was fascinated with the newcomers on the hill. The helpless, trusting nature of the white-fleeced babies as they tottered on shaky legs by their mothers' sides enthralled her — though she soon learned that mother-love from the hitherto trusting ewes could be a rough experience when she came too close to their babies.

It was during the lambing that Gael's usual freedom on the hill was somewhat curtailed, for, it being her first lambing, she was still learning the ways of sheep and her visits were disciplined so that the ewes were not unnecessarily disturbed. However, with the weather so wet in the early days, visits to the hill were frequent, for many a newborn lamb needed the extra nourishment and treatment of the medicine satchel in order to counteract the damp cold.

Although constant rain brought poor lambing conditions, the ewes were able to keep dry. They sent the water spraying from their bodies with a good shake of their fleece, and the rain rarely penetrated the dense undercoats. The lambs, with their thin, curly-woolled coats, were not so well clad, for constant soakings and the wet cold sapped their strength and spirit. Constant shepherding was the only way to see that each newborn lamb and its mother had every chance of survival,

Gael slips through the cripple-hole in the wall.

so that even when the rains ceased and the sun shone, visits to the hill were often and regular.

It was on one such visit in the sunshine of Easter Day that Gael met Tup Lamb. He was white curly-woolled, and his big ears stood out from his head like butterfly's wings. His face was black and white in the true tradition of his illustrious Lonk pedigree. He had shiny-black slotted feet, and two jet-black patches on the knee-caps of his white forelegs. When he bleated, his tongue was pink in a toothless mouth, for he was only three hours old. He was well bred and strong, 15 inches tall at the shoulder — the same size as Gael who was now fully grown and a handsome golden animal.

Gael met Tup Lamb when she trotted through the cripple-hole in the stone wall on her way to Scholey Pond. (Cripple-holes are openings left in the walls to enable sheep to pass from field to field.) The lamb bleated a pitiful welcome for his mother had wandered off across the hillside and he was lonely. A young shearling ewe whose first baby he was, she was grazing some 300 yards away near to where a lapwing covered two eggs on her ground nest.

The ewe was unaccustomed to the ties of parenthood, and felt no kinship for the woolly baby she had mothered. But Tup Lamb's querulous and persistent bleating, as he nosed up towards Gael's warm body — whilst she in turn joyfully welcomed a willing friend — awakened the dormant mothering instinct in the sheep. She lifted her head and listened. Suddenly realising that her firstborn was calling for her, she answered the call and ran towards the lamb.

Gael was enjoying the friendship of Tup Lamb, if a little surprised that he was allowed to be so friendly, for recent experience had taught her that the lambs were protected by bad-tempered parents who made no secret of their dislike for interfering collies. She touched noses with Tup Lamb and sniffed his warm scent, and thoroughly enjoyed an unexpected friendship although she was a little embarrassed at the lamb's efforts to nuzzle close to her.

So the mother ewe found Tup Lamb and Gael together. Angry, she lowered her head and stamped the ground with her forefoot. She called to her lamb, and it ran to seek her milk. Gael, recognising the signs of parental disapproval, dodged back through the cripple-hole in the wall, leaving the ewe to be with her lamb.

Unwittingly, Gael had completed her first practical test of shepherding in mothering the lamb. It was an old and tested trick of a shepherd to instruct his dog to threaten a rejected lamb so as to awaken the protective and mothering instinct in a wayward ewe.

Gael learned other tricks during those April days of the lambing on the hill. By the pondside she met a lamb which wore a coat. One of twins, it had been taken from its own mother and fostered on to another ewe which had lost its lamb, so that it would get a full supply of milk to grow strong. The coat it wore was the skin of its foster-mother's own dead lamb and, as ewes recognise their lambs by scent, it had been adopted quickly by the ewe as having the correct smell. This was another simple ruse of the shepherd to enable a bereft ewe to take on another baby.

Hill ewes on rough pasture are better suited to raising one strong lamb and

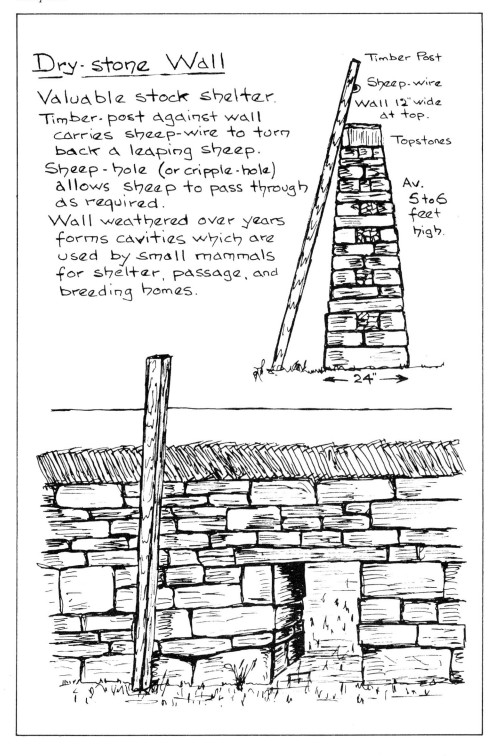

Dry-stone Wall

Valuable stock shelter.

Timber-post against wall carries sheep-wire to turn back a leaping sheep.

Sheep-hole (or cripple-hole) allows sheep to pass through as required.

Wall weathered over years forms cavities which are used by small mammals for shelter, passage, and breeding homes.

Timber Post

Sheep-wire

Wall 12" wide at top.

Topstones

Av. 5 to 6 feet high.

← 24" →

most farmers are content if each lamb has the advantage of a full milk supply. Twins are often born, however, and the ewes are of a quality to cope. They have been selectively bred over many years to a pattern that retains into the breeding flock only the gimmer — or female — lambs which conform to the true Lonk characteristics of outstanding hardiness, adaptability and good motherhood.

These were type-stamped, solid, good-boned sheep, with a grey fleece which was thick and dense enough to withstand the rainstorms and snow blizzards of the Northern climes. Their Roman-nosed faces were marked black and white, as were their sturdy legs, and they could range over high moorland and find food where other sheep breeds would perish. They were a flock evolved from stringent breeding patterns and good management through generations. Any animals which did not come up to standard were culled. By this policy, faults were bred out and the desirable characteristics were retained to produce hill sheep which had to live throughout the year on high land in the worst of climates.

The purity of their Lonk attributes had been maintained, and they were true to a breed that was one of the oldest mountain types in the country. They were strong, compact, even, and firmly woolled sheep, and handsome in appearance with distinctive black and white horned heads and trim, stocky bodies. They were ideal sheep for the barren slopes and peat moors of East Lancashire.

The lambs which were born on the hillside in that first year of Gael's life would

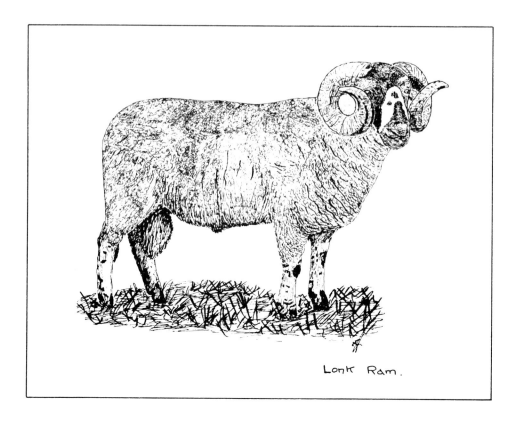

Lonk Ram.

SHEEP - AGE by TEETH.

"A sheep is as old as its teeth".

A sheep has molar (grinding) teeth in both jaws, but incisors (cutting) only in the lower jaw which bite against a hard pad in the upper jaw.

A lamb has 8 milk incisor teeth. oooooooo

At approx. 15 months, centre pair milk teeth replaced by permanent incisors - "two tooth" - oooOOoooo

At 21 months second pair change - ooOOOOoo

At 27 months third pair change - oOOOOOOo

At 3 years, the last change to full-mouthed - OOOOOOOO

Later (7.8 years) teeth loose and sheep is 'broken-mouthed'.

A sheep until weaned is a lamb (or until the end of the year of its birth).

Male terms - Ram. Tup. Heeder.

Female - Ewe. Gimmer. Theave. Chilver. Sheeder.

Castrated males are Wethers. Wedders.

Weaning to Shearing - Hogg. Hogget. Hoggerel. Teg. Pug.

After first Shearing - Shearling. Theave. Dinmont. Diamond.

Later - classified according to number of times shorn - Two-shear (sheep in its third year).
Three-shear. etc. etc.
Twinter is a two years old ewe.
Thrunter is a three years old ewe.

After fourth shearing usually Aged or Full-mouthed.

A ewe ceasing to give milk is a Barren, Yeld, or Eild ewe; and taken from the breeding flock she is a Draft ewe. Drafted (in milk) from the hill to the lowland, she will continue to lamb in easier conditions.

ensure the continuity and quality of the flock. Each year the best lambs were retained for the breeding flock, the remainder going to the butcher. They would be carefully selected and, when spained — weaned — from the parent ewes, would spend their first winter on the lower pastures to ensure a good and healthy start to their subsequent life on the hill. Hillmen never bred from the ewe lambs in their first year, preferring to give them the only pampering they would ever get in their lives by wintering them well.

The flock numbered 500 breeding ewes on the 2,000 acres of hill, and each year one third of the older ewes were replaced by the lambs. These ewes would have borne three crops of lambs by the time they were drafted from the hill, and sold to lowland farms where they would have another three or four lamb crops in easier climes and conditions.

An important part of each year's lambing was the breeding of top quality male lambs which would grow into ideal rams with big curly horns, strong limbs and aristocratic Roman-nosed heads, with inbred qualities to sire lambs true to the Lonk type.

Gael had come to know Lonk sheep from her first days on the Pennines, and as she grew in stature up to her first lambing season, in some small measure she played her part in their welfare. She learned that they were basically timid creatures, although inquisitive and enquiring, and that they were inclined to move fearfully away from interference, yet were transformed by motherhood into

Gael on hill—this photo shows walling and sheep-wires over the wall referred to in the sketch.

aggressive bravery. When with lambs at foot, even the mature collies were faced and often butted, though the stronger character of the dogs eventually prevailed.

Subject to sudden panics, the sheep were unpredictable, typical flock animals with moods spreading quickly from animal to animal. They felt safer en masse than as individuals and were thus more amenable to shepherding. But they were not stupid, and were able to find food on sparse, inhospitable hillsides where other farmstock would have perished from hunger.

There were days of warm sunshine when the sheep were able to leave the shelter of the walls and graze over the land, and the lambs were able to play together in groups. Lapwings and curlews dozed over their eggs, tadpoles swam in the warm shallows in Scholey Pond, and Silva, the vixen, played with her cubs in the woodland.

On those days it was hard to believe that the hill could be so fierce. On one such day, Ching, the reed-bunting, brought his mate, Nicas, to Scholey Pond. Gael was enjoying the warmth of the sun whilst stretched on the raised banking by the waterside. She was quietly peaceful, her nose resting on her white forepaws, her eyes closing dozily, when her ears pricked to the seeping calls of the buntings.

Ching clung to the upright stem of a pondside rush within 2 yards of the collie. Balancing on the swaying stem, one leg bent and gripping level with his breast, the other straight and rigid beneath it, he rode the pitching movement which his own weight caused. He was a handsome fellow, the sunbeams lighting on his jet-black cap and white collar, and Nicas, drably clothed by comparison in brown feathering, watched him with pride from her perch on the nearby wall top. She had already accepted his courtship, and come to the thickly-growing rushes to find a place to build their home. It was his smart appearance which attracted her, for his love song was poor, almost indifferent, with a weak, hissing finale.

Ching saw Gael, but as she was still lying quietly watching him, she was not to be feared. He saw the expanding circle of ripples spread, glinting, in the sunbeams over the pond water when a newt broke the mirrored surface to snatch a fly. He cocked his head to watch a wood-pigeon veer in flight when its timid eyes saw the golden form of Gael on the ground.

Nicas flew across to join her mate, but she, seeing Gael for the first time, swung away in mid-air calling 'chit-chit-chit' in sudden alarm. Ching followed her across the pond, taking a fly in his beak as he wing-bounded after her. Gael had not moved, other than having twitched her ears, and she dozed on.

Winter was still loath to relinquish a hold on the hill and, two days later, there was a white covering of frost on the ground. The early morning sunbeams were chasing it away when Gael rescued a lamb from a gruesome death. The youngster, a particularly good lamb, and the daughter of a ewe which had won show honours the previous year, had slipped into a crevice at the top of the hill pasture and was held fast between two rocks. It could neither move backwards nor forwards and its small, supple body was wedged, as though in a vice.

Sixty feet above, Kee, the kestrel, hovered, playing the wind over his feathers and peering down. Mirrored in the round dark pools of his eyes was the scene in every detail. He saw the trapped lamb, the parent ewe standing guard — and he watched Corbie, the carrion-crow, perched on the nearby wall top, and patiently waiting his opportunity to attack the lamb. The lamb was hopelessly vulnerable, and Corbie never missed an opportunity to prosper from some other creature's misfortune.

He had called to his mate, and when she arrived they could work together to outwit the guardian ewe. One could distract her whilst the other reached the lamb. They were adept at such cunning tricks, and had won food from other creatures in the same way. Carrion-crows and foxes were the natural predators on sickly — or defenceless — lambs in the sheep flock.

Gael was sniffing at the musk scent of stoat in the wall bottom when she heard a commotion of noise higher up the hillside. She lifted her head high and raised her ears to distinguish the sounds. The agitated bleating of a ewe, the less fulsome bleats of a lamb, were mingled with the raucous calls of Corbie, the black crow. Gael was interested.

She ran up the wallside for a hundred yards, stopping when she came within sight of the ewe. She lifted her left forepaw and stretched her nose to point, her almond eyes puzzled at what she saw. The ewe was running around the top of a narrow black cleft in the ground, running to the hole, bleating, turning away, then running towards the wall in most agitated manner. On top of the wall sat Corbie, bowing and calling 'kaak-kaak-kaak' to the ewe. His head was lowered, his strong black beak open, his whole attitude threatening as he plagued the ewe.

Gael was puzzled. She knew Corbie to be a dangerous and bad-tempered bird, but his present manner was frightening. Then, hearing the querulous bleats of a lamb coming from the hole in the ground, Gael reasoned the cause for the commotion. The ewe's lamb was trapped down the hole and Corbie was waiting his chance to attack the helpless youngster.

Immediately Gael ran forward to help the ewe — only to become a target for the ewe's wrath as it felt another danger threatening its baby. As the ewe swung on her, Gael side-stepped quickly to avoid her attack. Corbie flicked his wings in excitement and shouted further abuse. Was this his chance to attack the lamb whilst its mother was distracted? But Gael was to prevent such an attack.

To avoid the onrushes of the ewe, she leapt for the wall top. There was a flurry of black feathers and golden fur in the sunlight; a confusion of noise, the guttural squawks of the crow, and the annoyed barks of the collie. Corbie fell from the wall, his wings beating frantically to lift him up into the air before he could hit the ground. Gael missed her footing in the excitement and tumbled down the opposite side of the wall.

The ewe looked around in confusion when both bird and dog disappeared from her sight. Trapped in the hole which had been excavated by a vixen the year previously, the lamb called for its mother. From above, Kee, the kestrel, watched the enactment of the drama with interest. Corbie was an old enemy, and it pleased the hawk to see him routed.

Gael was not hurt by her tumble and she jumped to her feet, looking around for the crow. Seeing him flapping angrily into the air, she barked her derision at his retreat. Corbie was furious. He had been baulked of a possible feast, and

Gael with hill-hoggs on Scholey Hill grazings.

furthermore, his ego — he prided himself on being master of the hill — had been shattered by the collie's intervention. Seeing Kee, he swung round at the hawk. Here was a chance to vent his feelings and reassert his authority. Kee tilted his wings, slipped easily away from the crow's blundering attack, and climbed rapidly into the sky. Corbie knew his defeat, called a bad-tempered 'kaak-kaak-kaak', and when his mate flew to join him over the hill, he shouted his wrath at her.

Gael completed her rescue act by jumping back to the wall top and barking so insistently and loudly that I went across the field to see what was upsetting her. Lifted from its prison, the lamb ran to its mother, sought her udder, and wrinkled its tail happily in feeding. 'Good Gael', I said, and she wagged her tail in accord. All was well again on the hill.

Chapter 5

Inhospitable night

Gael finds a practical use for her keen sense of smell, and an injury forces her to spend a lonesome night amid the snow-covered wastes of the hill.

Hill sheep are vital to the economy of the Pennines, for they alone can turn the bleak upland acres into viable farming enterprise. Living among hill sheep, Gael developed into an intelligent and capable little collie, coming to know their moods and their ways, and playing her part in their welfare. It was during the following winter that she really earned her 'spurs', when she was found to possess a particular knack, coupled with a good sense of smell, of finding sheep which had been overblown with snow.

For over a week, snow blizzards raged across the land, trapping and covering many sheep when they sought the shelter of the dry-stone wall bordering the lower side of the moor. Most of the flock had been turned from the hill to the lower ground in the first days of storm, but not all had left the moor in the wild snow showers, and they sought their own salvation. They were tough enough to live in the open, but when they sought shelter against the wall, from the wind-driven flakes, they became trapped by the settling snow. In this icy trap they had been known to survive for three weeks, occasionally longer, but lack of food and loss of condition would finally kill them.

It was Gael's nose and her powers of scent which saved many sheep that winter. Gifted with a keenness of scent which was exceptionally reliable, she became indispensable in the task of locating the buried sheep, for the human method of finding buried sheep is the most back-breaking and soul-destroying task in the world. A forbidding task in the freezing cold of a white wilderness, the only way is to inspect physically, with a sense of utter frustration, the snow drifts piled against miles of stone walls.

The plan of seeking buried sheep is to walk slowly along the hard, piled drifts, prodding the deep snow at intervals with a shepherd's crook or pole in the hope of finding soft resistance — a sheep's body. Signs of air holes, caused by the ascending breath of the entombed animals, are sought, and melted snow from the heat of the sheep's body searched for.

Almost accidentally — or so it seemed at the time — Gael found the first sheep by snorting breath from her twitching nostrils into the cold snow mass over a tiny hole in the drift. She yapped her excitement at the warm taste of sheep scent, and

Gael with Eric Halsall in a blizzard on Scholey Hill.

Gael with Eric Halsall in a blizzard on Scholey Hill.

a probe from my crook confirmed her success. Dug from its icy prison, a Lonk ewe shook the loose snow from its fleece, stamped a forepaw at its rescuer, bleated, and trotted away down the hill to join the flock on the lower land.

Gael then scented another sheep — and another — and during that first day of search, she located 13 animals trapped under the snow, all living in igloo-like caves thawed out by their warm bodies under the snow. A still-frozen layer above prevented the roofs of the caves from collapsing, and air filtered through tiny holes in the snow and down between the stones of the wall. The sheep fed on the grass beneath them, and if with companions, even chewed at each other's wool. Gael pointed out sheep which were trapped three feet below the snow.

It was during the rescue operations of that time that Gael spent a night on the snow-covered moor. Unnoticed at the end of the day by the tired group of men and dogs, and as adventurous as always, she wandered down to the banks of one of the streams which drained off the hill. She scrambled over a wall by the stream, and yelped with pain as a big stone fell from the wall top and struck her forepaw. Loosened from its seating by the ice, snow and wind, the stone tumbled with her as she brushed against it. It trapped her paw to the hard ground before rolling clear to crunch into the deep covering of snow.

Cold and inhospitable in winter, Rack Clough was icy and rush-grown.

Hurt, Gael lay in the shelter of the wall and licked blood from the cut on her bruised foot. The sting of pain eased with the solace of her damp tongue over the white-furred paw. She rested, lolling the tension from her lungs through her open mouth. She rested in snow six inches deep, surrounded by a bleak white wilderness of high Pennine moorland. Snow flakes, individually dainty in that place of rugged grandeur, flurried to settle on her golden fur.

Unseen, Gael lay in a highland basin surrounded by the white hills. She was alone and injured. Frozen over, a narrow stream ran beside her to feed a large reservoir lower down the valley. So keen was the frost that the water in the stream and reservoir moved under a covering of ice. A blown white snowstorm hid the highest tops of the hills, and all creatures sought shelter.

As always, the wind, which even in the wall shelter whipped at Gael's ear-tufts, ruled over the bleak inhospitable land. This wind was ever-present on these open Pennine hills, and only did its strength and voice vary with the seasons; in summer, to a cold freshening breeze which whispered loneliness to the dancing bents and cotton-grass flowers; on that mid-winter day, coldly bitter in its touch and screaming mournfully of its power as it tossed the helpless snowflakes across the moor.

Gael licked the pain and blood from her injured paw, but she could not bear to put her weight on it. When she stood, it was on three legs. Limping, she walked from the shelter of the wall into the buffeting snowstorm. Wherever she could, she kept to a wind-blown route, or to the snow-trodden sheep tracks across the moor.

When she had to cross snow, it was slow and hard going. Whipped by the wind, she moved gently, her claws extended for grip, and her tail rigid for balance, so as not to break through the frozen upper crust of snow. She stretched forward to cover the ground with every step, but the action of partially carrying her injured foot gave more weight to her useful forepaw, and too often she floundered up to her chest in the snow. She faced a constant bombardment of ice particles which the wind whirled across the snowfield, and her sable fur was coated white. Born to the hills, she was not distressed, only impeded from a speedier journey.

She hobbled close to a brown-feathered meadow-pipit which crouched for shelter among the snowy hags. Failing to find sufficient food, weak from the mis-timed blow of a hunting merlin, and poorly from the cold of the last two nights, it would sleep unto death in the cold of the coming night.

A hungry hill stoat, intent on stalking the line of a grouse which crouched in the shelter of the hags, was surprised when Gael suddenly appeared out of the swirling snowstorm. It spat at her in annoyance and chakkered in defiance, but darted for the safety of a narrow peat runnel. The grouse, its senses alerted to the danger, burst from cover, frightened by the sudden movement and noise but a few yards away. Saved by Gael's timely appearance, it flew with the wind, sweeping on down-curved wings over the white moor and calling 'go-back-go-back' into the snowstorm. Gael faltered on her way.

When the snow shower ceased, she had reached the shelter of a woodland of stunted conifers which grew on the sloping bank of the reservoir. A female hen-harrier peered boldly at the little collie from its perch on the bough of one of the conifers. Gael sensed its presence and stopped, lifting her injured forepaw in a pointing stance, her nose questing for the scents in the air.

The bird watched her, staring unblinking with its brown-ringed eyes set liquid in the bold facial disc. Wings loosely held to steady itself in the wind, black talons gripping the bough of the tree, it did not take immediate flight, but when Gael moved closer it spread warm brown wings to a 30-inch span and sprang on to the wind.

Gael listened to the play of its wings on the air currents when it climbed up above the conifers. Her cocked ears lined to the sound. She settled down on the snow-covered ground, puzzled and alert at her meeting with the big hawk, a strange winter visitor to her land. The wind, whistling its song of loneliness through the trees, tossed her silky fur, patterning the hairs of her back to a fine knife-edge, probing into her thick, warm undercoat.

Overhead, the harrier, named Snecchen on account of its long snatching legs, sported with the wind, soaring in pleasure, its graceful wings canted upwards, flight-tips spread in buoyant and easy flight. Banking to turn, its broad, barred tail spread as a rudder, it glided down over the hillside. A party of reed-buntings skulked into the trees as the winged predator lazily beat the air above.

Gael heard their anxious alarm calls as the harrier swept low over the trees, its narrow-winged form silhouetted against the grey sky. It swerved, leisurely from side to side, calling a soft 'hek-hek', then turning, it floated back to quarter, closely and carefully, the white ground below. The reed-buntings were terrified into hiding in the trees, and their voices silenced.

Over Gael's couch, the harrier hovered to watch her. It was puzzled at the dog's presence and called a chattering cry of annoyance. Equally startled and puzzled, Gael jumped to her feet and barked defiance at the great hawk. The harrier careened gracefully aside, and went soaring from sight over the hill top. Gael settled when the bird had gone. She heard again the whisperings of the reed-buntings. There was relief in their voices at the harrier's departure.

Gael lay on the ground, sheltered from the wind by a drift of snow, her ears pricked to the talk of the buntings. The light began to leave the sky, the snow clouds were blown away and, over the cold hills, stars began to twinkle. Jack Frost was coming to hold the land in his icy grip. Soon his probing fingers reached where the wind-blown snow had failed to touch, and mere wind shelter was not enough for the wild creatures. The reed-buntings flew to shelter down into the valley where they crouched with feathers puffed for warmth. A tiny gold-crest crept into a niche in a wind-torn fir tree, and six jenny-wrens huddled together in a domed nest hung from the bank of the reservoir overflow at the bottom end of the plantation.

Whilst Gael was listening and watching, and resting between the trees, a white-furred stoat ran by. Its coat of ermine had not completely coloured white, and a chestnut head and back-saddle made it skewbald. It passed within two yards of Gael, its quick body weaving over the snow, but it did not see her, and was gone

Trogo,
the wren.

in a flash. The moon rose bright in the frosty sky, and Gael was some way from her home in the valley.

In her disabled condition and in the slowing ground conditions of the deep snow, Gael reasoned that the journey would take her too long, for she was over-tired with her three-legged hobbling. She decided to seek shelter in the woodland. She knew of a fox's den among the trees which had been deserted ever since a vixen and her cubs had been killed during lambing time. Holed up in there she would be dry and sheltered for the night.

When the brown owl flew on broad, soft wings between the trees in grey darkness, Gael was curled in a dry cave under the roots of one of the tallest of the fir trees in the centre of the woodland. The tawny-owl was a stranger to the plantation (its usual haunt was the oak and birch woodland on the lower land), but the search for food in the snow-covered wastes had widened its range. It flew away hungry, for the voles and mice of the highland kept to their tunnels and ran beneath the snow. They ran into Gael's cave, and fled back up their tunnels in fright when they smelled her, squeaking their terror of the stranger.

Gael lay warm, with her tail over her nose, asleep with that animal watchfulness which instinctively pricked her ears to the sounds of the night. Once they twitched to the bark of a fox. Over in the quarried area which had provided the stone for the reservoir construction, a big dog-fox barked once to the moon which hung, white and cold over the wilderness of snow.

The fox stood at the entrance to a den in a slit between two rock slabs in the quarry wall and shook itself like a dog. It had just awakened to the call of the hunting owl. Its nostrils opened wide, it tested the thin air. Listening to the sounds of the darkness, it heard the unsettled squawks of two gulls perched cold on the ice in the centre of the reservoir. The bark of a dog at one of the distant farmsteads caused it to raise the short red hairs on the nape of its neck.

When the hunting owl opened its beak in a cry of triumph at finally snatching a careless vole from the floor of the valley woodland, the fox started the hunt for its own food. Padding through the deep snow with its white-tipped brush carried clean, it left the stone quarry. Silent in stealthy tread, so that its movements over the snow were wraith-like, it ran to the side of the reservoir and bit at the ice for water. The cover was too thick to break, and it licked at the ice, lifting its head between each taste to listen for sound. Food was not easy to come by in the cold night, and the fox was feeling hungry after two nights of lean hunting.

A crowd of black-headed gulls was roosting on the ice, but too far from the bank to tempt the fox to risk passage over the doubtful cover. Movement could not be controlled to stalking skill over the slippery surface — and gulls were not that nice to eat. It turned towards a large pond in the centre of the conifer plantation in the valley below the reservoir. Moorhens roosted in the reeds, and the water-bailiff's ducks slept in semi-wildness, and here the fox had killed on previous occasion. It slunk under the low-branched trees where a goldfinch fell in its path, dead from the sharpening cold. Snatching the small corpse for food, the fox looked up for more, but the rest of the golden-feathered birds were hunched together above its reach.

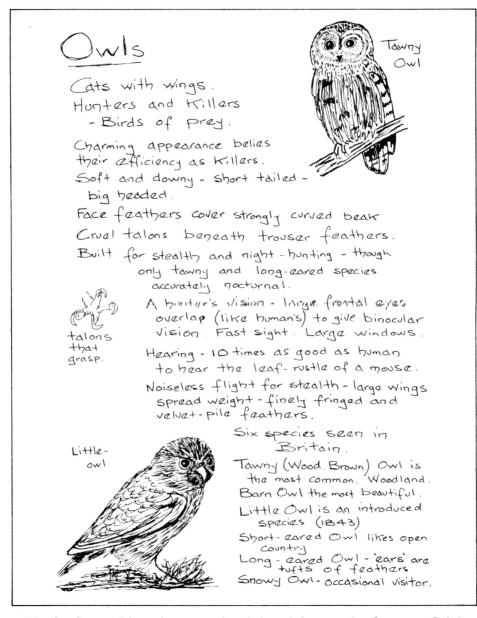

Owls

Tawny Owl

Cats with wings.
Hunters and killers
   - Birds of prey.

Charming appearance belies
their efficiency as killers.
Soft and downy - short tailed -
   big headed.
Face feathers cover strongly curved beak
Cruel talons beneath trouser feathers.
Built for stealth and night-hunting - though
   only tawny and long-eared species
   accurately nocturnal.

talons that grasp.

A hunter's vision - large frontal eyes
   overlap (like human's) to give binocular
   vision. Fast sight. Large windows.
Hearing - 10 times as good as human
   to hear the leaf-rustle of a mouse.
Noiseless flight for stealth - large wings
spread weight - finely fringed and
velvet-pile feathers.

Little-owl

Six species seen in
   Britain.
Tawny (Wood. Brown) Owl is
   the most common. Woodland.
Barn Owl the most beautiful.
Little Owl is an introduced
   species (1843)
Short-eared Owl likes open
   country
Long-eared Owl - 'ears' are
   tufts of feathers
Snowy Owl - occasional visitor.

The fox flattened into the snow when it heard the squeals of two rats fighting over the old, meatless carcase of a duck on the pondside. It belly-crawled towards the sound, but the rats took its scent in time to scutter to safety. A new scent crossed the fox's nose, a thin bird scent which thrilled it. Roosting low in a leaning alder over the ice-covered pond, a moorhen huddled, feathers puffed and senses dulled by the bitter cold. It lurched forward and twitched in an instinctive attempt at flight as the fox's teeth sank into its soft body, but it died almost instantly without knowing why. Hunger satisfied, the fox loped off on a prowl of the farm poultry-cabins in the valley, though its need was no longer urgent.

Gael awakened to a cold, grey dawn. Seen through the cave opening, the trunks of nearby trees were silhouetted black against the half-light. Tiny icicles hung from the roof of her shelter, and the silence was intense. Her damaged paw was covered with congealed blood, but the pain of the blow had gone. She licked the blood away, and lingered, in no hurry. She dozed again, and she did not stir until the morning was full, and the sun rose bright over the white countryside. Then she uncurled her warm body. Standing, she stretched her limbs, first her forelegs together, then each hind-leg in turn, her mouth opening in a wide yawn which dispelled drowsiness.

She walked into the open, and rolled in the crisp snow. Lying on her back, she rolled and rolled, enjoying the cold softness of the snow cushion. She heard the bugling of geese in the sky, and watched through a gap in the tree roof as a skein of seven pink-foots flew with slow wing-flaps high above her. As she watched, they changed the leadership of their chevron formation.

Refreshed, and able to take weight on her damaged foot again, Gael ran across the snow between the trees. She followed a path to the lowland which sheep's hooves had pressed flat and hard, and crossed and re-crossed the prints of magpies, crows, rabbits, stoats and the fox she had heard in the night.

On the open fields, the wind whirled fine powdery ice-flakes over the surface of the settled snow, and Gael's face and eyebrows became brushed white with snow, and her golden coat covered in a white wrap. She shook the snow clear in a shower of spray, and lay down to bite snowballs from the feathering of her legs and from between her toes. The brightness of the sun on the endless whiteness dazzled her eyes. She squeezed under a fence into a woodland clough. Finding the cast horn of a sheep, she tossed it in play, and two tiny blue-tits, their colouring bejewelled by the sunbeams, chided her frivolity. They found no pleasure in the snowfall as they searched every cranny of the hawthorn hedge for food.

Ruddock, the red-breasted robin, statuesque on a perch in an oak tree, agreed with the blue-tits, and called his displeasure at Gael's boisterous appearance. Having registered his complaint, Ruddock ignored the dog and flew down to the base of the tree trunk to scatter snow and peck at a mossy growth. Gael cocked her head to watch. She knew Ruddock, for it was he who usually greeted her visits to the woodland.

She sank into the snow, pricked her ears, and watched with interest for she welcomed familiar company in the quiet white world. Ruddock flitted round the trunk of the oak tree, picking his beak into the bark, then he flew up to the lowest bough of the tree. There he perched, puffed out his feathers to a round ball of insulation against the cold, and peered with dark, shining eyes down at Gael.

Gael continued her journey towards home. She arrived to a warm welcome, and when she held her paw up for inspection, she received the sort of fussy treatment and sympathy that she loved. She had, quite naturally, been missed when she failed to turn up on the previous evening, but she was deemed capable of looking after herself for at least one night on the hill.

Chapter 6

Strange friendship

Born blind and helpless in the dim world of her nursery sett beneath the woodland floor, Jena grows from an inquisitive cub to an enquiring young badger, and makes a strange friendship.

Jena, the baby badger, was born in the nursery sett in Brockholes Wood whilst the snow still covered the land and Gael was busy with her rescue work with the sheep on the hill. Jena was the second-born of a litter of three cubs and she was only five inches long and blind at her birth. She snuggled close with her two brothers, pushing her little black nose into their sparse fur, and she was warm and dry on a soft bed of grasses in the semi-darkness of her home, six feet below the snow-covered woodland floor.

Her mother, Zana, cared well for the family and, during their blind helplessness, suckled and nursed them with constant devotion. Whilst they suckled, she spoke to them in a low mewing voice, telling of her love for them and of the pleasure they gave her. It was a voice which Jena knew as the mother who would shelter and protect her whatever happened and, utterly secure, she dozed in the warmth of this affection.

However, Jena mewed in complaint when her mother washed her with her tongue. Badgers are the cleanest of creatures and Zana was true to her tribe. Never was the nursery allowed to get fouled; what she could not carry away to disposal, she ate. She constantly groomed the cubs, licking any soiling from the light grey hairs on their backs and from their soft pink-skinned tummies. She caressed them with a gentle tongue, and curled her body round to warm them.

Jena mewed when hungry, scratching with her clawed feet and snuffling her nose at Zana's body to find the milk teats. Not for long at any one time did Zana leave the cubs, uneasy to be away from the sett for any period of time. Her own feeding trips were short, but she never neglected to eat well, for her own health and the sustenance of her milk supply was vital to the strong growth of her cubs. Much of her food was earthworms, and these she obtained quickly by digging below the grass of the adjoining pastureland when patches of the snow had melted clear. When thirsty, she hurried down the direct track to the riverside, gulped her fill, and ran back to the nursery, printing the snow with her five-toed marks.

When it was bitterly cold outside the sett and snow blew to pile around the

Badger (Meles meles)

Male: Boar. Female: Sow. Young: Cub.
Home is underground sett.
Extensive system of tunnels.
Sleeping chambers: Nursery chambers
Bedding - Bracken. Grass. Leaves.
Regularly changed: Clean animal.
Personally clean. Grooms coat.
Digs latrines.

Of ancient origin. Nocturnal.
Very wary and secretive.
Active. Good senses of smell & hearing.
Eyesight not good.

Single litter of cubs. Av. 3. Born January - April.
Subject to delayed implantation.
Approx. nine months - two months gestation.
Cubs born blind. 5" long. greyish-white colour.
Eyes open around 10 days. Markings gradual.
Underground about 8 weeks. Weaned 3 months +
Learn quickly - forage - remain with family until
autumn - through winter - Great community livers.
Like to sleep - but not true hibernation.
Adults growl or bark a warning - Purr pleasure
Cubs excitable - high pitched voice - squeal.

R. Hind

A 'little bear' in appearance — weasel family.
2½ - 3 feet long.
12" high shoulder.

Sexes similar.
Sow sleeker.
Short legs.

Eyes small.
Ears Short.
Musk glands.

L Fore
L Hind
Overprint

Rough hairs
General colouring Grey

Strong jaws.
Striking black and white face.
Flexible Snout.

Large Pads 5 Toes.

Stumpy Tail.

R. Hind

entrance, none of the badgers ventured into the woodland. They carried winter fat on their bodies which enabled them to do without food for quite a long time. Jena's mother, however, preferred fresh food to freshen her milk so that her litter grew strong — although there were days when even she could not find food in the snowstorms.

Missing her company, her mate, Jan, joined another boar and together, when the snow became soft and started to melt away before the warmer air, they roamed and played in the woodland at night. Jan knew that Zana was busy with his family, but she was jealous of his interference, and he was content to listen to the snufflings and gruntings of his sons and daughter from an adjoining chamber in the sett.

When her eyes began to open on the tenth day of her life, Jena dimly saw her mother for the first time. Her gentle blue eyes followed every move of her parent in the glimmers of light which reached the nursery chamber. Zana was a handsome sow, two years old, strong and clean, and comely in the eyes of every boar in the woodland. Even with the responsibilities of her family, she never failed to attend to her own toilet, grooming her coarse grey fur to a tidy sheen with her strong claws so that each black-tipped hair lay neatly in place.

The distinctive black stripes on her face were even and symmetrical, contrasting sharply to the white hairs around them. It was by these sharply defined markings that Jena came to recognise her mother. Zana's ears were coquettishly flopped and tipped with white, her legs sooty with shiny, black claws, and her tail short and broad. She had no blemish or scar, for she was friendly and amicable with all her kin. Well-grown and lithe in movement, she weighed around 23 pounds and was 34 inches long, a handsome member of her tribe.

Only when her eyes opened did Jena move from the warmth of the tightly-curled bundle of her brothers' bodies. Waddling on her wobbly legs around her home, she poked her tiny nose into the couch of grasses, against the earth walls, and into the long hairs of her mother's coat. She found a tree-root growing into the corner of the chamber, and bit and tugged at it with her milk-teeth. Her nose and ears told her more than her eyes of the limited world around, for her sight was slow in strengthening to distinct lines, and would never be really good, although it was better than the general badger-range, so that she began to seek the light more than her kin.

The greatest pleasure of her babyhood was to lie in the half-light at the entrance to the nursery chamber, and wrinkle her nostrils and turn her ears to the smells and noises that drifted down the tunnel. The mysteries of the world above, into which her mother would disappear from time to time, fascinated the little badger.

She nosed the scent of damp woodland air with all its mysterious and unknown taints, the sourness of dead bracken, the acrid smell of fungus and tree-rot, and once the strong odour of fox which unaccountably — to her — raised the hairs of her body, and sent a tingle through her blood. Often she took Gael's scent, for the little collie knew that cubs had been born when, on a misty morning in February, she heard their tiny squeaking voices sounding up the tunnel from their nursery.

Gael knew the sett well, and had met the badgers on her travels through the woodland at dusk and dawn. On occasion, she had joined Jan and Zana in play, though she was always treated with some suspicion, and she in turn knew just how far her company was tolerated. At times testing their amicable relationship, Gael entered the sett, but was wise enough never to go into the chambers, content to stretch for scent from a yard inside the tunnel.

Badgers had lived in Brockholes Wood for many years. The population had never been great, but the conditions were right to support a small colony that lived in two main setts 100 yards apart. Jena's home was at the top of the woodland which rose steeply from the banks of the river. Its six entrances were hidden among the bracken cover, so that her parents and relations were able to come and go with some degree of secrecy, particularly during the shorter, lighter nights of summer and autumn when the bracken was standing tall.

The sett's tunnels were excavated into soil, which was mostly clay, in such a way as to turn water away from the living chambers and keep them dry. Planned with thought and executed with care, the subterranean home was safely bound with the roots of the trees to prevent any major collapse. Jena's nursery chamber was about three feet square and 18 inches from floor to roof, and the tunnel which led to the outside world was nine inches in diameter. A mild, though constant, air current kept the chamber fresh.

In Brockholes Wood and its surrounding lands there was ample food of one kind or another which satisfied the badgers. They were an adaptable tribe, and their tastes varied between the small mammals and various tree-fruits and plant-bulbs of the woodland, to the legion of worms, grubs and insects of the adjoining pastureland.

It was a land teeming with interest, and when Jena lay in the tunnel of her home to listen to its varied voices, she heard the whistle of the wind and the swish of swaying trees, the drip of rainwater which came to wash the snow from the land, the sudden cackle of a blackbird when alarmed by the discovery of Aluco, the tawny-owl, roosting in a tall sycamore, and, in the distance, the song notes of Ruddock, the robin. At night she listened to the call of the hunting owl, and heard a vixen yowl to her mate.

As the days went by, she came to like the light, which was unusual for one who was to spend most of her life in the dark, and when she tired of playing with her brothers, or with the pebbles she dug from the walls of her home, she often crawled a little way up the entrance tunnel and lay, listening and nosing, facing the light-source.

She was unafraid, and one day in February, when the light was strong with winter sunshine brightening the tunnel, she explored further than usual and found an earthworm wriggling down the tunnel. Other than the spiders and similar insects she found in her bedding, the worm was the first stranger she had ever met. She was not afraid, for badgers eat earthworms, and she grabbed it in her teeth and bit it — just as her mother came down the tunnel. Zana was a cautious parent and did not yet want her family to get the wanderlust. She pushed her erring child none too gently with her nose so that Jena lost her footing and rolled down into the nursery. The worm fell to the floor and was snapped up by Zana. Unconcerned — for mother knew best — Jena yawned, curled on the grass couch, and went to sleep.

Sleep was something that badgers enjoyed and, like most young creatures, Zana's family spent two-thirds of their time dozing and dreaming. As time passed in days of cold sleet, heavy rainfall, white hoar-frost and bright sunshine, with the bewildering uncertainty of the East Lancashire Pennines, the baby badgers grew in strength. Towards the end of February, they were five weeks old and Zana found them quite a problem to keep in order. They could now move around quite easily, wobbling a little on unsteady legs at times, but were quite frolicsome and playful between themselves.

Jena in appearance was now a smaller edition of her mother. The black and white stripes on her head were cleanly distinct, her nose was jet black, and her ears were tipped with white. The hairs on her body were thickening to a coarse grey coat which darkened down her legs. Sharp, black, unworn claws tipped each five-toed pad.

With every new awakening, she became more adventurous, and led her two brothers up and down the passages of the big sett. They visited the various chambers and, not always welcomed by their elders, were met with grunts of annoyance, and sometimes a nip from sharp teeth. They chattered to each other like young piglets, squeaking and whickering their voices in high-pitched excitement.

When they behaved like naughty children, Zana was upset, for she was a proud mother, and she sternly rebuked them, and none too gently hustled them back to

Zana was a comely badger.

their own nursery chamber. There, Jena would lie quietly on the warm couch for a while. Becoming restless, she would seek one of her pebble-toys and push it around with her paws. She bit at it and tossed it in the small space. She found that digging into the side of the nursery was easy and great fun. Her strong claws gouged a lump of clay from the smooth wall, and she rolled it into a ball to form another mobile plaything. When she tired of the lack of response — and if mother had left them again — she mewed to her brothers and harried them to play. Together they would play a biting game, nipping each other on legs and nose, and chattering their excitement.

On one of her expeditions through the sett, whilst her mother was out in the woodland, Jena met Jan, her father, for the first time. He was on his way to clean his claws on the trunk of a large sycamore tree, which the badgers used for a scratching post, when she waddled from the nursery passage into his path.

There was no recognition as neither knew the other, though Jan knew his family was growing up, for Zana had come back to him on her visits from the sett. They had mated again and Zana would have another family in 12 months' time — for the female badger was subject to delayed implantation and the unborn youngsters would not start to form in her womb until November.

Jan was a strongly-grown boar badger, and whilst his family were none of his concern, he purred his pleasure at seeing Jena, nosing her body, and licking her face. But he did not linger. He eased her to the side of the tunnel with his leathery nose, and ambled up towards the twilight.

Jena was so surprised. She blinked her eyes and wrinkled her nose after the disappearing boar; sat on her bottom and scratched an irritation behind her ear with a hind claw. So vigorously did she scratch that she overbalanced and rolled down the tunnel until a bend at a large stone in its course stopped her.

There was another occasion, even more important, when she made her first outing above ground — her greatest adventure. It was during the second week in March and the night was lit by a full moon casting ghostly shadows between the bare woodland trees. Zana had left her cubs, to go foraging by the riverside in the valley bottom, when Jena led her two brothers towards the circle of wan light at the top of the tunnel. Cautiously, she nosed her way into the open air for the first time in her life, stopping to wrinkle her nose to the exciting scents and pricking her ears to the sounds of the night. Her scenting powers were keenly developing and her hearing was acute enough to identify the slight rustle of a rabbit in the bracken on the bank by the sett.

Bravely, she walked up the mound of excavated earth on her doorstep and, catching her air of confidence, her two brothers followed. Together, the three youngsters sat and stared around at the land of shadows into which they had adventured. Moon-dappled patches of dead bracken formed a mosaic carpet from the bank of the sett, white frost glinted with dim uncut sparkle in the moonlight, and a prickly tangle of brambles looked gaunt and black — and a little scary.

Suddenly, Aluco, the tawny-owl, called to the moon as he hunted on silent wings through the trees — and the three little badgers bolted for the safety of their home, tumbling one after the other into the sanctuary. There they stayed curled together for protection and confidence on the warm couch until Zana came home, and they rushed to greet her with more fuss than usual. Each sought one of her six teats and sucked her milk with noisy gulps, the quiet warmth of her presence driving away their fears.

Jena even lay still whilst her mother licked and cleaned her, a routine to which she usually objected most strongly. Zana was rearing her family in the true badger tradition of cleanliness, and they had already learned to lick clean their own pads and forelegs. Whilst she regularly objected to the washing routine, Jena always enjoyed the nights when Zana changed their bedding, for, with the new pile of bracken, grass and leaves which was brought into the sett were spiders and other tiny creatures to be hunted and eaten.

Feeding was an important part of the youngsters' lives, and under Zana's devoted attention to their welfare, they thrived and grew quickly. All the cubs ate well and liked their food, but Jena had an exceptionally keen appetite and she grew quickly, from suckling her mother's milk, to gulping the regurgitated worms and beetles which her mother scattered over the floor of their nursery chamber. She especially liked the remnants of flower bulbs — snowdrops and bluebells — which Zana offered. She never went hungry, and the glow of health showed in her sturdy young limbs, strong sharp teeth, and thickening and darkening fur sleeked with gloss.

Two weeks after the three cubs had made their first adventurous sortie to see the outside world, they were taken back up to the woodland under the motherly care of Zana. Their education towards weaning had really started. Aluco, the tawny-owl, who had given them such a fright, and whose mate, Tui, had that night decided on her home in the hollow of an oak tree, 50 yards from the badger sett, saw Zana's family leave their home. Zana came first, emerging from the sett with her nose questing the air and her ears lifted for even the slightest hint of danger. She was very cautious and careful, and hesitated when a large russet-feathered bird swished its wings between the trees.

Long stout beak pointing the way, Wudu, the woodcock, saw Zana with his big eyes. He was gone like a wraith, and Zana recovered her composure. She heard the dreamy chakking of a fieldfare which, with ten others of its kind, roosted in a tall sycamore on the woodland fringe. She accepted the thump of rabbit feet on the trodden badger track through the bracken. She sat down and lifted her right hind paw to scratch viciously at an irritation behind her right ear. She was relaxed. She called her cubs, and throwing aside all the caution that had marked their first venture, they left the sett entrance with bounds of delight, sure that all was safe when mother called.

It was a mild night. The air was scented with the smells of a new season, for the snowdrops held their dainty white heads in the lower valley, wood-anemones held their purple-tinged white flowers closed on nodding stems, and a mole's energies formed a sweet pyramid of newly-turned earth crumbs. All the scents were new and exciting to the cubs.

For ten minutes Jena and her two brothers showed caution in their actions, pushing their pointed noses into the leaf-mould on the ground, scraping the bracken-rooted earth with sharp claws, biting tentatively at a low branch of thorn bush, ever-ready to arch their backs when some sudden movement upset them. Their confidence grew, and the three youngsters erupted into a disordered frenzy of action. Round and round, in a revelry of excitement, they romped over the open clearing by the entrance to the sett, chasing each other, biting at each other, rolling over each other.

Nervously, Zana watched them at their play, fearful that such exuberance would attract attention, yet happy to indulge their game. Only when they started to scream and chatter in rising excitement did Zana lose her patience and drive the three cubs back down into the sett.

On that night the cubs were above ground for half an hour, for as long as it took Aluco to catch his first vole, and Zana was relieved to see them safely back underground. Tired, they immediately curled together on their bed and went to sleep — and Zana was content to leave them and return to her own affairs in the night air.

On subsequent nights — after the three cubs had expounded their initial energy in pointless romp — Zana taught them the woodcraft they would need in order to stay alive in the days to come. She showed them round their woodland haunt, leading them along the maze of badger tunnels which all led to somewhere of practical interest through the bracken and bramble. She took them along the river bank to the safest drinking places and showed them how to blend their colouring in camouflage on moonlit nights.

In the early dawn she interpreted the blackbird's call of warning when their neighbours were making their final hunting kills. Anxious that the cubs should survive their dangerous youthful days when they were vulnerable to any trick of the more experienced woodlanders, Zana disciplined them to regular nightly lessons, though she was wise enough to cover much of her teaching in play.

She played hide-and-seek with them, making them use their noses to locate her. They learned to taste the air for clues, to stand quite still and listen, to stalk with care in placing their feet in the right places. She showed her family the power of their claws to break away bark from trees to seek beetles, and to dig into the earth to uncover the juicy bulbs of snowdrops and bluebells. She taught them the fun of grubbing their sensitive noses through the rich, moist leaf-mould to find grubs, spiders and worms, and to surprise voles.

One night was spent in showing them how to turn cow-pats to get at the beetles which were always hiding there. True to her practice of cleanliness, she taught the three cubs to dig and use latrines.

By the beginning of April, by the time that the lambs were arriving on the hill, and lapwings covered eggs, Zana started to leave them for a spell during the darkness to give them confidence. Jena was unworried by her mother's disappearance, but her brothers were not so confident. They had a fear of getting lost — and instinctively they learned to musk. By discharging the smelly, oily liquid which their bodies produced in abdominal glands, they could mark a route which they could always follow home. It was these marked routes which Gael followed on subsequent mornings.

Jena was not so fearful of losing her way through the woodland darkness. She roamed far too freely for any young badger. On one trip through the bracken she met Spiny, the hedgehog and, it being her first experience of such a prickly-looking neighbour, she was frightened. She snorted, lifted the hairs of her body in mock bravado and stood tall on her legs. Spiny did not hesitate. He ran. He knew that one bite from a badger's mouth would cut him in two.

The following night, Jena crossed the scent of a doe rabbit and her senses tingled with excitement. Nose down, her keen sense of smell interpreting the ways of the rabbit like an open book, she followed — and got lost! Failing to musk her route in her excitement for the rabbit, Jena was well beyond her normal known territory when she stopped to consider her surroundings. She was still in the woodland, but the tree trunks around were unknown; the bramble patch under which she stood was strange; the trod, from which the rabbit scent teased her nostrils was new.

Darkness was leaving the land and the light in the eastern sky was brightening. It was decision time. Unconcerned, and suddenly tired, she sought a hollow in the ground and curled her body in sleep. Some time later the sun rose on a bright day.

A golden light, though nice and warm to her body, dazzled Jena's eyes, and even when she tucked her piggy nose away in an attempt to cover her eyes beneath her hindparts, she could not hide from the strong light. For one who had spent almost all her life in darkness, the brightness of the sunbeams was startling. Sniffling and snorting in a restless mood of unease and annoyance, Jena tried to curl further down into the ground hollow.

She coughed and spluttered, and the woodcraft she had quickly learned in the past three weeks of growing up was cast away, when Gael, leaving the haunts of the rabbits beneath the rhododendron bushes on the woodland slope, came towards her unusual noise. Gael was wary of the strange noise — the groaning and nose-snuffling—and pricked her ears forward as she approached stealthily, her pads placed gently on the ground, her attitude the slinking, concentrated crouch of her breed.

Tentatively, she extended her nose to the little creature in the hollow between the grass tussocks in the bracken clearing. A bumble-bee buzzed over her head, and a bright-winged tortoiseshell butterfly, sunning on the ground, took flight. Gael knew the scent of badger, she had taken the musk odour many times, but it was her first meeting with one so young and she was a little unsure. Jena did not worry at all. She continued to splutter and grunt, and wriggle her body to try to find some comfort from the blinding light. She was annoyed and tired and quite prepared to indulge in baby tantrums — particularly if she had an audience.

With the slight breeze stirring her ear tufts, Gael stood over the youngster, her head on one side, her attention completely held by the little stranger. Ruddock, the robin, singing to his mate from a perch 40 feet high in the sycamore tree, suddenly stopped his notes of love, to a rush of wings and some harsh chakking calls, as a flock of a hundred fieldfares flew over the trees heading to the north-east and their summer home in Scandinavia.

PLASTER CAST

Erect "wall" of
thin card
around track.

Gael's
right
fore-
paw

Paper-clip
holds card.

Clean track as
much as possible.
blow away light
debris -
(without
upsetting
track.

(Choose as
dry a print
as possible.

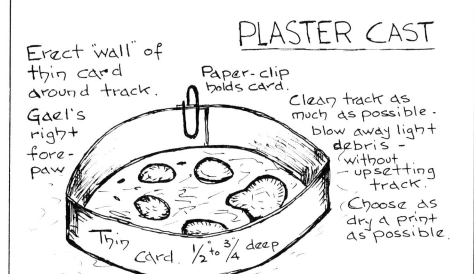

Thin card. 1/2" to 3/4" deep

Use Plaster of Paris for detail - not building
plaster. Mix - adding the powder to the water -
to a consistency to remove air bubbles.
Gently pour into frame. Whilst setting a
paper-clip can be inserted
to form hanger.
Drying time is
dependent on weather-
conditions - never
less than 15 minutes.

Black drawing-ink,
colour to pad-marks
emphasize the
detail.

Scrape flat on
back and label
- animal, pad,
location, date
etc.

Scrape
flat
around
print.

To an exploratory flick of Gael's tongue over her black and white striped face, Jena uncurled, lifted her wet pointed nose, looked at Gael through gentle blue eyes, and stretched. On unsteady legs she walked under Gael's questing nose and rubbed her grey body against the collie's legs.

It was a sign of friendship, one springing from her loneliness and discomfort at having lost — if only temporarily — the warming presence of her mother. It was a sign of the fearlessness and the trusting innocence of such young creatures, though Jena had been well schooled to the dangers of the world.

Gael was not sure whether she should accept the responsibility of this adoption on such a short aquaintance, and she stepped away. She stretched herself on the ground some three yards from the cub, and pondered the situation. Jena was a portly, well-nourished youngster — and, apart from her obvious characteristics and colouring, was not unlike Gael had been when she was also 12 weeks old. Gael felt a kinship for the youngster.

Fully awake, Jena sought her new acquaintance again. She walked with more steadiness to where Gael lay on the ground. She thrust her nose to Gael's nose in a token of greeting, rolled on her back, and purred her pleasure. Such total lack of restraint, such confidence and trust immediately strengthened kindred spirit in the collie, and Gael accepted the friendship. She mouthed Jena's short legs, bit the thickening muscles of her neck in play, then jumped to her feet. Trotting away along the badger track with Jena following behind, Gael led the youngster home. Some 200 yards from their meeting, Jena found the dark tunnel leading to her home in the damp earth, and went waddling from Gael's sight.

Chapter 7

Respectful neighbours

Bufo inflates his body to increase his size when faced by the little collie who finds less problems, and more interesting activities, with her neighbours — the moorhens and reed-buntings on the hill pond.

It was kindergarten on the hillside as curly-coated lambs gathered in playful groups. In parties of three, five, and even eight, they played with chosen mates or any other lamb that cared to join in. They chased and gambolled across the short grass, encouraged by weather which, for the moment, was kind and mild to foster their jollity. Unpredictable in action, for new, gangly legs didn't always follow the mind's dictates, they bounced sideways, skipping on sharp split hooves which marked the soft earth on landing. They nuzzled each other with pink tongues licking from black lips.

One of the group of eight made a dash alongside the fringe of rushes, and seven others followed in a tireless game of tag. They shied in sudden alarm when their frolics sent a snipe from its couch in the rushes. They stood still, tails flicking, innocent eyes watching the zig-zagging flight of the bird, flop ears hearing its shriek of protest. A bumble-bee buzzing close across the grass diverted their attention, and a wheatear bobbed to them from a tussock of ground. A skip and a hop, and the lambs forgot all about their sudden alarm. They ran round the fringe of pond rushes, caring little for the whereabouts of the mother ewes. In a band of excited happiness, they wandered like any group of mischievous children with little thought of danger.

But a few days old, the white of their wool was as pure as snow, the black of their faces as dark as coal. Chases and frolics, pushings and shovings for superiority were all part of their growing-up. As with the young of all creatures, so much of their play had the purpose of strengthening their bodies, adding muscle and bone, of keening their thoughts, and of co-ordinating brain and limbs. At that age they had a pathetic vulnerability which, allied to their innocence and inquisitiveness, belied a confident air of self-sufficiency. No two were alike, neither in marking nor in nature. The evenly-marked black-and-white-faced lamb was confident and unafraid at three days old; its more white-faced playmate was gangly and unsure at five days old.

Much of their true nature showed when Gael came to watch their frolics. When the little collie came through the sheep-hole in the stone wall, some of the lambs ran towards her, some ignored her, and the timid, so tested, bleated for mother. Those that welcomed her appearance appeared to regard her as a potential playmate, those that ignored her were unsure of her role in their lives, those that shouted for mother were surprised and wanted to play safe.

Gael knew all their moods, and she kept a wary eye on the ewes that came in answer to the calls of their offspring. Parent ewes at that time of the year were truculent and unfriendly, even to a known neighbour, for maternal possessiveness made them suspicious, brave and bold, and they would not tolerate interference.

As quickly as she was able, Gael left the friendly lambs. Among the thick screen of brown rushes in Rack Clough she came suddenly upon a baby rabbit, so suddenly that the rabbit, even with its extreme sense of caution, failed to hear her approach. Maybe the continuous rustle of the wiry rushes moving against each other in the breeze had covered the light noise of Gael's pads on the soft ground. Maybe the baby rabbit, with little experience of life, had been too engrossed in nibbling at a patch of sphagnum moss. Now it was too late. It tensed with fear of the dog, and crouched unmoving to the ground.

Gael pushed it with her nose, with an invitation to play — fortunately for the rabbit — for she had no malicious intent. With heart beating visibly through its soft, brown fur, eyes wide and fearful, the rabbit tried to press itself even closer

Charming and cuddly, the rabbit was very vulnerable, and had large eyes to watch for its enemies.

More intelligent than frogs, toads carry a poison in their skin which is distasteful to a dog like Gael and can cause some distress.

into the mossy ground. Only when Gael poked her nose right under the rabbit's body and forcefully moved it, did the baby totter to its feet. Then, with the hypnotic fear broken by movement, it suddenly regained its inbred urge to survive and darted into a burrow only two yards away. Gael let it go, a playful humour on her face.

Close by where she stood, a soft tuft of brown and white fur marked the spot where one of the baby rabbit's family had not been so fortunate. Ruso, the fox, had surprised the rabbit's brother and snatched it for supper.

Taking a last scent from the rabbit's couch, Gael turned to follow the sheep-trod which wound across the solid ground between the tall rushes. Treading the yielding ground which oozed water between her toes, she pattered across soft, black peat and, nose to the earth, followed the weak scent of hare for 30 yards.

Instantly recognising Bufo when she came face to face with the toad, she quickly and instinctively lifted her nose away from the wart-covered creature. Past experience had taught her the nastiness of those warts. The friendly flick of her tongue over his skin on an earlier meeting had scalded her mouth with the acrid white discharge from his warty glands, and she had learned her lesson.

Assuming Gael to be an enemy, Bufo also took action, inflating his lungs to increase his size, stretching out his hind legs, and dropping his head to face her with the most distasteful appearance he could muster. Gael shied from the toad with a sideways leap which frightened two meadow-pipits. They flew up from the rushes in straight upward flight, twittering to each other as they dropped on fluttering wings which seemed too feeble to carry them far. Riding the breeze whilst Gael passed below them, they dropped back to the jungle of rushes.

Capella, the snipe, was the next creature to be disturbed by Gael, but there was no indecision in his retreat. He leaped to flight, and darted speedily on a sharp, irregular line away over the hillside. Weak sunbeams broke through the greyness of the cloud cover, and a skylark rose across them on trembling wings to sing its song of liquid joy.

Two curlews flew up from Gael's coming, and floated on the air above her head. On spread and hollow wings they glided, opening long-hooped beaks to trill their wild music. The spirit of the hill was reflected in the voices of the curlews, and Gael lifted her ears to its bubbling power. Leaping a deep ditch, she sank her pads into the wet peat on the opposite bank. The peat stained the whiteness of her leg feathering to a murky brown.

Following the water channel, Gael ran between the fringe of rushes, treading across green moss patches and splashing through brown water. A flock of chaffinches flashed their white wing patches in the sunlight as they rose before Gael's crossing of the pasture, and when she ran through the sheep-hole into the next field she was mobbed and screamed at by diving lapwings. Following the bottom of the wallside, she ran round a group of playful lambs which gambolled

Moorhen.
Kurra.
Scholey Pond.
April.

towards her and, pushing under the bottom rail of the field-gate, ran to seek a peaceful rest among the rushes by the hill-pond.

Lulled by the protesting and constant clucking of Kittic, the moorhen, who distrusted her presence, for his mate was brooding eggs in her nest in the rushes, and encouraged by the monotonous buzzing of a bee, Gael crossed her forepaws, lowered her head, and closed her eyes. She dozed on the couch of rushes until the restless voice of Kittic became annoying in her ears. She opened her mouth in a wide yawn, stood to stretch her muscles, and decided on a game of tag with Kittic.

Gael had a good nose and it was rarely deceived, so that the scent-line of Kittic was plain and distinct for her to follow. Nor was the seclusion of the thick brown rushes by the pondside sufficient concealment for the bird when the line led Gael directly to him. There was only one way to kill the tell-tale taint, and Kittic took the plunge. With Gael's nose snuffling the black feathers of his back, he dived into the water, plunging, with no pretence at secrecy, into an environment in which he was superior to the dog.

Swimming below the surface, Kittic kicked forward with strong leg strokes, the air bubbles trapped in his feathers giving an ethereal delicacy to his body. The airy form shattered when he rose for breath some two yards from the bank where Gael eagerly awaited his reappearance, for she knew the ploys of moorhens.

Kittic left the cover of underwater obscurity and, with no attempt to fool Gael in his retreat, he scuttered across the pond surface, wings and legs pumping in a half-flying, half-running dash for the opposite bank.

Gael watched Kittic go, and she saw him disappear into the brown mass of thick vegetation with a final flick of his white under-tail feathers. She could prolong the game of hide-and-seek by running round the bank of the pond to reach Kittic's hide, but she conceded to the moorhen, having shown him her own powers of detection.

From the depths of the rushes came a quiet croak of 'kurruk', a satisfied chuckle of relief when Kittic realised that Gael had conceded. It was also a note of relief for Kurra, Kittic's mate, who was becoming anxious at the frantic sounds of her mate's scramble across the pond. Kurra relaxed her tension, and sat quietly and quite composed in the secluded safety of her nest amid the rush tangle. She shifted her position over six red-and-purple-spotted, clay-coloured eggs on the well-woven nest platform to which Gael had to wade until the murky water reached up to her shoulders.

Kittic and Kurra, of a breed which set great store on territorial rights, had claimed Scholey Pond as their home — even though Gael went with the property, for they had quickly come to an understanding with her. Kittic had known Gael for some time, the pond being one of her regular haunts, and, apart from the ice-bound days of winter, he had kept to its locality and the shelter of the adjoining clough. Kurra, after accepting the role of Kittic's mate, had quickly learned the ways of the little collie and her harmless interest (although she ran them in fun), so that the moorhens and Gael had become tolerant neighbours.

Gael lingered by the pondside, for the wind's ruffle was blocked by the rush-screen and, without the wind, the sunbeams had the warmth that promised summer heat. She returned to her couch by the edge of the still water, and stretched her body on the dry ground. Probing fingers between the brittle rushes, the breeze stirred her fur so that the sunbeams played across the sable waves of her coat. Her eyes were closed, but flickered open momentarily to the fleeting shadow of Krark, the heron; her ears were laid back, but twitched to the bleat of a lamb across the hill.

Hidden from the ground, she was easily seen from above, and the heron veered away when he spotted her, his great grey wings slowly swinging him back over the hill. Kee, the kestrel, hung on quivering wings in the sky, tail fanned, head down, watching Gael. Often the collie had sent mice and voles scurrying into open sight, hastening unwarily from her passing, but right into the full, deadly stoop of the kestrel. Gael was content to doze, only the blink of an eyelid, the turn of an ear, the twitch of a nostril keeping her in touch with the happenings around her. She heard the drumming of a snipe high above her head, the bleat-like noise coming with the rush of air through open tail feathers every time the bird dived earthwards. She heard the piping music of a redshank, and the twittering notes of a party of twites that flew over the pond.

Only when the noise of air across larger wings came louder down the breeze did Gael raise her head from her paws to seek the cause. Between the rushes she saw a strange black and white bird skid to a halt on the mirrored surface of the pond, and settling, float quietly on the water.

It was a tufted-duck, a strikingly handsome black and white drake, his head-crest graceful in line, his golden-yellow eyes bright in the sunlight, his flat beak slate-blue in colour. A wanderer, Curra had not yet found a mate, and had pitched on to the pond for food. He slipped silently beneath the surface of the pond, an upsurge of bubbles marking his submersion. The bubbling surface following his underwater progress, the duck nipped the choicest growth from the aquatic weeds growing in the mud of the pond bottom. He surfaced to breathe, and continued his diving sorties, each of about 15 seconds duration, until his hunger was gone.

Curra floated lightly on the water, enjoying the warmth of the sun on his back. He lifted a webbed foot and scratched his head. Leisurely he preened his feathers, rolling on his side to show his white breast, oiling the feathers from the gland on his back. Stretching his head backwards on to the preen-gland, he stimulated the oil flow.

Kittic, the moorhen, followed the duck's example, and now fully relaxed with Gael's presence on the bank, stood on a rock from the water, and drew his black feathers through his brightly-marked red and yellow beak. Kurra, his mate, dozed in complete trust over her eggs.

Gael dozed — although the keeness of her scent and hearing, even when at diminished interest, kept her completely aware of what was happening on the pond. She heard the arrival of Nico, the black-capped reed-bunting, to his summer home. Twitching an ear, she heard his voice — 'tweek-tweek-tweek-tititick' — welcome his mate, Riza, to her home.

Gael remembered Nico as the one who fooled her with his broken-wing act to decoy her from his family of four baby buntings the previous summer. She had quickly tumbled to the ruse, and had ignored it ever after, quietly visiting the four youngsters to suck their scent during the 13 days they were in the nest. She never harmed them, and whilst always anxious of her presence, Nico and Riza ceased to fear her.

Now the reed-buntings had returned, and Gael listened to Nico's song. The bird saw her and, for a moment, hesitated. Quickly flicking his tail from side to side as he grasped the reed stems, one leg bent, the other straight beneath himself for balance, he stuttered his notes. Flying into the air, he fluttered, almost hovering above a rush clump three yards from where Gael lay. Joining him, Riza uttered notes of doubt.

Short, jerky flight took them some ten yards away from the collie, and they settled back to perch on the rushes, fluttering balancing wings to counter the downward tilt of the fragile stems when they alighted. Neither bird was particularly skilful in flight, bounding through the air as many finches did, but they were adept and clever in balancing on the light stems of soft bogland vegetation.

Another bird had but recently returned to Scholey Hill. Chacka, the wheatear, had flown all the way from Africa to join Nico and Riza, and Gael, on the high pastures. From his perch on the stones of the wall top, he bobbed curtsies and called to Gael in a grating voice.

'Chack-chack-chack', the wheatear called his return to his nesting haunt. Gael

Riza, the hen reed-bunting, blended with her surroundings to keep her babies warm.

Food for hungry mouths. Nico, the cock reed-bunting, brought a snack.

pricked her ears to the voice she remembered from last summer, and when
Chacka flitted down to the ground to perch on a dried cow-pat, she lifted her
head from her forepaws.

Chacka stood boldly erect, unafraid at the nearness of the dog, and watched her
with dark, round eyes. He was a handsome fellow, tight-feathered in clear grey
and buff, with a distinctive black tail tip and prominent white eyestripes. He sang
a few squeaky notes then, as a shaft of sunlight spread over the hillside, he danced
into the air and puffed his feathers. His first practice courtship display was for
Gael's benefit — for there was yet no female wheatear on the hill. Gael jumped to
her feet and ran towards Chacka who flitted airily to the sanctuary of the wall top.
Chacka was home.

It was the time of year for home-comings, and the time for family duties. The
first swallows and house-martins were completing their long journeys from the
tropics. Feeka, the kestrel, guarded eggs on the rocks across the valley; Zana, the
badger, had weaned her cubs; and Silva's fox cubs were opening their eyes in the
darkness of their underground nursery in the woodland.

Gael, enjoying a game of hide-and-seek with a nimble weasel along the bottom
of the field-wall, stood to listen to the drumming of Capella high above her head.

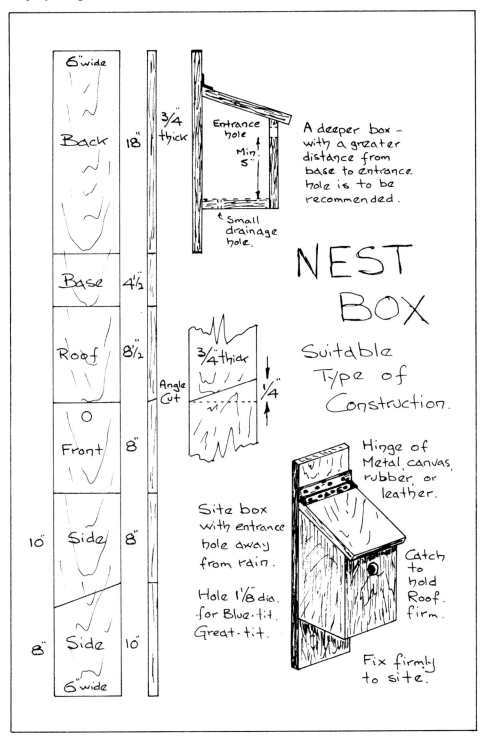

6" wide

Back 18"

¾" thick

Base 4½

Roof 8½"

Angle Cut

¾" thick

¼"

Front 8"

10" Side 8"

8" Side 10"

6" wide

Entrance hole

Min. 5"

Small drainage hole.

A deeper box – with a greater distance from base to entrance hole is to be recommended.

NEST BOX

Suitable Type of Construction.

Hinge of Metal, canvas, rubber, or leather.

Catch to hold Roof firm.

Site box with entrance hole away from rain.

Hole 1⅛ dia. for Blue·tit. Great·tit.

Fix firmly to site.

The snipe, a tiny speck in the sky beyond Gael's vision, climbed to a peak of flight, turned, and diving with tail outstretched, vibrated the rush of air into a goat-like bleat. Couched between covering rushes on the ground which hid her completely, Capella's mate listened to the sound which told her where her husband was. She listened until Gael pushed a way through the vegetation, then she leaped to flight, zig-zagging on fast flying wings to join Capella.

Gael nosed the scent of hares and ground birds between the rushes, treading warily and noiselessly between the tangle, in the hope of surprising some creature. A pair of redshanks screamed their sudden departure with a ringing 'tu-tu-tu' as they swiftly left, long red legs trailing, sharp-pointed wings quickly clipping the air. A pair of golden-plovers, beautiful in spangled gold and black plumage, were more trustful, and quietly winged to a stretch of mud 20 yards in front of Gael. When she persisted in annoying them, they pattered with wader-like strides over the mud before opening their wings to fly.

Crossing the open hillside, Gael was immediately mobbed by Vanus and his mate. The lapwings swooped down, rolling and banking over her head on rounded wings, the humming of the wind through the webs of the feathers adding to the clamour of their weeping voices. When Gael crossed to their ground nest and flicked her tongue over the three mottled eggs, their agitation increased, and they stooped lower, almost brushing her ears with their wing-tips. Gael yapped a protest, and ran from the field. The clamour ceased at her going, and the hillside was calm again.

When she roamed the riverside, Gael found plenty of interest.

Chapter 8

Not wanted

Crahen nervously broods her four eggs high in the branches of a silver-birch tree;
Chook defends his home and puts Pyat, the robber magpie, to flight; and Gael finds
she is an outcast.

Cocking her eye skywards, Crahen, the female carrion-crow, saw the flock of 30 fieldfares fly into the trees of the woodland clough. She was relaxed and broody, snuggling her body warmth over the four darkly-marked eggs in the saucer of her nest. Raindrops splashed through the leafless twigs of the birch canopy above her head, the water dripping over her glossy feathers, and running safely away from the precious eggs into the stick foundation of her home. She was proud of her new nest, and zealous in the brooding of her eggs, the last of which she had laid that morning.

Crahen, wife of Corbie, the dominant crow and undisputed leader of his clan in the locality of Rack Clough and the lower valley, had built a new nest, refusing the previous year's nest site on the rocks of the Cliviger Gorge, in spite of her husband's wishes. She had chosen the top fork of branches, 30 feet high in a silver-birch tree on the fringe of the woodland in the clough. The site was well chosen for it commanded a clear view, and there were good observation perches in nearby trees from which Corbie could keep his watchful guard on the nest. Staid in his ways, the older crow had demurred at her choice, but Crahen had her way.

With patient labour, the birds had gathered sticks, many snapped with their strong beaks from the trees in the wood, and carried them to the nest site, placing and weaving them to form a solid and well-anchored cradle in the fork of branches. They had lined the cradle with dried grasses and sheep's wool.

Crahen stirred in the nest, easing the eggs into her warm breast feathers. Her tail cocked over the lip of the nest, and with raised head she watched a fieldfare, perched on a branch above her home, preen its feathers. Suddenly, the bird took flight, followed into the air by the whole company of Scandinavian thrushes, their going marked by the harshness of chakking voices. Crahen's heart-beat increased. Something had disturbed the fieldfares. She listened intently for the cause.

Corbie was away over the hill, and not dutifully able to allay her fear. The abrupt and explosive flight from the ground of five wood-pigeons, their wings cracking through the tree branches as they rose, sent Crahen's heart racing even faster, and her beak gaped a little. Though of an intelligent and independent breed, Crahen always tended to be nervous when brooding eggs, and imagined danger to her unborn family at the slightest untoward occurrence.

It was the familiar and confident 'Kaaah-kaaah-kaaah' greeting of Corbie, as he sailed over the hill crest on outspread wings, that calmed her anxiety. His call, thrice repeated, dispelled all her fears, and when he flapped into the topmost branches of the sycamore which grew next to the birch, she relaxed once more over her eggs.

On the ground Gael, the little collie, trotted between the tall trees, her nose to the scent of rabbit. It was her approach which had sent the fieldfares and wood-pigeons away, and caused such unnecessary distress to the brooding crow.

Momentarily, Crahen was disturbed again when Corbie, seeing Gael beneath his nest site, called down abuse upon the little collie. Gael, familiar with the ways of the black rogue, lifted her head to watch him dance from foot to foot in his rage. Her lips curled in a noiseless snarl, and she trotted away with slight heed of Corbie's language.

The rain shower passed, and sunbeams pierced the grey clouds to warm the countryside. A bee, buzzing and hovering by the face of the field-wall, sought a home in the cavities between the stones; a colourful tortoiseshell butterfly danced up from the grass in front of Gael's feet; a spider quickly disappeared between the leaves of the grasses.

Gael turned through the sheep-hole in the wall and surprised a lapwing from its nest. She took the scent of the two eggs in their frugal nest, flipped her tongue over them, and continued her journey. Swooping low in order to see her, one of the first swallows to return to her land twittered a few song notes before gaping its mouth to snap at a crowd of flighting midges. Whaup, the curlew, flew up from the mud by the side of Scholey Pond. He had been probing for food with his long, curved bill.

The grass carpet which Gael trod was brightened by the orange-eyed white daisies and the splashes of orange dandelions. By the hedge, yellow celandines sparkled, and, between the budding trees down by the shallow stream, the banks were white with wood anemones.

Gael followed the trickle of the stream down towards the River Calder, and met another summer visitor to her land. From the tangle of green rhododendrons a willow-warbler sang a sweet, wistful song which ended in a gentle murmur when Gael came along the narrow, earth-trodden track. It was a song which would dominate the whole woodland during the coming weeks when the tiny olive-green and yellow warblers settled into their summer quarters.

Delightful visitors to the area from April to September, the willow-warblers came from the savanna and scrublands of Africa. They came to rear their families, and took up residence in every woodland in the locality, even up into the sparsely-wooded cloughs of the upland areas. They were among the smallest and most abundant of Gael's summer friends and she liked them because they built their nests where she could find them on the ground — partly-domed nests of grass and moss, constructed among the winter litter on the woodland floor.

The voice of the little warbler was sweet; it was peaceful among the trees; and the dainty white petals of wood anemones were opening to the warm sunshine when Gael watched a familiar friend skip daintily over the River Calder.

Her friend was Motator, the pied-wagtail who had only one leg, and was so christened because of his continuous movement. Gael had first met the wagtail when she was a puppy, and his ability to dance such rhythmical movement on his single leg had fascinated her ever since. Motator had never really had two legs, for his left leg had withered after becoming caked with dirt in the wet, crowded nest of his birth. When he left the nest, he learned to hop, instead of to run like his brothers and sisters.

Gael watched him flit from stone to stone along the bankside, bouncing sure-footed on his one leg at each landing, perching with black and white tail dancing. His agility in no way impaired, he had learned to use his long, feathered tail as a limb of balance.

He fluttered out above the water to take a fly in his beak. A blunt-nosed water-vole, stretching from its feeding hole to reach a stalk of grass, frightened Motator, and, calling 'tschizzick, tschizzick', he flew on undulating wings to a pebble-covered bank at the bend of the river. There, he feasted on the gnats and insects which were out in the sunshine, bobbing on his one leg, supporting a sudden turn of the head with a thrust of his tail to the pebbles as he snatched up his food. The suppleness and strength of his single leg was shown in his speed and agility when he thrust his pointed beak between the pebbles to chase and grasp the tiny beetles.

Motator chased flies over a sandy bank, leaving single-footed imprints and tail-tip impressions to puzzle whoever followed, as he hopped to the water's edge. He sipped at the water, running the liquid down his uplifted throat, before taking the breeze under his open wings to rise into the air. He flew high above the tree tops, out over the pasture at the side of the clough, to the grey stone wall on the hill. There he slanted down, and alighted on a rounded stone on the wall top, still bobbing his tail and balancing easily on his single leg.

He called softly to his mate who brooded five speckled eggs in their home in a hole in the wall. She quietly answered him. All was well, and he settled to rest on the wall top, crouching on the sun-warmed stone to rest that strong, but sometimes tired, single leg.

With the sunshine lighting up his feathers, Motator was a handsome bird of black and white plumage. His tail was long and dainty, and he wore a white mask with two black eye-holes which gave him a clown-like facial expression. A rook flew overhead, and Motator raised himself to alertness, cocking his head to one side to watch the bird with one of his black eyes, but there was nothing to endanger his peace, and he settled down again to rest.

In the nest in the wall his mate, Motal, dozed over her eggs. She was far more comfortable than Philo, the song-thrush, whose family was so virile that she could not rest at all comfortably over them. Jostling and wriggling beneath her, five strong youngsters made rest an uneasy affair.

Even a fat, juicy worm could not be stretched round the whole mistle-thrush family.

A devoted parent, the blackbird was keenly alert whilst baby-sitting.

Philo sat high over the mud-lined cradle, brooding her newly hatched family, her feathers ruffled and spread warm over their featherless bodies. One baby pushed up under her feathers and gaped — the splash of open mouthed orange colour bright in the artificial dusk of the holly bush where the nest was slung in Rack Clough.

The helpless family had hatched from the five sky-blue eggs (each with a cluster of black dots on its broad end), which had been guarded jealously and successfully by the parent thrushes. Concealment had not been easy, for the trees were only showing tiny sprouting leaves, and the holly bush, one of many in the clough, was the only full-leaved tree.

In the next holly bush, some 15 yards away, a blackbird brooded four greenish and brown-mottled eggs, cradled in a grass-lined nest. Gael knew both nests, for neither was high from the ground, and when the birds had begun to sit tight they had come to accept her daily visits. Momentarily nosing to take the scent of Philo as she sat over her babies with beak and tail pointed high, and dark eyes unwinking, Gael wandered to a nearby bankside where Rubor, the robin, sat on five red speckled eggs, and, equally bold in staying on the nest, stared fearlessly at the collie.

From the bankside, pierced with curling fronds of new bracken, Gael walked down to the river to drink. The water ran cool and clear, leaping along its rocky bed and splashing green banks which were massed with yellow celandine flowers, forming pools on which gerris insects skated.

A rabbit sensed Gael's approach, and it sat up like a squirrel, the sunbeams shining flesh-pink through its upright ears. The sunbeams danced on the shivering leaflets of the fairylike silver birch trees; they brightened the yellow-anthered white faces of wood anemones which grew from the wet land; they gleamed on the red, yellow, blue and black colours of the tortoiseshell butterflies which danced over a clump of nettle plants.

Whilst Gael played at chasing the butterflies, an angry chattering sounded through the woodland. Chook, the blackbird, had caught Pyat, the magpie, too close to his nest, and he was annoyed and frightened. The magpie was a robber and a destroyer, and would eat the blackbirds' eggs — or the neighbouring song-thrushes' youngsters — with relish, if given the chance.

Chook was far from being a coward in the defence of his home, and, fearlessly, he flew at the bigger black and white bird. Pyat chuckled at the consternation his presence was causing, but he had to duck his body smartly and, changing his tune, swear in annoyance as the fury of Chook's attack made him hastily flutter his wings to retain his balance on his perch in the oak tree above the blackbird's holly bush.

In the nests of blackbird and song-thrush in the twin holly bushes, Merle and Philo stirred nervously over eggs and family as they listened to the noise of battle in the tree tops. Aggressively posturing with head high, eyes bright, tail elevated, and orange bill open to call, Chook stood ready to attack. He had the advantage of manoeuvrability through the branches. He flew at the magpie, striking it quickly on the head with his feet as he swooped past.

His temper rising at such action. Pyat's mood changed from one of pleasurable baiting of the lesser bird to one of serious fight, and when Chook flew at him again, he stabbed with his strong black bill. Chook had to side-slip quickly to avoid the blow. Disgruntled, Pyat retreated. Hopping from twig to twig, he climbed to the top of the oak tree and flew away. He was followed by Chook's loud screams of victory.

The sounds of victory were heard by Tudo and Chicha, the mistle-thrushes, who were building their home 30 feet above the ground in the fork of branches of a sycamore tree by the riverside. They had already lost one nest (owing to shoddy building and a sudden windstorm) a few days earlier, before Chicha could take up residence. Their second nest was none too tidy, with a string of white sheep's wool blowing in the breeze like a flag from the nest. This nest had already been noted by Pyat who had marked it for a future raid, although Chicha and her mate were as bold as Chook in defending their home.

For most of the day, the thrushes had pulled dead grasses from the ground and carried them in beakfuls to the nest. They had tugged sheep's wool from the wires of the wood-side fence and carried it to the nest. Each beakful of building material had been woven into the cradle, the long grasses twisted into the bark and twigs of the tree to anchor the nest safely to its lofty site. Chicha had formed the hollow of her nest by pressing it to shape with her breast.

Above left *A Tawny-owl is catholic in its choice of nesting site, and will readily take to a well-sited box.*
Above right *Trogo, the tiny brown-feathered wren.*

The building was almost completed, and Tudo had already assumed the role of defender. When a starling, whose mate was covering five pale blue eggs in a hole in the oak tree across the stream, alighted in the sycamore to watch the nest-building, he was immediately put to flight, Tudo flying at him in anger at the intrusion.

Tudo was tired of nest-building and, leaving Chicha to form her cradle, he flew down to the ground to feed. Sunlight between the trees burnished the brown feathers of his back and brightened his handsome white breast which was marked with the conspicuous oval dark brown spots of his breed. Flashing the spotted tips of his tail when he settled his feathers, he stood alertly still in the grass and lifted his head to see if all was safe for him to forage on the ground. He saw nothing to disturb him. He cocked his head sideways so that he had full vision to examine the ground with one dark eye. Wings loosely held by his side, he stood to watch for movement. Nothing stirred in the grasses so he ran three strides and watched again, equally alert to the possibility of food or danger.

A worm pushed out of the ground soil, and Tudo tensed. Then he struck to grasp the worm in his pointed beak and, worrying it from the safety of its hole, he swallowed it with gulps of pleasure. Happily chasing a fat bumble-bee between the trees, Gael frightened Tudo. Startled, the thrush tightened his feathers and flew from the ground, still gulping at the worm in his crop. Gael stopped her play as Tudo flew low over her head, and she watched him go up to perch on the topmost branch of the thorn hedge. There, as Gael sat down on the grass and

Above *Alauda, the skylark, had won his mate and together they would rear a strong family on the hill.*

Below *Blue-tits find a man-made nest-box most acceptable as a safe home.*

peered up at him, Tudo screeched scolding notes at her intrusion, jerking his wings the while in anger. His calls brought Chicha from the nest site to see what all the commotion was about and, seeing Gael, she added her notes of annoyance to the scolding.

Gael was never very popular with her bird friends once they had turned their thoughts to family matters. She suddenly got in their way, for they distrusted every creature around their nests. Even so, she visited, for it was really the one time when they were static and she could approach them. She found their nests took many forms.

Bronda, the lapwing; Numa, the curlew; and Tringa, the redshank, formed little more than a scrape in the ground with a lining, and on this sort of nest, their eggs were laid. Although Bronda was content to sit on open, often bare, ground, Numa and Tringa preferred to hide their nests among rushes or tall grasses. Their chicks lived to mature in the egg for up to a month, and were able to leave home almost immediately on hatching.

In contrast, the babies of Merle, the blackbird, and Philo, the song-thrush, were born naked and helpless, and grew in the nest for a fortnight before being able to leave, so that their cradles were built strongly and well-hidden and well-founded in the branches of a tree.

Helpless babies were also hatched to Rubor, the robin; Vena, the skylark; and Lita, the meadow-pipit, and Gael knew these best of all for they were on the ground, and thus of her world. They were reared in strongly-constructed cosy nests, well woven with tough grasses, and built into private and secluded hollows.

It was usual for a species to keep to a pattern, small birds rarely building high off the ground; and Trogo, the wren, and Pyat, the magpie, added a covering dome to their homes.

As with every happening in the countryside, the weather played a vital part in nest-building, determining the time to start building by its effect on the feelings of the birds, and by its effect on the materials of construction to be used. Frozen material could not be fashioned, wet sheep's wool and cow hairs and feathers were messy, and brittle leaves were unmanageable.

Actual construction varied from species to species, but the female always took some part. The male's share of building ranged from none (as with most ducks), to the building of the main structure (as with wrens). Once started, birds did not linger at house-building. A 'repeat' nest could be built in a day, and a busy starling could have a home in a few hours.

Birds related their nest-building to the standard required to protect their eggs and youngsters. Birds like Tui, the tawny-owl, just used a hiding place like a hole in a tree-trunk; Philo, the song-thrush, lined her nest with hard mud to stand the rigours of a growing family; the kingfisher and sand-martin drove a tunnel into an earth banking; the woodpecker chiselled out a hole in a tree-trunk; swallows and house-martins hung their mud-built homes on brackets; and Kurra, the moorhen, rafted her nest in the rushes of Scholey Pond.

Chapter 9

To the rescue

Gael saves a water-shrew from the beak of a herring-gull, prevents a wood-mouse from becoming bottled, and encourages a fox cub to play truant.

In all her years of wandering the Pennine Hills, Gael never killed any creature, she never even harmed any creature, indeed, she saved many a creature from injury and death, though often inadvertently. On a bright sunny morning in May, she saved what was probably the rarest little animal in her homeland from being killed. She interfered, simply by arriving on the river bank at the right time, at the precise moment to save a water-shrew from being taken by a herring-gull.

It was a pretty morning, sunlight piercing the waters of the Calder and lighting the undulations of the river-bed, casting rock shadows and dappling the stone-covered mud. Two small water-shrews, shrouded in the silver air-bubbles which stuck to their furry coats, twisted and turned through the water in a love chase.

Like two tiny torpedoes, driven by the full thrust from broad, hair-covered hind feet, they played follow-my-leader between the stones, through the circle of a submerged barrel hoop, and under the drowned branch of a tree. Darting round the edge of a rock, they scattered a shoal of sticklebacks, sailed through a waving tangle of moss, and rose to gulp air above the surface.

Nose to tail, they bobbed to the air every half-minute, sometimes leaping clear of the water in their frolics, then dived again, delighting in their aquatic prowess. Playfully, they overturned small stones on the river bed, chopped at a caddis worm, and rose to chase a red alder catkin which floated on the mirror of the water's surface.

Motator, the pied-wagtail, bobbing to the marsh-marigolds on the edge of the water, flipped into the air when startled by the sudden appearance of the shrews and flighted to a close-by alder bough, causing a hawking swallow to dart aside.

Motator watched the shrews run from the water over soft bankside mud. Each was about three inches of black, shiny, velvety fur, and they chased each other under the exposed roots of the bankside grasses, and between heart-shaped celandine leaves. They explored a hole which ran between the roots of the alder tree. They chirped together in their game, and a coal-tit answered them. They returned to deep water to play in their natural environment.

Wriggling with fish-like movements, they forced air-bubbles from their fur,

Rats, Mice, Voles, Shrews

Rats: Public enemy No.1 as a destroyer of food and a carrier of disease. Versatile and clever.

Brown Rat.

Water -Vole : None of rat crimes. Charming. Inoffensive. Timid. Simple and unassuming. Strong swimmer Uses four feet. 3 m.p.h.

Water Vole

Mice: Bright, beady eyes.
Large rounded ears.
Pointed nose.
Scaley, sparsely-haired tail.
Pest- destructive.
Rate of breeding is means
of survival.

Wood Mouse

House Mouse

Voles: Smart little animals.
Smaller ears. Rounded muzzles.
Shorter, hairy tail.
Bulkier and larger than mice.
Pest-agricultural produce.

Short-tailed Vole

Shrews: Primitive. Much maligned.
Tiny eyes. Small ears.
Odd-looking snout.
Mole-like fur.
Farmer's ally - eats grubs.
Slugs, snails, insect pests. etc.

Common Shrew

floated on the underwater currents, and rose for air. Their appearance on the sunlit surface was seen by a large herring-gull flighting at tree-top height. It flew lower, and when the shrews surfaced again, it dropped at them, neck extended, beak agape, to take one.

Two feet above its quarry and the prize within grasp, the bird's concentration was broken by a movement on the bankside. For the fateful second which saved the shrew, the gull faltered, uncertain, and it veered away to rise in flight as Gael pushed through tall rushes on the riverside.

Even more opportune, a few days later, was Gael's rescue, from a lingering death, of Mulos, the wood-mouse, who at the time had a helpless family of five plump little babies totally dependent upon her. Bare-skinned and blind, the newly-born wood-mice huddled together in the cradle of their home on the ground, a cosy nest of chopped grasses which Mulos had twined into the growing grasses and nettle stems to blend from the sight of Kee, the kestrel, and Aluco, the tawny-owl.

Ever fearful of the terror from the sky which could snatch her and her family to instant death, Mulos was also conscious, in her tiny brain, of the danger of ground predators. Easy prey for stoat, weasel, fox and the roaming farm cat, her family depended entirely for their safety on her ingenuity in concealing their presence. Her nest, round and tight, and with two small entrance holes, was sited to attract the least attention. It was some distance from the bottom of the dry-

The crumbs left by picnickers provided a banquet for Mulos, the long-tailed field mouse.

stone wall which was the natural route for skulking predators and, with the hastening growth of the nettle patch, was well screened from above.

All was serene and quiet, and the baby mice squeaked in pleasurable satisfaction as Mulos suckled them. A bumble-bee buzzed in leisurely flight over the nest, and Mulos tensed her body in sudden anxiety until the drone was recognised and placed as harmless. The bee flew up and away, passing among six tortoiseshell butterflies which danced together above the nettle leaves, darting and twisting in strong and rapid flight, and flashing their upper-wing colouring in the bright sunbeams. For the butterflies also, the nettles were a nursery; their eggs laid on the leaves would hatch into hairy caterpillars which would feed on the plants.

Her suckling finished, Mulos slipped from her nest and quickly darted away, scurrying along a narrow tunnel between the grass and nettle stems so that the glint of her sleek brown fur was not caught in the sunlight. Her actions were fast, her movements purposeful as she followed her tunnel. Some 20 yards away from the nest, and through the stone wall on the bank of the river, Mulos had a favoured feeding area. In it was food of infinite variety, for the bankside was used by picnickers. Scattered in the grass, Mulos was able to find crumbs of many tastes, provided she was there before her neighbours, robin, chaffinch, starling and dunnock.

Mulos ran her route from the nest — out of the nettle clump at the upright stem of a horsetail plant, to the right of a dainty tall-stemmed mayflower, between the pale stalks of bluebells and under the broad sceening leaves of a dandelion — until she reached the wall.

It was a section of wall in which she knew every tunnel and crevice between the stones — some tiny in which she alone could find refuge and along which only she of minute stature could travel; others huge and cavernous in comparison to her own proportions.

Nose twitching for every scent, jet-black eyes peering short-sightedly, Mulos

The house-mouse is a scavenger, and pretty as it can look, its dirty habits spread disease.

ran into one of the gaps between the stones on her way to her feeding ground. It was when she came through to the other side of the 20-inch thick wall that she found the pint-sized milk bottle wedged upright between stones, placed there by some untidy picnicker. She sniffed the interesting scent of souring milk coated round the rim of the bottle, and stretched her mouth to taste. It was good, and she licked the rim-edge clean.

Gripping the bottle-rim with her tiny hind-feet, Mulos balanced, and hopefully stretched her head into the bottle. There was more milk in the bottom, and she slid down the glass to reach it. She fed until the bottle was licked clean, and it was then that she found she was trapped. The bottle sides were too smooth to climb, the narrowing neck did not permit a leap, and she could not reach any higher than stretching upright from her hind feet, and that was not high enough. She tried to leap and to scramble up the glass. She struggled to reach the round opening above her, and her energy became exhausted. She was hopelessly trapped.

She had been bottled for ten minutes, and her young family were in danger of becoming motherless, when Gael arrived to save the mouse. Nosing for rabbits at the bottom of the wall, Gael took the scent of the mouse through the mouth of the bottle. She savoured the smell, pushing her nostrils on to the top of the bottle. Dislodged by the push of Gael's nose, the bottle rolled on to its side on the ground — and Mulos darted out to safety.

Gael saw her go, and playfully pounced on to the grass into which Mulos had disappeared. Nostrils blowing along the line of the mouse's run, Gael quickly followed the scent to the wall when, defeated in her quest, she turned away from the hunt to see a fledgling song-thrush watching her with bright round eyes.

Clean and immaculate in his first spotted feathering, the short-tailed youngster was puzzled by the antics of the dog. Perched on the top of a sheep-post which jutted above the wall, he watched with the cocky independence of youth, both interested and wondering at Gael's purpose. Fearless to the point of negligence, the thrush saw no danger in Gael's activities, but a cock chaffinch which joined the youngster on the next post was not too sure.

Splendid in colours of blue, pink and chestnut, the chaffinch, whose name was Coelebs because much of his life was spent in bachelorhood, was doubtful because he had taken a mate who brooded eggs in a nest 50 yards away, and he was always extra cautious at such a time. He sang to keep his confidence high, though his notes were a little monotonous. His eyes were never still, and when Gael looked up at his perch in passing, he panicked and changed his song to a note of alarm. Coelebs was silly to cry alarm. The creatures of the countryside were relaxed and content about their business until his 'chink' call rang out. It upset his wife who became unnecessarily fearful for her eggs. A mallard duck called hastily to gather her happy brood of cheeping ducklings from their games in the riverside grasses. Ten of them, they ran to their mother's voice, and she hurriedly shepherded them into the water.

Their loud cheepings finally disturbed the confident song-thrush into flight and, testing his wings as a bee buzzed by, the youngster managed to keep level

The chaffinch was one of Gael's most colourful neighbours in Rack Clough.

flight away over the pasture from the riverside — and straight into the chaffinch's interpretation of danger!

The young song-thrush pitched into the twigs of a hawthorn bush under which Gael had decided to stretch her body in rest. Gael noted the bird's arrival, but was more interested in the voice of a cuckoo which perched in the garb of a hawk, and called its name from the top of the hawthorn whose buds were on the point of bursting white.

In the field, house-martins darted low over the backs of ewes and lambs, snatching in their open mouths the dancing insects on which to feed. Between food-flights, the martins gathered up tiny pellets of moist soil from the grass-bare earth in the gateway and carried them to the under-eaves of the farmhouse where they were moulding their cup-shaped nests. Their family rearing was only just starting, whilst, two yards along the gutter-line of the building, a squawking brood of six young starlings called continuously for food from their nest in a hole by the gutter-bracket.

Bluebells were in flower on the bankside where Gael rested beneath the thorn hedge and, dotted in damp areas across the pasture where the lambs played, were lilac-coloured mayflowers — the flowers of the lady's smock. Among them were deep butter-yellow king-cup flowers, and a cluster of primroses struck a paler yellow blotch in the green of the grass.

Dainty wood-sorrel flowers lifted mauve-veined white blooms above pale green heart-shaped leaves; yellow buttercups, white daisies and orange dandelions jostled their growth. Tall horse-chestnut trees grew their large white candles of flowers, and sycamores were bright with new leaves.

Well hidden in the tracery of thorn twigs not far from Gael's head, a dainty dunnock covered five small eggs, as blue as a summer sky, in a neat hair-lined nest and, a little further along the hedgerow, a blackbird warmed eggs which were on the point of hatching. Gael rested quietly on the ground, and the young song-thrush dozed in the tree.

Straying from the waterside, a blunt-nosed water-vole nibbled the leaf of a

Trim and smart in subdued feathering, the dunnock built a hedgerow nest to match.

dandelion plant. It lingered, stretched a hind-leg and scratched behind its ear, before becoming uneasy when two tortoiseshell butterflies danced too close. Quickly the vole ran back between covering grasses to the riverside.

The butterflies, a male and a female, delighted in a carefree skirmish, danced over Gael's golden coat, then skipped away to a more practical clump of nettles. On the terminal leaves of the nettle plants, the female tortoiseshell would lay her eggs, and the clump would become a nursery and food supply for her caterpillars.

It was a pleasant day and, after the false alarm which Coelebs gave to his neighbours, all had settled back into a warm and ordered life, busy though it was with family duties to attend to. Gael was not so inhibited — nor was the young thrush which perched above her head — and they both went to sleep. Gael laid her head on her white forepaws and dozily closed her eyes; the young thrush tucked its head under its left wing and dozed.

It was that instinctive sense that is held by all animals, but denied to humans, which opened Gael's eyes after some five minutes of doze. Without any movement of her head, she opened her eyes to see that she was under close scrutiny.

Light in the sunshine, two pricked ears, a small neat pointed face and bright eyes looked at Gael without fear. The fox cub was little more than a month old and had not yet learned to fear, and its eyes were wide with innocence when it peeped at Gael from the side of a sycamore trunk.

Gael did not move to frighten the cub; she too was interested and friendly towards the young fox which she knew to be some way from home. (Its home, along with four brothers and sisters, was away up the side of the clough among the tangle of rhododendron bushes.) Gael lay still, watching.

The cub was wearing a patchy coat, the red fur of growing-up mottling the brown of babyhood. Its nose and ears were fox-pointed; its eyes were bright with fun. To the inexperienced cub, Gael looked very much like one of her own kind, although the scent was wrong. The fox cub whimpered with excitement and, though a little unsure and unsteady on puppy legs, walked boldly towards Gael.

Bright eyes without fear.

Gael waited as the cub came at her with a playful humour; she waited until the cub reached her and bit at her ear; she rolled on her side when the cub tried to nip her nose. Over and over the dog and the fox tumbled in a playful ecstasy, the cub squealing in excitement whilst Gael growled her mock threats.

The song-thrush had left its perch above Gael's head in hurried confusion. It was a wild and carefree romp which the fox cub had with Gael, for the little collie accepted the game, and her mouth was gentle in the mock battle. Over and over they rolled on the leaf carpet beneath the hedge, the cub snapping and biting at Gael's ears with its needle-sharp puppy teeth, whilst she tried to dodge each sortie.

Gael played the mother-role, allowing the cub the privileges which were granted to all young things, whilst making sure that she did not catch the pain of its sharp teeth. The grip-and-pull technique which was the natural bite of the young fox could be a painful experience. Gael and the cub enjoyed a heedless roistering which took no account of the normal relationship between their kind, for the cub at little more than a month old was too young to fear, and Gael too wise and gentle to do any harm.

It was dangerous play for the cub to accept, with total confidence and trust, the good nature of a strange creature, however like in form Gael might be; it was the normal type of activity for a growing fox cub with its own kind.

Fox cubs, like so many young mammals, grow their strength and learn their early woodcraft in play. Ducking and weaving, darting and swerving, snapping and biting, the fox cub attacked Gael with all the ferocity it could muster. With legs still awkward to control, body swaying with tubbiness, and tail wagging in pleasure, the cub showed its teeth in a snarl whilst trying to bite Gael's ears and nose.

Suddenly the cub tired and flopped on the leaves of Gael's couch, its energy used up in the total assault. Gael settled down by the cub's side, wrinkled her nose at the baby's strong odour, yet flipped her tongue over its red coat. It twitched its tail in liking, and closed its eyes in absolute trust of its new and strange bed-fellow.

Trogo, the mousy wren, saw the strange partnership and could not contain his surprise. He churred resounding comments so that he was quickly joined by many of his woodland neighbours. Ruddock, the robin, perched on the thorn over Gael's couch; Coelebs, with something really to shout about, alighted on a twig of the same tree; and Chook, the shiny-feathered blackbird, came to see the strange sight.

Only when Pyat, the magpie, who involved himself with everything which happened in the woodland, flew to a perch in the tall sycamore so that he could look down on the scene, did the other birds disperse. They had only hatred, and some fear, of the magpie who bullied their lives whenever he could.

Gael heard the interest with which the birds viewed her friendship with the cub. She heard Pyat make his entrance, for though her eyes were closed in a half-sleep, her ears were open to the comments of the birds. The fox cub was not yet experienced in having a watchful 'cat-nap' and, totally dependent on its parents — or their substitute — slept deeply in ignorance of the happenings around.

Pyat poured typical call and abuse down upon the dog and cub from his safe perch above their heads, and Gael opened her eyes and curled her lip in a gesture of scorn. The cub barely moved, sleepily pressing closer to Gael's fur in a long, relaxing yawn.

But there was a surprisingly sudden and different reaction in the cub when a sharp and resounding yap echoed down the valley of the clough. As though charged with a surge of energy, and barely taking time to open its eyes, the cub ran from Gael's side as fast as it could. Tottering on unsteady legs, it disappeared round the corner of the sycamore trunk from whence it came. Mother had called — and mother must be obeyed — immediately!

Gael did not move to follow. She knew the cub's home with the rest of its family up at the top of the clough, and she knew something of the wrath of Silva, their mother, when she was displeased. The cub would get a very sharp reminder that it had strayed much too far whilst she had been away from the den. Gael lowered her head on to her white forepaws and closed her eyes.

Chapter 10

Lapwing anxieties

Through the trials and tribulations of raising a family on the ground, the lapwings view Gael with mixed feelings when she licks their eggs, noses their babies and guards them from enemies.

Gael was fascinated by the lapwing's antics. She lay flat against the close sheep-cropped grass, nose resting on her white forepaws, almond eyes fixed on the bird. She was close, only four yards from the bird which stood on a slight ground hillock, but her presence was seemingly ignored.

Standing on one leg, the lapwing bobbed and bowed, tilting and turning its body whilst combing its plumage with its other foot. Twisting with the agility of a contortionist, it stretched back its leg, bright red against the white feathers, to comb the feathers of its tail into position. Under and over its tail, under its wings, its nails groomed the feathers into place whilst it balanced easily on one leg.

For two minutes it preened then, satisfied, it combed its head feathers, up and over the dark crest feathers, closing one eye whilst it scratched at an irritation. Finally, when the lay of the feathers felt comfortable, it shook them into place and tightened them to its body. Only then did it turn to watch Gael whose flattened immobility had caused not the slightest concern.

The darting, zipping flight of a swallow, skimming low over the heads of lapwing and collie, broke the understanding trust. Gael lifted her head to the swallow's line and, not liking the dog's sudden movement, the lapwing spread its wings and climbed leisurely into the air.

Gael jumped up, and following the low flight of the lapwing, bounded over the ground. Close to the field-wall she startled Chacka, the wheatear. He called 'weet-chack-chack' and flitted down the wallside, his distinctive white rump catching a ray of sunshine, and attracting Gael's attention. Chacka called partly in annoyance and partly to inform his mate of Gael's presence. She was safely hidden in a cavity between the stones of the wall, gently brooding her six pale blue eggs.

Chacka alighted on the wall top some 20 yards away, and immediately winged off again, suddenly seeing that he had landed too close to Kew, the little-owl, whose motionless colouring blended almost into invisibility against the stonework. Kew slightly swivelled his head, no sudden movement betraying his presence, and watched Gael cross the corner of the field. His round yellow-rimmed eyes were unblinking, and not a ripple of movement marked his perch. He saw all, and patiently waited for some item of food — a small bird, mammal, or glossy beetle — to come along.

Gael squeezed under the bar of the field-gate, and trotted down the rough tussocky slope of Rack Clough to visit Lita, the female meadow-pipit, who brooded five mottled brown eggs in a secluded grass-woven cup by the edge of the bogland. Stealthily though she moved in her approach, each pad carefully placed without noise on the ground, as Gael pushed her nose between the long grasses which hid the nest, Lita darted away. Gael sucked the warm scent from the cosy cradle, flipped her tongue over the eggs, and left them undamaged.

Between the rushes and mossy growth of the bog, Gael played her daily game

Lapwing
Vanella
Scholey Hill
May

of hide-and-seek with six moorhen chicks, chided the while with harsh croaking protests from Galla, their mother. Ugly-looking little downy creatures, with vivid blue and red crowns contrasting their black body colour, the youngsters were a match for Gael, darting in an out of cover on long, spindly legs until sinking into hiding. When Gael did nose one out of cover, she left it after a thorough scent search, and when she went from the swampland, Galla reassembled her brood unharmed.

The bogland and the high pastures above Rack Clough were a favourite haunt for Gael during May days, for she enjoyed the company of so many young creatures. Lapwings were particular favourites, for she was able to join in their daily lives so completely. From the arrival on the hill of the parent birds and their ritual mobbing of her, right to the final flighting of their youngsters, she shared their fears, anxieties and satisfaction of family rearing and, on occasion, saved their eggs and youngsters by scaring away predators.

Although they came to accept her regular visits, she was often the target for their displeasure, particularly in the early stages of their nesting stint. Vanella, the female lapwing, had eggs on the ground, and though she had often seen Gael in the pasture, she was still nervous of the collie's intrusion into her domestic affairs. Diving in flight, she almost brushed Gael's head with her wing-tips, braking, then zooming upwards before collision. She swooped down again, calling her annoyance with plaintive voice, and rolling and banking above Gael's head. The air sang in the webs of her rounded wings, a throbbing, humming sound which christened her scientifically after *vannus*, the fan.

Since her first egg was laid, Vanella had mobbed and harried every creature which had entered her territory. With her mate, Puit, she had attacked crow, gull and magpie which had sought her eggs for food. Together, they had beaten down on Grey, the fox, with such fury that, rather than have the whole countryside know of his whereabouts on the hill, he had slunk quietly away. They had also startled away the playful lambs from the nest.

Gael simply ignored Vanella's mobbing tactics. She flipped her pink tongue over the three eggs which lay, warm and neatly grouped, on the grass-lined cradle-scrape on the ground. Her interest was cursory and, her inspection of the eggs completed, she trotted away across the close-cropped grass. Vanella followed her until she left the field, before returning to settle back over the eggs and continue their incubation.

It was an anxious time for the lapwing. The incubation period was four long weeks, and ground-laid eggs were so vulnerable. Only their marvellous camouflage markings of blotched, black-streaked pattern over dull olive-green shells made them difficult to find, and their cradle blended into the general ground cover of dead grass, wisps of hay, and the spread manure of the field.

Gael left Vanella's field, and was immediately accosted by another lapwing, Vanella's neighbour, who flew up from his guard-post to mob the collie and call a warning of impending disturbance to his mate, Bronda. She also incubated three eggs, as Corbie, the black crow, had stolen her first egg as he had done with Vanella's first-laid.

Mobs
interfering
visitors
during
breeding
season.

Both male
and female
wear crest.

Difficult to sex
male and female
similar in appearance

Lapwing

(Vanellus vanellus)

Friend of sheep-farmer - destroys the
water-snail host of the embryonic
form of liver-fluke in sheep.

Eats insects, snails, wireworms, and
    other creatures generally harmful
        to agriculture.

Social bird outside breeding
    season - spends nine months
        of life in flocks.

Slow "wobbly" flight action.
Dancing flight in courtship.

Generally boldly
black and white
plumage.

Nests on ground.
No cover - relies on
camouflage. Single brood
of four pear-shaped
eggs. April - May.
Chicks mobile and move
away quickly after born.

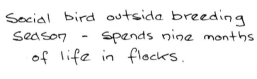

A lapwing, relaxed in the brooding of eggs.

Bronda's nest was small and compact on a dry patch of earth amidst an array of water puddles in the wet field, and Gael sank her white feet into black mud when she walked to it. This nest contained eggs of differing colours, one being of a clay-coloured background, the other two of olive-brown. Gael flipped them with her tongue and ran off to her next point of call.

The wild bugling of Coorli rang bubbling notes across the hill to tell his mate that Gael was approaching her nest, hidden in the vegetation beyond the bog, and the curlew's warning was also heeded by Tringa, the redshank, whose three brown-spotted and blotched buff-coloured eggs were the best hidden on the hill. Entering the territory of a third pair of lapwings — each pair occupied about two acres — on her route, Gael visited their nest which was the neatest of the three.

Some two yards from a ponded depression in the field, it was set on a good vantage point, was comfortably lined, and its four eggs were neatly arranged with their pointed ends to the centre in a warm brooding pattern. Each of the eggs was a marvellous self-contained nursery for a young lapwing, and a much stronger container than was generally surmised.

An egg gives a young bird, at the initial stages of its development, all that it needs to live and grow in a sheltered environment. By what could be termed a pregnancy outside the body, it also enables the parent bird to remain unencumbered in its daily task of living.

The protective shell of the egg is immensely strong in its construction owing to the setting of the particles of which it is formed. These are arranged rather like the stones of an archway which bind together when outside pressure is applied. Yet, whilst the particles interlock under external force, they are easily broken open from inside, thus enabling the young, weak bird to emerge at hatching time.

Bird's eggs vary as much in shape as in colour, and the lapwing's eggs are sharply pointed at one end, and round at the other, somewhat like a pear. The strongest shape for an egg is to be completely round like a ball, but nature has to get sufficient size into the egg to provide maximum nourishment for the chick, and also to proportion this to the size of the bird which lays the egg. Thus nearly all eggs are elongated and tapered at one end. The lapwing's eggs are approximately two inches in size to the bird's size of 12 inches.

There has to be space inside the egg for the chick to grow and, in the lapwing's case, the chick remains in the egg until it is down-covered and is able to run around almost immediately after hatching.

The chick develops from the germ cell which is contained at the top of the yolk and, as it grows, it feeds on the yolk which is full of nutrition. To prevent damage, the yolk is held in suspension on two twisted membranes attached, like springs, to the inner ends of the shell. The yolk is surrounded by the 'white' or albumen which also provides food, and which acts as a cushion. All is contained in covering membranes lining the inside of the shell, and together, whilst permitting oxygen to enter, these prevent harmful germs from entering the egg. External colouring on the shell plays an important part for the safety of an egg in many cases — particularly so for the lapwing's egg, its black-blotched olive-brown markings blending perfectly into the background of the nest which is little more than a grass-lined scrape on the earth.

The long hooped beak of the curlew was used like a drinking-straw to suck food from soft ground.

The Egg supplies everything

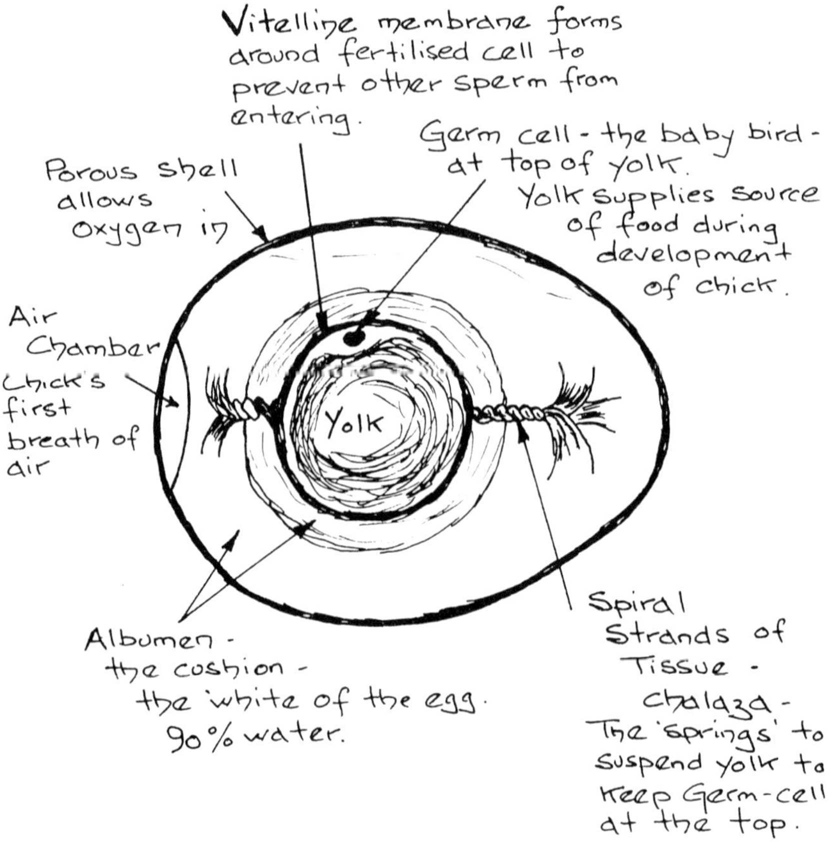

Vitelline membrane forms
around fertilised cell to
prevent other sperm from
entering.

Germ cell - the baby bird -
at top of yolk.

Yolk Supplies Source
of food during
development
of chick.

Porous shell
allows
Oxygen in

Air
Chamber
Chick's
first
breath of
air

Yolk

Albumen -
the cushion -
the white of the egg.
90% water.

Spiral
Strands of
Tissue -

Chalaza -
The 'springs' to
Suspend yolk to
keep Germ-cell
at the top.

Yolk contains nutrition
of fat and protein for
growing chick.
Amount varies in type of bird
as does length of incubation.

Shell strong from outside.
Weaker from inside to enable chick
to break-out using 'egg-tooth' chisel.

By the pondside where there was a fresh green colouring about the bur-reeds, Gael stretched to rest in the warm sunshine. She was quiet in her arrival at the pondside, and Krark, the heron, who was dozing on one leg in the shelter of the rushes across the water, was late in seeing her. His lack of vigilance annoyed him, and he called his anger in a loud, croaky voice as he slowly opened his great wings to let the breeze carry him into the air.

Angling the large span of his wings so that the breeze held him almost stationary, Krark watched Gael, and for a moment considered whether to harry the collie to teach her a lesson in manners. But Gael was too large for him to tackle, and there was no point in a useless display of bad temper. Krark spent his life going from one place to another, and rising higher into the sky, he slowly beat his wings and flew off down into the valley. Gael pricked her ears to the heron's departure, then swivelled them to cup the croaking notes of Kurra, the moorhen, who, knowing the collie to be there, did not venture from the reeds.

Gael watched a white butterfly dance across the reed tops, and when Kee, the kestrel, came to hang over the pond on hovering wings, she saw him mobbed by Teuk, the male redshank, and by Puit, Vanella's mate, both brave in the face of any imagined threat to their home. Such a waste of energy on such a warm day! Gael watched Kee simply glide from his attackers, and then she rested her head on her forepaws and dozed.

It was the following day when Gael helped her lapwing neighbours, Puit and Vanella, to defend their eggs against Corbie, the black crow. Corbie had managed to amble, by picking at the recently-spread manure clumps as a decoy, to within 20 yards of the lapwings' nest. Even though Puit was standing between him and the nest, and the three eggs which were his target were covered by Vanella, he was always prepared to try his luck. Hitherto he had always had to retreat under the fierce defensive assaults of the lapwings, but he did not accept defeat easily. Then there appeared another complication — which might turn to his advantage — when, keeping one eye on the guardian lapwing, he spotted Gael with his other eye as the little collie crossed the field.

She immediately presented a quandary for the three birds. Corbie was bold and arrogant and only flew from her path at the last moment; Puit normally winged into the air and dived to mob her; and Vanella usually slipped from her eggs, so as not to attract attention to them, before joining her mate in mobbing the intruder.

All three birds watched Gael's approach. Puit had the biggest problem. If he flew to divert Gael, would he let in Corbie who might outsmart Vanella. Gael solved his problem. Seeing her old adversary, Corbie, strutting on the ground, his thigh feathers pulled by the breeze so that he waddled like a portly clown, she chased towards him. The crow had no alternative but to fly, though with a protesting croak, and only as far as the boundary wall of the field, to the top of a post which held the sheep-wire in place. There, he stabbed his polished beak savagely against the post in anger.

Puit spread his black and white wings above his back and rose on the air, climbing to wheel in a throbbing dive down over Gael's head. Vanella quietly left her eggs and joined her mate in mobbing the collie. Almost brushing Gael with rounded wings which hummed as the air sang in the webs of feathers, both lapwings banked and rolled above her head with no measure of gratitude at her dispersal of the crow.

Unnoticed, a skylark slipped from covering three brown-mottled eggs lying in a cow's hoof-print in the ground which she had used for a nest. Living within ten yards of the lapwing's nest, she had used Puit's early warning system to Vanella as her own warning of danger.

Gael followed Corbie's flight-line to the wall. The crow watched her, cocking and twisting his head to look down at her. He was annoyed with her, but such was his nature that he would try to outwit the lapwings again — and the closer they got to hatching, the more delicious would be the eggs if he succeeded.

Corbie breasted the light wind, lifting both his wings to the air currents. He ran the primary feathers through his beak, stretched his leg under a wing, and shook the whole of his body feathers into a comfortable lie. Gael called his bluff with a yap, and Corbie leaped lightly from the post, slowly beat his wings four times and glided on outstretched feathers down the hillside. Gael followed him, stalking a black-capped reed-bunting through the rushes by the pondside until a cock mallard burst from cover beneath her feet and made her lift her head in sudden surprise.

She was welcomed into the woodland by the anxious pinking of a hen chaffinch, and the sweet, simple, song notes of a willow-warbler. A wood-pigeon wing-slapped from the safety of a new nest, built on the old structure of a crow's, when it heard Gael rustle the ground leaves. A great-tit, not so panic-prone as the pigeon, called 'zi-zi-zi' to warn its mate of the dog's presence. The female great-tit brooded seven tiny eggs, each white shell delicately pencilled in red, in a cleft in the trunk of an oak tree.

Although its plumage flamed with a blaze of chestnut-red in the green light beneath the trees, it was the constant fluttering movement which attracted Gael's attention to a restless bird. Weetic, the redstart, had returned from his winter home in the North African savanna.

Back on the hill, with another threat to their eggs safely met, Puit and Vanella quietly relaxed. Their lives were a constant, somewhat fatalistic, contrast of climax and anti-climax, despair and joy. Vanella returned to her nest, gently settling her body to warm the three eggs in the softness of her under-feathers. She watched a crowd of midges dance over water which lay stagnant in a deep rut gouged by the wheel of the farm tractor.

She dozed back into anti-climax. Her eyes closed, her head plume lowered as she relaxed, and the sunlight burnished the metallic green colours of her back feathers. The whites and blacks of her chest feathers contrasted above the rough rim of her nest. She was content. Some 30 yards away, Puit took up his look-out position on a slightly raised tussock of ground, ready again to call a warning of the next upset. Every creature which came within his eyesight was carefully examined to determine its role of friend or foe. So the days passed.

When the day of hatching came, although it was not the first time that Gael had

Weetic, the redstart, soon found a mate to mother his family in a nest between the stones of the clough-wall.

heard cheeping eggs, they never failed to puzzle her. She stood over the three eggs in Vanella's nest and tilted her head in perplexity, first to one side, then to the other, her ears pricked and cupped as she pondered the mystery of the tiny voices. She bent her neck and flipped her tongue over the eggs, feeling the tiny prick of an egg-tooth from one of the eggs.

Watching closely, Gael saw the white-tipped beak of one of the unborn chicks enlarge the tiny hole it had already chipped through the shell. The white tip on the baby's beak was the egg-tooth, so called because its sole purpose was to chisel a way through the egg-shell before it was discarded.

Gael squatted on her haunches, fascinated by the cheeping eggs and the tiny hole which was being pecked from within into the shell of one of them. She was not left in peace to solve the strangeness of the eggs, for Vanella and Puit, having failed to misguide her from their nest by initial mobbing tactics, returned with renewed assault.

They swooped through the air to harry her, coming so close in their agitation for the safety of their unborn chicks that their wing-tips brushed Gael's head, and the rush of wind from their feathers stirred the silky hairs of her ear tufts. The lapwings clamoured their alarm, and turned and twisted above Gael's head, swooping down upon her in their anxiety. Always active in mobbing any possible predator, they were now wildly excited and distressed, with their chicks so close to emergence from the eggs.

Gael crouched as Vanella dived wildly towards her, flipped her tongue again over the eggs, and then, still puzzled, she retreated under the barrage of flailing wings and rushing air. She trotted away to the boundary wall of the field, leaped lightly to the top of the stones to disturb a buff-feathered twite and, squeezing under the sheep-wire, disappeared from the lapwings' territory. Vanella immediately planed down to the nest with its precious contents, called the 'all clear' to the chicks she had not yet seen, and settled carefully over the three eggs as a spatter of cold raindrops fell to the ground.

It was at this time, when the chicks began to cheep within the eggs, that their parents took an extra interest, talking to them as though they realised for the first time that the eggs were alive. Chicks usually emerge from the eggs all together as a complete family, although this is not always so, and the period of hatching from commencement of egg chipping appears to be very variable.

When Gael visited the hill on the following morning, she surprised Puit who was standing over the nest, fascinated by the sight of his babies. Two chicks had hatched, and the third was coming through the remaining egg. Gael was just as fascinated as their father, though, heeding the loud cries of warning from their mother, Vanella, who twisted and turned in anxious flight above their heads, the two baby lapwings crouched motionless.

Their stillness puzzled Gael for they were warm to her questing nose. She flipped her tongue over their downy bodies, but still they laid unmoving. She pondered the mystery of their stillness. Even a gentle push from her nose failed to stir them. Again she flicked the babies with her tongue, smoothing their softness with dampness.

With no visible signs of fear at the collie's intrusion, the babies completely ignored her persuasion and heeded the alarm notes of their parent without question. Orders were to crouch low and not to move — and the reaction to command was so strongly ingrained at birth that not even the pushing nose of Gael could break it.

Gael appeared to take the same commands and crouched low beside the chicks, but hers was an instinctive reaction to the desperate mobbing of Vanella. It was an impulsive crouch to avoid the rush of air from the bird's wings which brushed the tips of her ears. Vanella was really annoyed at Gael's interference; Puit even more so for he had suddenly found a real interest in his family. Together they swept down on Gael.

Under such an attack, Gael gave way, deciding to humour her belligerent neighbours, although she was still baffled by the inactivity of the babies. Flipping her tongue over the two chicks in a final gesture of friendship, she turned and walked away across the field.

Some time later, when the third chick had escaped from its egg, Vanella's family left home. Skilfully camouflaged in black-marbled downy-brown colouring to protect them, the chicks did not linger in the nest. Although also marked with conspicuous white collars, possibly to attract their parents' attention when against a sombre background, they were completely hidden when crouched, the collar colouring tucked into the fold of brown.

As they were able to run as soon as they were dry from the egg, Vanella led her chicks away from the nest. Initially they would lead precarious lives, their sole defence being their colouring when they crouched into the grasses of the field on the instructions from their wary parents. Immediate reaction to the alarm call was imperative for their safety. They must crouch immobile, and under grass cover if possible. They were zealously guarded and cared for by their parents — Vanella, brooding and warming them with her own body heat; Puit, on sentry duty and always on the watch for possible danger.

Foraging round Vanella like domestic chicks in the farmyard, the babies were able to feed themselves almost immediately after leaving the nest, and they wandered completely unafraid until called to order. For some six weeks, until they became fledged and able to fly, they would be dependent on the vigilance of their parents.

During the six weeks that Vanella's family were on the hill, Gael met them

Lapwing chick.
Vanella's first-born.
Scholey Hill.
May.

often, and she played her games with them. She used her keen nose to find them, for they gave off little scent and the grass grew to give them good cover. Each time she found them, they used the same ploy to try to outwit her, crouching close in the grass, relying on a motionless cringe, but chiefly on her kindly nature.

After the perplexity which she had felt at their still attitude on their first meeting at the nest, she did succeed in getting them to move. One day, when the youngsters were well-feathered at three weeks old, and dispersed for safety over the field area, she flicked her tongue over the baby feathering of one of them. It had grown the distinctive crest of its kind, though a little raggle-taggle, and its sleek brown feathering blended, like a clod of earth, with the ground. Its eyes, a beautiful bilberry blue set in rings of rich brown, were well shadowed so as not to attract attention.

It still listened to the 'lie still' commands of Puit and Vanella who flighted the air above, but who were not now so agitated at Gael's regular appearances among their family. The youngster accepted Gael's quizzing nostrils without fear. She nosed the youngster, but only when she persisted did it deign to move, jumping on to its long legs and running away between the grasses.

Gael watched it, and, her playful spirit rising, she trotted after it. For five minutes she shepherded the baby from point to point across the field, flanking to turn it, heading it into retreat, with all the skill of her breeding. Above her head, the calls of protest from the agitated parents grew to crescendo as they watched the startling scene. Finally, Gael took their message. She settled on to her haunches, her tongue lolling in the heat of a blazing sun, and watched the young lapwing scurry away.

Chapter 11

Decoy acts

Why Gael is surprised by a hare, spat at by Kew, scolded and bamboozled by pipits and buntings, and why, after meeting two charming babies, her unpopularity grows.

Although light and gentle, the wind was fresh in the heat of mid-day sunshine and Gael sought its touch to cool her blood, standing on the top of a small hillock above Rack Clough. She panted the heat from her lungs, her pink tongue lolling from her gaping mouth. Her wet nose took the message of every ripple of air, her nostrils probed the layers of the wind currents to read the numerous tales for something of interest.

She stood quite still, facing into the breeze, her handsome head held high. Sunbeams danced across her fur, burnishing her beauty, shimmering the deep golden sable of her flanks, lighting the whiteness of her chest. She was trim and graceful, the slight fingers of the breeze stirring the silkiness of her coat to stream the feathering of her lines. Ears pricked, head moving slightly, she listened to the voices of the wind, the call of a gull in the cloudless sky above, the bleat of a lamb from lower down the hill, the cheerful notes of a willow-warbler from among the trees of the woodland clough.

Chacka, the wheatear, flew to the nearby wall top to watch her. Gael closed her almond eyes in rapt concentration, sorting the scents of the air, the mixed perfume of mayflowers, bluebells, buttercups and daisies, the heavy odour of sheep, the faint trace of hare. It was the taint of hare which interested her, and she moved up the line of scent.

Lievre, the female hare, her cleft nostrils sifting the breeze, her long ears erect to every sound, sat poised and alert, her head above the stalks of the thick grass growth on the fringe of the field. She saw Gael coming towards her, but made no move to hide, nor did she prepare to flee. On other occasions she would have crouched low in the grasses or bolted from the dog, relying on camouflage or her speed to take her to safety.

This day she waited, openly showing herself as if indeed to attract Gael's attention, for this day she had the safety of her family to consider. Gael was moving down a line which would bring her upon three young leverets which were couched in the grass. Only one day old, the three babies lay hidden by the thick grass growth. Open-eyed, with short, furry coats, they crouched together, sheltered from the direct rays of the sun by the breeze-bent grasses over their backs. Unmoving and silent, they were helpless in their extreme babyhood, totally reliant on their mother's protection.

Leveret.
Son of Lievre.
Scholey Hill.
June.

Brown Hare
(Lepus capensis)

Long, black-tipped
ears.

The speediest
animal on the
hill

Fore-
feet

Hind-feet

Feet over-lap
at speed.

Strong hind
legs.

Gael saw Lievre. Ready for a game, even in the heat of the sun, she raced towards her. Strangely, the hare did not flee, and suddenly realising that this was not their usual pattern of play, Gael hesitated, a little perplexed. She was more surprised when Lievre ran at her, the hare grinding her big yellow teeth in anger, and only dodged aside when hare and dog almost bumped into each other.

Startled, Gael watched the hare leap round and rush back at her, and this time leaped right over her back when the collision again seemed inevitable. Only when Lievre kicked out with her strong hind feet and caught Gael a glancing blow on the head did the little collie become annoyed at the unprovoked antics of the hare. This was not their usual game. Gael curled her lip and snarled her displeasure, rushing at

Lievre with a hint of venom in her own action. Lievre spurted away, and raced from Gael, hoping and expecting the collie to follow. Gael did so — so fast that she kept pace with Lievre until they were a field distant from the leverets.

Lievre was satisfied. Dashing through a sheep-hole in the stone wall, she increased speed in a curving, right-hand turn so that she was out of Gael's sight when the collie came through the wall. Gael had to follow her by scent, a much slower and more laborious task. Returning over a wide arc of ground to her babies, Lievre took all her inbred precautions, approaching their couch warily, breaking her line by sideways leaps, and by re-tracing her tracks with scent-baffling care. When she crept quietly into the nest, Gael was three fields away and no longer interested in the hare. Lievre suckled her family, and she was content.

Gael lost interest in Lievre when a baby blue-tit fell to the ground in front of her stalk of the hare. It was sudden, unexpected, and it surprised her. Casting for Lievre's scent by the wallside, she had heard a faint rustling in a hole between two stones of the wall, some 12 inches above her head. Looking up, she had seen a tiny blue and yellow feathered jewel appear on the lip of the hole, and had stared into the black unblinking eye of a baby blue-tit.

It was doubtful which had been the more surprised, the collie, wise in the ways of the

Young Blue-tit.
Scholey Hill.
June.

countryside, or the fledgling bird, taking its first step into the strange world.

Whichever, the bird had reacted first. Unimpressed with its first venture from the nest in the wall, it had turned to retreat from the strange creature before it. But the stone which was the letting-board of the parent blue-tits throughout their family rearing had been made smooth by their coming and going and, tiny claws scraping for a hold, the baby bird had slipped, and cheeping in alarm, had fallen to land in the grass between Gael's front paws.

Undismayed by this first frightful adventure, the baby peered up into the eyes of the dog. If dogs laugh, Gael opened her mouth, curled back her lips, and did so. She bent her head and flicked her tongue in a gesture of friendliness over the fledgling — much to its annoyance as it started to loudly chirp for help.

From the top of the wall, two frantic parents scolded in anger. Anxious days were beginning for them for they had another five youngsters ready to leave the hole in the wall. The baby fluttered and scrambled up against the stones of the wall, and Gael left it to its struggle to return to its home.

She tossed a stick in her mouth, trapped it under her forepaws, and broke it in her teeth. An empty shotgun cartridge packet intrigued her, and she tore it to shreds in her play.

She hunted flies and snapped a blue-bottle in her jaws, then spat it out with distaste. She blew a crane-fly, spreading its tracery-wings to the sunbeams, from its perch on a dock leaf. She snatched a small soft pellet from beside Kew's resting rock, threw it in the air, caught it, and worried it to fragments of tiny mouse bones, colourful beetles' wing-cases, and fur and feathers — the indigestible parts of the little-owl's meal. Gael often played with the tasteless pellets which she found scattered around the lichened rock on which Kew liked to perch. Jutting up through the soil of the hill pasture, the rock gave the little-owl a good view of his upland territory.

Meeting her at the rock, Kew often joined in Gael's fun, safe in knowing that he would not be molested, for they had been tolerant neighbours on the hill for some time. Kew's part of the proceedings was to mew encouragement from his perch whilst jigging in excitement from foot to foot, a fluffy, bouncy ball of feathers no taller than a thrush. Gael always accepted the owl's company; Kew always welcomed her visits until she became too friendly and approached too close with her questing nose.

For the most part, their relationship was one of mutual regard, although whilst Gael was always willing to regard the owl as a companion, if Kew had had poor hunting, he would turn his round yellow-rimmed eyes to her with a look of intolerance and quit her presence. Dog and bird played together in individual roles, for they never touched each other, each drawing on the other's presence as a sort of participatory audience.

Kew was not at his perch on that visit, and it was the fearful notes of Prato and Lita, the meadow-pipits, which told Gael where he was. The little-owl was threatening their family of four half-grown baby pipits which lay in a couch of finely and strongly woven grasses beneath an overhanging tussock.

Even as a baby the kestrel had strong cutting notches on its oversize beak.

To the peace-loving pipits, Kew, squat, flat-headed, and taloned, was a ferocious-looking creature perched on the wall top but ten yards from their home. Puny though they were in comparison, they were not lacking in courage, and they twittered and scolded on fluttering wings around the owl's head. So strong was their parental instinct that they braved their mobbing to within a yard of the owl's deadly hooked beak.

Kew took not the slightest notice, indeed he took their agitation as a sign that food in the form of tender young birds was a distinct possibility. Testing his theory, he jumped from his perch and flew his bullet-headed body 20 yards to alight on a patch of banking. Frenzied calls from Prato and Lita when they followed his flight told Kew that their nest — and his food — was somewhere close by. He stood upright on the ground, and extended his ear-openings, listening intently for the slight sound of a tell-tale cheep from a young throat. Instead, his keen hearing took the sound of scampering feet as Gael came to investigate the cause of the pipits' prolonged alarm calls. When she came over the lip of the banking, Kew spat two staccato yaps into her face, and quickly winged his retreat.

For the time, the baby meadow-pipits were safe, although Gael caused continued distress to the parent birds by seeking out the nest and nosing their family. Prato and Lita fluttered over her head, then dropped to the ground three yards away. Seeing them alight, Gael bounded playfully towards them. They rose in confusion, and fluttered a further ten yards. Gael followed, and the pipits drew her from the nest. It was not a true decoy-act, but it succeeded in taking the collie from the nest.

Decoy-acts had often fooled Gael. Nico, the reed-bunting, had fooled her, drawing her away from his nest by throwing himself at her feet in feigned distress. Firstly she had heard the 'chit-chit-chit' notes of warning which Nico called to warn his mate and four young buntings of her coming. They were cradled in a home on stilts, their nest of cow hairs and grey sheep's wool slung between waving rush stems.

Gael had moved closer to the nest which she had known for some time, and where the baby buntings had gaped pink-mouthed to her twitching nose. (They interpreted any noise and presence as the arrival of food.) Within a yard of nosing the babies again, Gael had been distracted by Nico's stuttering wings hovering within a yard of her head. She had then been astonished to see the black-capped bird throw himself in a seemingly reckless action to a bare patch of ground by the nest-clump of rushes. She had watched, puzzled by his faltering wings and helpless behaviour on the short wet moss and turned to seek his problem, but when she had almost been upon him, Nico had fluttered up from the ground. Cleverly controlling his flight, he had risen no higher then Gael's head, and had moved no faster than a yard in front of her pace. Intrigued by the bird's actions, Gael had followed him. To encourage her, Nico had again flung himself to the ground, one wing outstretched as though uncontrollable, beak open as though gasping for breath. The ruse had succeeded and Gael accepted it. She had followed Nico away from the nest.

Clinging to a rush stem, one leg bent, gripping level with her breast, the other straight beneath her, Nico's mate, Riza had applauded his bravery with a low 'seeping' call — interspersed with 'chitting' notes to her babies to continue lying low in their nest.

Gael became familiar with the reed-bunting's decoy-act, and subsequently ignored it, but the decoy-acts she was most familiar with were those of Kurra, the moorhen, and Hyncha, the mallard duck. Kurra used to slip from her nest, cluck a warning to her chicks, and when some ten yards from the nest, openly scuttle between the rushes half-running, half-flying to scatter water in a noisy splash which attracted Gael's attention.

Hyncha's method of drawing attention away from her ducklings was similar to the moorhen's. It was a June day of warm sunshine and Gael was dozing on the side of Scholey Pond when she heard the weak, though clear and penetrating 'cheep-cheep-cheep' of a baby duckling coming from the rush cover. Tired of waiting for the 'all-clear' after its parent had led it with its five brothers and sisters to hide in the rushes at Gael's coming, the baby, a downy bundle of yellow and brown, sailed with confidence and poise into the open water of the pond.

Gael rose to her feet and walked into the shallows, her pads sinking into the

Cuddlesome baby owls belied their savage and bloodthirsty nature.

black mud, and the still water lapping her legs. Her head tilted, quizzically she mused over the little bright-eyed bundle of energy which sailed so confidently on the water — and quite cheekily to within two yards of where she stood.

The baby mallard was four days out of the egg, but perfectly happy in its wild surroundings, propelling itself over the water with determined strokes of its leathery-skinned webbed feet. Without a hint of fear, it cheeped to Gael, though they were the calls of communication with its own family. Unconscious of any danger, even the presence of Gael, it called its brothers and sisters to come and enjoy the fun of the smooth water.

The duckling was foolish to have ignored its mother's order to stay hidden in the shelter of the pond rushes, like its brothers and sisters, until Gael had left the area. Gael was harmless to its safety, but the next visitor could be Ruso, the fox, who had already snatched two of the mallard duck's family.

Hyncha knew this full well and, couched in the covering rushes, into which her mottled buff and brown feathering blended to hide her, she feared for the safety of her baby. She had but one course of action. Her heart thumped as she considered it. Her decision was made when, lured by the happy sounds of its brother on the water, another of her chicks broke from hiding and swam into the open. Like naughty, erring children, the two ducklings sported on the open water.

The most intricate and cleverly constructed of all nests was the home of Rosac and Sisee, the long-tailed tits.

Hyncha splashed from her hiding place, leaving her couch with an intentionally noisy clatter of wings and calls to distract Gael's attention from her babies. She flopped on to the water by the side of Gael, threshing spray with her feet and wings. Her brave ruse worked. Gael turned, startled, to the new interest, and the two ducklings, suddenly fearful of the confusion, dashed for the shelter and safety of the tangled rush growth.

Trailing her wing as though stricken, Hyncha played her decoy-act to perfection, switching all Gael's interest to herself, and drawing the collie through the shallows. It was a ruse which Gael knew, but which always had the desired effect, sending her scampering, water spray flying, after the supposedly crippled bird. The duck flopped through the rush bed and on to the grassy bank, teasing Gael after her. When the collie was well enough away from her family, Hyncha rose into the air, flighting quickly up over the hillside.

Gael watched her go, knowing that once again she had been fooled, yet she did not return to the ducklings. She scampered across the breast of the hill where the grass was springing high, and ran towards the woodland clough. By the time she was passing down the nettle-grown ditch, Hyncha had returned to the pond. Quacking her family together, she gathered them and led them in safe paddling on the pond water. Yet another anxious incident was passed, but life was full of hazards for the chicks, and she would be fortunate to see them all survive to maturity.

Young birds of every species are most vulnerable to predators immediately after hatching from the egg. It is sad, but very necessary that some, indeed many, young birds must die and never reach maturity. The slaughter of the innocents by predation, accident, hunger, sickness and adverse weather is the only way that nature contains the population, and of all other creatures as well as birds.

If a pair of great-tits averaged ten eggs each season, and all their nestlings survived to breed at the same rate, in ten years the original two birds would produce over 120 million offspring.

Mulos, the wood-mouse, had several litters of up to nine babies a year, and the earliest-bred of those youngsters would breed the same year. A female rabbit is sexually mature at four months, and has four or five litters of between three and nine youngsters a year. So it is essential that many young creatures must die before reaching maturity. This is really in the interest of preserving, not only their own species, but also others, for the weakest die and the strongest survive.

Chicks, such as the baby duckling which leaves the nest almost immediately on hatching, have less than a 50/50 chance of surviving to adulthood, being most vulnerable in the early downy days whilst wandering about the bogland. At that stage weather conditions are vital to their well-being, rain-soaked ground and grasses bringing on chills and pneumonia.

Nestlings of the nidicolous 'nest-attached' birds, such as the blackbird, robin and great-tit face perhaps even greater hazards than the duckling, for they are born — after spending less time in the egg than the mallard — blind, naked and helpless, and entirely dependent on the flow of food from their parents to keep them alive. It is such nestlings which suffer most deaths if there is a sudden and unnatural shortage of food under unusual conditions. Whilst helpless in the nest, they are also the target for nest robbers like magpies, jays, crows, stoats and weasels.

Nestlings need a lot of food which they convert into rapid growth. A baby robin increases in weight from one-fourteenth of an ounce to seven-tenths of an ounce in 12 days, so that the parents are under a great strain to provide food. Adult birds take more risks, and are less wary in seeking that food, and are consequently at their most vulnerable to predation.

So the fittest and the most cautious survive, particularly so when the youngsters leave the nest and have to compete with the adults for food. At the end of summer and into autumn, when food supplies begin to diminish, competition intensifies, with the adult having the advantage of knowing from experience the sources of supply, and the juveniles being the ones which perish.

It has been estimated that only three out of every ten baby great-tits reach maturity, and nature balances the population, with the number of juveniles surviving equalling the number of adults which have died in the year. The average life-span of a blackbird has been estimated to be just under two years, for a robin little over a year, for a starling one and a half years, and Gael's friendly duckling would have a life expectancy of around two years, though individuals in all species have been recorded as living to a much greater age.

Chapter 12

False impressions

How youthful inexperience keeps the population stable; the mystery of soapy bubbles in a place beloved of butterflies is explained; Gael discovers a lizard which is too quick, and a creature which has a misleading appearance.

High mortality among young creatures is due mainly to lack of experience, to a lack of woodcraft which is so vital in the wild, and, in many ways, to the over-confidence of youth which tends to shrug away all the problems. Living is from hour to hour, from day to day, a great adventure after the confines of home have been cast aside.

To the young cock starling in the farmyard, none of life's fears, near-escapes, or survival struggles had yet marred his experiences. Trimly dressed in dark, sooty feathering — his first full outfit — everything lay before him, and he had all the exuberance and optimism of his breed.

Passed was the quickly-forgotten and helpless period in the nest, shared by three other squawking brethren, when every morsel of food, brought by indulgent and industrious parents, was competed for. Forgotten was the time spent in the confined space of the crevice between the grey stones of the barn wall, a home hot and stifling in the days of sunshine, and damp and chilling when the rain seeped down between the stones and into the nest.

Now, perched on the top of the wall which surrounded the farm paddock, the starling felt the warmth of the sun on his feathers, and shouted his independence to all who cared to hear. He was one of hundreds of young starlings loose in the countryside which had been reared successfully, but had yet to meet the dangers of immaturity. Typical of the optimistic fussiness of their breed, they would learn the pitfalls of their country life in the hard school of experience, and many would not survive to maturity.

However, life was good at the moment. The youngster had found that he had a loud voice, a large mouth and a universal taste in food, and that he was big enough to bully the sparrows in the farmyard. He was brazen, cocky, and full of the energy of youth, with no care in the world. But still a baby at heart, he could not resist a pleading gape on the arrival of an adult bird on the wall top, and his mantle of dignity slipped away with his open-mouthed, raucous appeal to be 'spoon-fed'. The old bird ignored him and flew away.

Spreading his wings, the youngster followed, flying steadily and in full control,

White was beautiful in the delicate and fragile wings of a butterfly.

across the paddock to the bird-table in the farmhouse garden. There, a fresh delivery of scraps had been thrown out, and he alighted on the board, bouncing a little on touch-down. He gobbled, gulping down pieces of bread that were too big, but jealous that others might steal his share.

He squared-up to another young starling, stabbing with his beak, fighting unnecessarily for his food. He scared off the youngster and, full of power, turned to an older bird. There he met his match, and it was he who retreated, again losing his pride, before he gaped to be fed. The adult bird pushed bread down his throat, and he was happy to revert to babyhood.

Gael found starlings such noisy birds, and her delight for a peaceful time at that period of the year was to leave the farmyard for the hill meadows where the sunbeams and gentle warm breezes brightened the light green waves of moving grasses. There, she was almost hidden by the growth of the grass, only the tips of her ears showing above the stems of timothy, meadow and cocksfoot grasses. Their seeds caught in her coat, and she was speckled with their small fruits, and yellow pollen from buttercups stained the whiteness of her chest. A seed stuck in the corner of her eye and she wiped it away with a sweep of her foreleg.

A swallow swooped low to see her, a spider slipped from the top of a cocksfoot stem into her silky hairs, and a black beetle fell from its hold on a dock leaf when she brushed past. Insects, drawn by the warmth of the sunbeams from their

Gael seeks water-coolness in the wind-sheltered heat of the bowl-like clough.

hiding places in the mass vegetation, were busy on grass stems and in the warm air above the seed heads. Small tortoiseshell butterflies danced over the clump of nettles by the wallside, a bumble-bee droned lazily on to a lilac cuckoo-flower, ladybird beetles sought succulent aphids on which to feed. A damsel-fly hovered so that the blue of its body was brilliant in the light.

Scattered, like loosely fallen snowflakes among the grass, were small masses of white bubbles — cuckoo-spit — although they had no connection whatsoever with the bird. Each blob of soapy froth was caused by the breathing of a tiny insect which lived in the centre of the bubble. The green-coloured nymph fed on the sap of the plant to which it clung with its legs and, in breathing, expelled the white bubble to protect itself from predators. Later in the summer, the insect would leave the stem on which it fed and would move about in leaps and would be known as a frog-hopper.

When Gael walked through the rank vegetation of Rack Clough, she avoided patches of thistles because their needle-sharp spines pricked her nose. The wind-sheltered heat of the bowl-like clough was beloved of butterflies. Dancing up into the sunbeams, the white butterflies were the most numerous and conspicuous. They comprised large-white, small-white and orange-tip varieties.

The large-white is the gardener's pest because of the damage which its caterpillars do to such vegetable plants as the cabbage; nor is the small-white to be encouraged in the garden, although its caterpillars live on the leaves of watercress in the bogland; and the orange-tip is the prettiest of the three. Attracted by the violet blooms of the mayflowers which grow in the bogland, the orange-tips fly a rather weak, fluttery flight with seemingly purposeless direction. Only the male of the species is marked with the orange tips on the white forewings.

Small-heath butterflies liked to flit in slow flight over the rush-grown area of Rack Clough. Pretty, active and interesting, the small-heath is probably the most numerous of all British butterflies, and lives wherever there are grassy places, at sea-level on dunes, in country lanes, grazing pastures, rough meadows, heaths and downs, and even up the hill to a height of 2,000 feet.

Around an inch in wing-span, it is basically brown in colour on the face of its wings. There is very little difference between the sexes, the females being slightly larger than the males, and a little paler in colour. The butterfly has a slow flight, flitting just above the grasses. On alighting, it closes its wings, and the eye-spots near the tip of each forewing are prominently displayed. This is a protective marking; many an insect-eating bird pecks at those eyes instead of the butterfly's head, and the butterfly can often get away with merely a torn wing.

At the best — should it escape every enemy — the small-heath only lives, as an adult, for between two to three weeks, although its life-cycle can be relatively long for an insect. In the short adult life of the small-heath, the weather conditions are vital. Butterflies, always linked with brightness and sunshine, can spend their whole lives without ever seeing the sun in Gael's locality. Britain in general is not an ideal country for butterflies because the weather is notoriously unsettled, and it is not surprising that the indigenous butterfly population is rather limited, with the southern half of the country far richer in varieties than the North Country.

The small-heath is a double-brooded butterfly, the first generation flying over Gael in May and June, and the second appearing from August to early October. The caterpillars, hatched from eggs laid on grasses in early summer, do not feed at the same rate. Some produce an autumn generation of butterflies, while other caterpillars hibernate, the butterflies emerging the following spring.

The female lays her eggs singly on any type of grass, and those that are going to produce second-brood butterflies feed up very rapidly, while others lag behind, and when half-grown, cease feeding and retire deep down into tussocks for the winter.

Gael enjoyed butterflies for their erratic flight, running and bouncing after them in playful romps, yet never mouthing them. She chased them across the sunbeams until she panted in the heat and flopped down on the ground to rest, her tongue lolling from her open mouth.

After one such doze, she opened her eyes to find a strange creature basking in the sunshine on a nearby rock. It was a brown-tinted lizard, marked with dark spots and lines. Five inches long, it was a common-lizard, a male, for its shape was graceful and not so heavily built as the female of the species.

Gael lay still, only her deep almond eyes watched the strange creature. With no movement to frighten it, the lizard remained basking in the sunlight. It lay with its body flattened to the rock and its limbs extended, the soles of its feet upturned to feel the warmth.

Although local to the area, these viviparous lizards of the family *Lacertidae* are uncommon, and it is difficult to assess their population as they are so quick to dart unseen to cover at the slightest unusual disturbance.

The common-lizard could live almost anywhere in the countryside, in hedgerows, in woodland, on open pasture, and high on the hills, and Gael had met it on high ground. It moved sharply, yet was graceful, proceeding in a series of short dashes from cover to cover, and seldom going about leisurely.

With the cover of heather, rough grasses and rocks, it was away into hiding before it could normally be spotted. It ran with a nimble, gliding motion, its body and tail seeming to slide over the ground like a shadowy streak. It could run equally well over heather, its long delicate toes spread to cover the plant stems; it could climb rocks without difficulty, gripping tiny footholds with sharp claws; and it could even swim and submerge to escape detection.

Lizards live chiefly on insects, and spiders are their particular fancy, so that they are readily satisfied in the summer months. In winter, when the frost hardens the land and the insects either die off or seek shelter, the lizards hibernate. They begin their rest in October and come out again to an active life in March, but this depends on the weather conditions. The mating period is between April and May and the young are born in July or August.

The wind ruffled Gael's fur, and the movement was seen by the lizard. It quickly turned the soles of its feet to the rock, and raised its muzzle, turning its head to one side, its eye towards Gael. She moved her head slightly, and the lizard darted into the cover beneath the rock and was gone.

Leaping to her feet, Gael was only the blink of an owl's eye behind the lizard, and she blew her nostrils for scent into the hole beneath the rock. Her stalking interest kindled by the loss of the lizard, she moved quietly away through the rushes, placing her feet carefully, her nose probing, her eyes alert to every movement, slinking up the wind. Gently, and ever so slowly, she stretched her neck towards a sway of the rushes. Her black nostrils sifted the slight air movement, and took a faint scent, the musk-taint of Craber, the water-vole. Her pads, lost from sight in the deep ooze of the bog, gripped to balance her straining body.

Gael was very quiet, on her best stalking behaviour, for she knew that the chubby vole who was enjoying a feed of grass behind the rush screen was the most timid of creatures, and would bolt at the least hint of her presence. Craber's vigilance was his only chance of life in a hostile world.

Slowly Gael nosed to within two feet of the vole who, his back to her, was quite unaware of her presence. Squatting on his haunches, a beam of dappled sunshine lighting the reddish hairs of his soft coat, he held his food in his hands like a squirrel.

The air movement was in Gael's favour so that Craber, though his whiskers twitched often to test for scent, did not find her. His round, black eyes had poor sight, and though his power of hearing compensated, Gael had made no noise. Only when she became too ambitious to make friends, and tried to nose even closer, did Craber suddenly become aware of her presence. Even so, he did not

The boglands of upper Rack Clough where Craber, the water-vole, made his home.

flee, though his muscles tensed, and he dropped his food, lifting his head to twitch his nose.

Then as Gael, encouraged by the vole's stay, pushed her aquaintance even further, Craber was off. Sleeking his fur, he slipped from the tussock of rushes into the brown bog water, and, swimming beneath the surface, was quickly gone from Gael's sight.

To Gael, Craber's disappearance was a challenge, a chase, a game of hide-and-seek in the wet and squelching bog. But Gael did not see Craber again. Although she dashed around, splashing and floundering in water and mud until her golden beauty was besmirched with black mud and green weed, she could not find the vole. Craber was safely hidden in the solid earth of the bankside, his underwater swim of but three yards having taken him to the underwater entrance to his tunnelled home.

Nico, the reed-bunting, chided Gael's behaviour, for her splashing around between the rushes upset his family; a snipe hastily pulled its long beak from the food-laden mud and sped into the air; and a host of insects left the scattered rushes.

Tiring of her fruitless chase after a will o' the wisp like Craber, Gael splashed to the banking and stretched out on the grass. She lay beside a hole which she knew to be one of the land entrances to the water-vole's home, and contented herself with the faint taint of musk which filtered from the tunnel.

Then Gael rolled on her back, squirmed against the wiry grasses to clean the mud from her coat, and settled to the warmth of sunbeams which, dodging the grey fluffy clouds of the sky, brightened the valley with brimming light.

In the darkness, some four feet below Gael's couch, Craber rested on a bed of dry grass in a rounded chamber. He was calm and settled after the excitement of his hasty retreat from Gael's attentions. He groomed a spatter of mud from his coat, and combed the fur of his head with his hind foot. He stopped, his foot lifted to scratch, when he heard the squeaks of his family.

They were cradled in the adjoining nest chamber, five sturdy babies watched over by his mate. They were ten days old, their eyes just opened, and their fur thickening to a lovely shade of golden red. Like all his kind, Craber was proud of his family and ever mindful of their safety. Their future depended so much on luck, for water-voles are very vulnerable and defenceless creatures, so often mistaken for water-rats and destroyed as such. Rats they are not — they are charming, warm-furred, inoffensive creatures without malice, and of no threat to man and his interests.

Gael had been gone from the banking above Craber's nest chamber for some time when the water vole ventured out again. Cautiously, he peered from the entrance hole in the bank, swivelling his head to listen to the sounds in the bogland clough. His whiskers twitched to take the scent lines. Neither sound nor scent carried any hint of danger and life had settled to normal after Gael's departure.

Craber slipped into the water of the bog, swimming easily with his nose held high to push a vee-shaped wake over the surface of the ponded stretch of bog. There was no apparent danger to his safety, and he was relaxed and lazily content with life. His ears were pressed back to his reddish-brown coloured fur, his body was floating well out of the water in typical water-vole fashion. Craber's passage in the water was screened from all but the darting swallows and house-martins by the high growth of brown rushes which grew from the soft ooze of the shallows.

Nico, now content, balanced with feet one above the other on the slim stem of a rush, and cocked a bright eye to the vole, before answering the call of his mate to cease his philandering and seek food for his growing family.

Craber swam to a bank of mud and, spreading his feet to grip into the ooze, walked from the water. He shook himself to send droplets of water showering from his body in a tiny rainbow as they passed through the sunbeams. Sitting on his haunches, Craber groomed his close-grown fur. He was fastidious in his cleanliness. He used his teeth to scrape the mud from his chest; he used both fore and hind claws to comb the fur on his sides and back. To complete his toilet, he used his tongue to smooth his coat.

Comfortable, with his fur sleeked and clean of irritation, Craber sat quietly by the waterside. He was one of the most interesting and distinctive creatures which Gael met in her travels. His fur was waterproof and smart, his blunt-nosed face at once distinguished him from a rat. Around 11 inches long from the tip of his nose to the end of his thick tapering tail, he was of chubbier build than his mate, whose time was taken up with her growing family. His ears were short, rounded, thickly furred, and had a skin-flap to keep out water when swimming. On his flanks were the oily musk glands which prevented his pelt being used commercially. Craber's feet were not webbed like those of most swimming animals, although the hind feet were finely haired between the toes to add to his swimming proficiency.

Craber was content to sit and be lazy until a movement among the rushes disturbed him. A mallard duck led five baby ducklings on to the water and Craber was immediately alert. He cocked his ears, his short-sighted eyes stared, his whiskers twitched. He grunted his doubts, and, when a swallow skimmed low over his head, he took fright and dived into the water, pushing himself downwards with a kick of his hind feet. Scooping into the mud of the stream bed, he stirred up a screening water cloud.

Happier in the water which was his natural habitat, he swam fast, streaming his body to a slender length and using his strongly-muscled feet to thrust forward. A change of direction was made by a push of his forefeet, not by a bend of his tail. His coat was silvered by tiny air-bubbles which clung to the fur. Rising after 20 seconds to fill his lungs with fresh air, he found that all was well and that his fear was unfounded. He spread his legs and drifted on the surface of the slow-moving water, sailing relaxed to gather speed under an arch of drooping rushes where the main run of the bog water narrowed to a faster current.

Chapter 13

Making hay

Full of fun at haytime, Gael romps the birds to flight, plays hide-and-seek with the moorhens, gives a hedgehog a ducking, stalks the rooks into panic, and is hissed by a baby cuckoo.

It was a sudden, startling crescendo of noise which brought Kew quickly from his doze. Heart pumping fast, the little-owl swivelled his flat-topped head to face the outburst of sound, and his round, yellow-rimmed eyes watched the tractor leave the farm-lane and enter the meadow. The peace of an early sunlit morning was shattered by the clank of a mowing machine making its first cut.

From his perch on a weathered branch of the lone sycamore tree at the north-east corner of the meadow, Kew saw the tall grasses fall in an orderly row to disclose the brown, yellow and light-green colours of the base crop. Grass conservation was vital in Kew's land of East Lancashire in order to provide food for indoor stock, mainly milk-cows, during the winter months. The summer's bountiful grass harvest was collected and conserved on the farms in the form of hay, dried-grass, or silage.

Fresh growing grass contains around 80 per cent of moisture, and if this can be reduced to no more than around 20 per cent, the grass is sufficiently dry to prevent mould, and it can be stored under cover to be fed to winter stock.

Traditionally, farmers used to 'make hay' in East Lancashire, but always it was a hazardous process because of the vagaries of the weather, so that alternative methods were sought. Alternatives are dried-grass and silage, although hay is still made. Dried-grass is produced by passing the harvested grass through a heated chamber, and it is probably the most efficient method of conservation, but it is also the most costly.

Growing in popularity over the years is the conservation of the fresh grass into silage, a compromise between the cheap, but risky, method of haymaking and the expensive, though safe, method of grass-drying. Haymaking in the traditional sense uses sun and wind to draw off the surplus moisture when the grass is cut and lying in the field. In the East Lancashire climate, the accepted rain showers not only lengthen the process but cause a loss of soluble nutrients within the herbage.

With silage, the grass can be cut and carted from the field while still green. It is packed tightly in a pit, tower, or stack silo where the air can be excluded. The cut

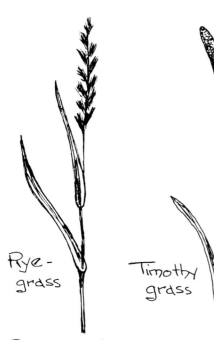

Grass - the most important crop.

Rye-grass

Timothy grass

White clover

Rapid growth - enormous bulk. / Very palatable / Yields well. / Improves yield and palatability.

Together make a reliable long term ley of high quality for grazing or conservation for both sheep and cows. (if cultivated properly)

The three essential plant foods are —

Nitrogen (N) for colour and size of leaves, rate of growth and yield.

Phosphate (P_2O_5) to stimulate root development, early establishment, and early maturity.

Potash (K_2O) to encourage health, drought and disease resistance, and improvement in quality.

grass begins to warm up immediately it is stacked, and by the process of bacterial and chemical action, organic acids are produced which act as a preservative for the vegetable mass.

There is skill in the making of both hay and silage, and there is skill and experience in deciding when the standing crop of grass should be cut. When grass flowers it reaches its maximum weight without the plant becoming too fibrous — and the feeding value of grass is in the leaf and not the stem.

An hour after the mowing machine had left the field over which Kew watched, regimented rows of heaped grass crossed its surface, and the little-owl found a feast of black beetles scurrying among the grass stubble — their tall, covering screen suddenly gone.

Nor was the owl alone in his appreciation of the bared land of plenty. A swarm of black-headed gulls descended upon the land to squabble and fight over every uncovered morsel of food, be it beetle, worm, insect or baby mouse. They were joined by the rooks gliding in from the trees of the woodland clough, by a group of lapwings which, their family duties completed, were gathering in social parties. Corbie, the black crow, and his new family of four took over the half-acre of land by the gate, driving away any interloper by their aggressive selfishness.

The freshly-cut meadow provided a clean new and unexpected source of food which was exploited by the predator birds until the beetles and insects, suddenly naked of their covering grass-screen, had adapted to the changed habitat, and burrowed their way into the short, remaining, uncut stems.

The gull-chuckles of satisfaction at easy pickings were silenced when Gael came into the field. The freshness of the bruised grass on her nose, she knew that all rabbit-cover was destroyed. She romped in the sun between the lines of piled grass, enjoying the chase of every bird that dared to remain earthbound in her sight.

Corbie spluttered his usual crow-abuse before leaving his flight to the last possible moment, and Kew gave Gael a welcoming mew before he silently flew to the top of the stone wall, his crop stuffed with black beetles. Gael scattered all to flight in her run to the drain opening where rabbits lived. She squeezed her shoulders into the now gaping hole, her nostrils savouring the scent of the rabbits. She struggled back, and stood over the drain, her tongue lolling in the growing heat of the sun's rays.

Beyond the rabbit drain, by the field-wall, grew tall thistles which had escaped the chop of the mowing blade. Their flowers were clusters of purple, and their freshness attracted a dozen tortoiseshell butterflies to add their red, black and orange beauty to the tall flower-heads.

Pushing through the rushes by Scholey Pond, Gael frightened two young moorhens to instant submersion below the weed-covered water. She cocked her ears to their slight movement and to their mother's alarm calls, then she lowered her muzzle and lapped the cool water, sending pond-skater insects scattering over the ripples she caused. Much to the annoyance of Kurra, the parent moorhen, Gael was becoming too efficient at the game of hide-and-seek which the little collie played regularly with the bird's family.

Neither of Kurra's two surviving youngsters, fully fledged in their greyish-black feathering and really independent of their mother, worried unduly about Gael's visits to the pond. They rather enjoyed the fun, and learning to avoid her was good training for more serious escapades. They could dart between the soft stems of the pondside bur-reeds, part swimming and part running over the floating vegetation, much more quickly than Gael could flounder through the mud in pursuit.

But Gael had become much more adept at finding them than in the first weeks of their lives, matching their woodcraft by a growing knowledge of their ways, and it was that skill which worried Kurra, who throatily croaked her frustration.

Normally the defence of the moorhen against predators was camouflage and stealth. Now that Gael could find and nose them from the reeds, they had to dodge her in a running game of hide-and-seek and, in the final act to avoid her, to dive below the water surface of the open pond where she could not follow.

It was only a game, for she meant no harm, but others of their brethren had died in the snapping jaws of Ruso, the fox, when caught in the reeds. Gael nosed the back of one of the youngsters as it weaved a way between the fleshy burs. She was up to her chest in the mud, the slimy black ooze staining and matting her silken fur, but she was too engrossed in the game to care for such trifles.

Realising that Gael was so close, the moorhen discarded all semblance of stealth and, the long, slightly flanged toes of its feet pattering the floating pond weeds for

At rest—the long slender body of Aeshna grandis, *and the intricate network of veins in the wings.*

a hold, it scuttled for the open water. Six yards out from the rushes it sank like a stone under the surface, safely away from Gael's pursuit. Cautiously, the bird lifted its beak above the water to breathe, otherwise remaining quietly immobile so that Gael could not see it.

Gael scrambled from the mud and lay on the solid bank of the pond. She closed her eyes and dozed in the warmth of the sunbeams, and a bright blue dragonfly came to see her. A common aeshna, the insect was brilliantly coloured over its three-inch long slender body. Its head had large prominent eyes and thin, short antennae. Its four whirring wings were silver in the sunlight and membranous with many veins.

Aeshna was born in the pond, hatching from an egg laid by an unknown mother into the mud. In nymphal stage it developed into the most fearsome and vicious creature in the pond. Carnivorous, it lived on other insect larvae and frog-tadpoles, catching them by striking out, from its lower lip, an extensible limb, at the end of which two hooks like lobster claws grasped the victim.

Sluggish in habit, coloured to blend with its background, it skulked in the pond mud until prey approached. Then it darted to feed. For two years it terrorised the pondlife, then in the early summer of the year it climbed out of the water up the leaf of a reed. Its nymphal skin split away and, after expanding its wings and drying in the sun, it flew from the reed as a fully-formed insect. Aeshna would mate, enjoy the full life for a month or so, but would not survive the winter.

As an adult insect, the dragonfly is equally as fearsome as when a nymph. It is an efficient hunter of prey, patrolling backwards and forwards across the pond and seizing other flying insects in grasping legs, eating them whilst in flight.

Smaller relations of the dragonfly, the damsel-flies, were also common to Scholey Pond. Unlike the dragonfly which holds its wings open at rest, the damsels close their wings rather like butterflies. They are equally colourful, though more delicate and weaker in flight than their larger relations.

Aeshna spent little time in inspecting the sun-washed silkiness of Gael's sable back, and darted out across the water to plunder the busy insect life above the rushes of the far bank.

Igel, the hedgehog, was pushing his way through the bottoms of the rush clumps on his way to the edge of the pond water. He was thirsty. Forcing a path through the tangled growth, his tiny pointed nose bending the tall rushes which grew 30 inches above his head, he disturbed a host of insects for Aeshna.

A bright blue damsel-fly lost its hold on a leaf, and flew away over the water, flashing its brilliance in sunlight. Nico, the reed-bunting, flitted cautiously from stem to stem through the tops of the rushes. He was wary of the unnatural swaying of the rush tops, but was attracted by the easy feeding on the insects. When he ventured close enough to see that Igel was the cause of the disturbance he relaxed and enjoyed the feast the hedgehog was providing.

A beetle scurried across Igel's path and he snapped it up. He grunted his way to the water's edge and lapped his drink. He nosed the scent of a large grey feather which the playful breeze floated to his side. Krark, the heron, had earlier preened the feather from his plumage.

Igel was rambling to no particular purpose. He had left his mate, Furze, to care for their family of four youngsters over by the hedge of Rack Clough. The young hedgehogs were four weeks old, and their baby spines had hardened. They had been born in a hollow in the ground under the roots of an oak tree in the woodland and were just weaned. Furze was busy teaching them where to find the beetles, worms and slugs on which to live. When the cold weather came in November they would be three-quarters grown and would hibernate and not be seen until the following spring. Igel walked over the soft mud by the pondside, his five-toed imprints marking his route.

Capella, the snipe, watched the hedgehog with a wary eye whilst pushing his beak into the soft ooze to feel for worms. Igel stopped to watch a bumble-bee explore the rushes, listening to its buzzing flight. He was in no hurry, and quite content to linger by the pondside.

He lifted his pig-like snout to test the warm air, and his keen sense of smell picked up Gael's scent. He tensed his muscles. His one and only means of defence, should there be danger from Gael, was to roll into a ball of prickles. It was a static defence, often effective for hedgehogs, but useless against the creature's more wily enemies. The badger could crush it at one bite without fear of the spines; the clever fox, and some dogs, had learned to open up the soft gap in the prickly ball.

It is this static defence which makes the hedgehog such a familiar road casualty, for instead of running away at the sound of an approaching car, it rolls into its

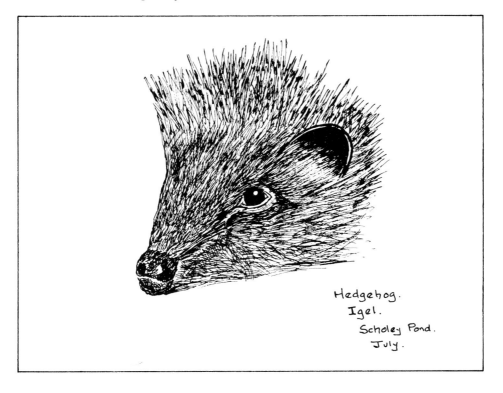

Hedgehog.
Igel.
Scholey Pond.
July.

Every way as beautiful as a dragonfly, the smaller and more delicate damsel-fly closes its wings when at rest

defensive ball and is crushed when the wheels of the car go over it.

But Gael was no real threat. Indeed, she had a healthy respect for Igel and his kind ever since her puppyhood when her inexperience had resulted in a sore and bleeding nose.

'Cat-napping' as always, with her senses alert, Gael was aware of the hedgehog's nearness. Rising from her couch, she carefully stretched her nose towards Igel, and he immediately lowered his head to face her with a spiny array. Gael was in playful mood, but had no desire to be pricked by the sharp spines of the hedgehog. Tentatively, she stretched a paw towards Igel, and he completed his defensive posture, his powerful muscles drawing together his head and legs in a complete ball. In that position every part of Igel's body was protected by sharp, erect spines.

Gently, Gael touched the rolled hedgehog with the leathery sole of her pad, and light though her touch was, it rolled Igel over in the mud. It was then that the hint of mischief came into Gael's eyes. Again she gently rolled the hedgehog and, a canine smile opening her lips, she pushed Igel into the water.

With a snorting and bubbling, Igel unrolled and swam out into the pond, strongly paddling across to the opposite bank from where Gael sat watching him with great interest. It was the first time she had seen a hedgehog swim. Igel scrambled on to the mud bank, and disappeared into the rushes, and Gael turned to other interests.

Leaving the water's edge, she walked through the cover of tall grasses which, because of their inaccessible position, were not cut by the mowing-machine. Their feathery tops brushed her face, their seeds littered her fur until she came clear into a meadow where the cut grass had been cured and heaped in parallel rows in readiness for the wrapping-up action of the baling-machine, prior to carting to the barn.

She shook the litter from her coat, and pawed a seed from the corner of her eye. Then she trotted away between two rows of the heaped grass. Stretching up and playing her ballet game of balancing on her hind legs, Gael peered over the piled grass to see a flock of rooks picking and poking for worms and grubs in the newly-bared ground. She was hidden from the birds, and it would be fun to play the stalking game.

The wind was right, blowing into her face and carrying the scent of the birds towards her. Her approach would be screened by the hay. Head up, nostrils quivering, she took the line of three birds which were foraging over the first row of hay, and some 20 yards up-wind. Pads placed carefully, body crouched, feathering streaming in the breeze, tail low, she stalked along the hay line with all the skill of her primitive ancestors.

Judging the position and the distance of the rooks by scent alone, Gael came to the point. The birds were exactly opposite her, only the pile of hay between. She bounded over the hay and landed right beside the three rooks. Madly, they scrambled to flight, calling out in fear and surprise, but they were slow and had Gael wished to strike them as a fox, they would have paid for their lack of caution.

Well pleased with the success of her stalk, Gael sat back on her haunches and watched the rooks wing slap into the air, the three joined by their companions as they also took alarm, the panic spreading through the whole flock. Calling loudly, they retreated down the hillside.

Full of the exuberant spirit of her prank, Gael leaped lightly over the stone wall into the adjoining meadow and sent a flock of over 200 lapwings on the path of the rooks, though theirs was a more leisurely retreat.

The lapwings were happy to be back in company. Sociable by nature, they gathered immediately together after their family rearing duties were over. In communal gathering for nine months of the year, the post-breeding flock which flew over Scholey Hill included many lapwings which had been born that year. Not all young birds were so advanced in age in July as to be independent of their parents; not all parent birds were free to relax and go their own ways.

When Gael left the hill for the woodland valley and pushed her way through the thorn of the hedgeside, she heard a hiss of defiance and disapproval from above her head. Raising itself on its legs from the under-sized nest it dominated, a young cuckoo protested at the noise of Gael's passing.

Puffing its feathers, and raising the feathers of its head to form a frill of anger, the cuckoo squatted belligerently in the misshapen, but delicate, hair-lined nest of a pair of dunnocks in which its unknown mother had chosen to lay her egg. Unwittingly, the trim dunnocks had been chosen to foster the grotesque over-sized parasite in their home.

The abundance of cover from the hawthorn branches, heavy with green haws and a tangle of white-flowered bramble shoots, screened the young cuckoo from view, and it sat safely protected in the thickness of the hedgerow. Its feathering blended in perfect camouflage with the thin, intricate branches of thorn and bramble, and only when it gaped in the heat of the day, or to accept the food from its hard-worked foster parents, did its mouth show a vivid crimson flash against the brown-barred, white-tipped feathers of its colouring.

The nest was 12 inches above Gael's head and, hearing the hiss of objection, she raised her nose to the scent-line, but her intrusion on the cuckoo's privacy was brief. She squeezed past the clinging bramble, leaving tufts of her white ruff hanging, and, not facing a bank of stinging nettles on whose leaves curled the blackish caterpillars of a red-admiral butterfly, she turned down the deep-cut ditch.

Gael passed from sight in the tangle of greenery, her going marked by the scolding churr of a wren, the angry 'tics' of a robin, and the flapping, branch-striking retreat of a wood-pigeon. The wood-pigeon had two down-covered squabs on a platform nest in the top of the thorn hedge.

Immediately Gael went, the cock dunnock darted into the bush to cram a beakful of grubs into the gaping mouth of the wheezing youngster. The hen dunnock followed, both foster parents unceasing in their task of rearing a nestling which was already towards three times the size of themselves, and which had murdered their own legitimate family by tossing them from the nest.

The young cuckoo had been a renegade from birth, endowed by nature for its role of dominating the lives of the parent dunnocks. It had no intention of sharing either the nest, or more important, the food supply with the young dunnocks, two of which had hatched, the other egg being infertile.

Nature had shaped the cuckoo nestling with a hollow back which enabled it to wriggle under each young dunnock in turn and toss it over the rim of the nest. It had likewise cleared out the addled egg from the nest. The dunnock youngsters had quickly died, their agonised cheepings ignored by their parents who, as long as they had one gaping beak to feed, were satisfied.

From that day onwards the young cuckoo had taken over the lives of its two foster parents, demanding that its apparently insatiable appetite be satisfied. All day long, from first light to nightfall, the dunnocks flew backwards and forwards to the nest, bringing flies and caterpillars for the cuckoo. In three weeks, the nestling increased in weight from one-fourteenth of an ounce to three ounces.

From across the Cliviger Gorge came the mature gobbling call of an adult cuckoo, but the young cuckoo's own parent had not the slightest interest in its offspring. She had succeeded in the greatest confidence trick in birdland, that of finding foster parents who would work themselves to a shadow if necessary to rear her child. The dunnocks would still be devoted to the whims of the outsize youngster when it left the nest in the hawthorn, and they would only be truly rid of it when in August or early September it left the area to fly south towards its winter home in Africa.

Chapter 14

Life is perplexing

Hard lessons for a baby grebe, while Gael ponders the flightless ducks, sees the curlews away, jumps a grasshopper to its death, and tests the alertness of a rabbit.

Even the black-headed gull, a member of a hard-hearted breed, protested at the treatment by the mother little-grebe of her own chick. The gull flew up from the reservoir and called its protest. It wore a cap which was mottled white and was only partially coloured. But Dabs, the female little-grebe, was teaching her youngster to dive, in order to overcome the fear of submersion. Her action looked almost ruthless as she flew at the chick over the reservoir surface, and forced it under the water with her beak. The chick, one of her family of six, resurfaced in a splutter, blowing water from its mouth and nostrils, showing a downy-white breast as it bobbed up like a cork.

Little-grebes lived by diving for their food — small fish, beetles and other water insects — and although much of nature was by instinct, certain lessons had to be learned by young creatures. Diving for their food was a lesson the grebe chicks had to learn.

The chick, however, was rewarded for its persistence in following its mother out over the deep water, whilst the other five chicks stayed in the shallows with Dowka, their father.

Dabs dived, and came up with a tiny minnow in her beak. She worried the fish into insensibility, the light glinting on its silver belly, and then she set it before her chick so that it floated. The chick snapped it up, and learned the lesson that food had to be caught.

Down again went Dabs through the still water, thrusting with lobed feet to intercept the escape of another minnow. She caught it, and resurfaced, all in a matter of seconds. Number one youngster had been fed, so she set off towards the rest of her family.

Her progress over the water surface was extremely fast. Water spumed from her breast, swirling behind her in an increasing trough, making the progress of two mute-swans and three mallard ducks, which were leisurely swimming some distance away, seem cumbersome by comparison. Reaching the rest of her family which were grouped around Dowka, she laid down the dying minnow before one of them, and the initial lesson of hunting was taught to another chick.

Dowka swam off, followed by the only chick of the family which had learned to upend itself like a dabbling duck, the preliminary stage to its learning to dive. Up and down, with scarcely a splash to mark his going and coming, Dowka brought up beetles which he fed to the youngster. It was early morning and the air was mild and warming to the growing heat of a summer sun.

A red-speckled trout streaked up through the green water, arched its back, and leapt into the air, a silver arc in the bright light. The plop as the fish fell back into the water turned the heads of the two mute-swans. A light breeze blew swan feathers from the birds' preening bank, sailing them like miniature galleons with cream sails billowing over the water. Two white-beaked coots poked around in the rushes, and swallows hawked the insects which they disturbed.

The grebe chicks cheeped among themselves, concerned when first one parent, and then the other, disappeared below the water. Dabs surfaced and her brood flocked towards her. She dived again when Dowka surfaced, and the chicks swam towards their father. It was a bewildering world.

The chicks were charming creatures. They had downy black and buff-barred heads with dark red colouring at the base of their beaks. Their parents were quietly beautiful. They were dark brown in general feathering, with warm chestnut face cheeks, and distinctive white beak patches. They were wonderfully aquatic, staying underwater for up to half a minute, capable of floating at different levels in the water, and speeding after prey with powerful strokes of paddle-shaped toes.

Gael had come, warm with exercise, off the high moor, and was lapping the coolness from the water on the edge of the reservoir when she saw the grebes. Beyond her reach, they were consequently of little interest, and she knew not of their rarity in her area. She lifted her muzzle from the water, sun-jewelled droplets falling from her lips, tiny ripples spreading across the calm surface of the reservoir from her intrusion. She lifted her head to the noisy, constant twitter of a host of small birds which flew above her head.

Led by an old cock linnet whose breast was splashed crimson with colour, a flock of some 50 twites wheeled and danced on the warm breeze. A post-breeding flock of the moorland finches, the birds flashed white wing-bars in their restless, indecisive flight. Some settled to perch on the top of the stone wall which bounded the reservoir, some alighted on the pebbles and sparse grass-growth around Gael, others flipped down to balance on the red heads of the thistles which grew by the wall. All kept a close eye on Gael, unworried yet unsettled in her presence.

The cock linnet perched on a gritstone boulder which jutted from the ground by the water. He puffed his crimson chest, cocked a bright eye, and in his paternally protective way to his associate flock, challenged Gael with his attitude.

Ignoring him completely, Gael walked towards the stone wall. She lifted her head and sniffed at a bee, its pollen-baskets swollen orange, which was clinging to a thistle flower. Buzzing annoyance, the bee flew from her twitching nostrils.

The linnet lifted a foot to scratch an irritation on the back of his head, then suddenly he spread his wings and jumped into the air as Gael, attracted by the movement of the bird, ran back towards him. 'Twe-ee' he called, and led the nearby twites in retreat. Others ignored the call, and pecked at thistle seeds with their stout yellow bills, balancing, striped streaky brown in plumage, on the swaying plants.

Having lost the linnet stalk, Gael turned to the remaining twites, treading lightly with her white feet over a low growth of white daisies and yellow buttercups. Each twite in turn was too quick for her, though one felt the flip of her tongue on its back feathers.

Patiently waiting for the collie to leave the reservoir bank, a pied-wagtail, her beak crammed with insects, sat on the wall. She had five youngsters to feed in a nest built low down between the stones, and ever cautious, she had no wish to reveal its siting, even to Gael.

Gael left the twites to their own indecisive flighting, and the wagtail was happy to see her go. She trotted down the wallside, splashed through mossy water which ran from an open moor drain to the reservoir, and crossed the pebbles and stones of the banking to where rushes grew in the shallows.

Keen senses told her the close-growing vegetation held something of interest, though she was more than a little puzzled at the reluctance of eight ducks to flight from her appearance when she pushed her way into the rushes. So slow were the ducks to leave the shelter of the tall rushes that she actually pushed the last bird on to the water.

Hesitancy and trust were not their usual nature, and Gael cocked her head in quizzical surprise to watch the ducks paddle slowly over the water surface with little concern for her presence, and without the slightest sign of fear. It was surprising, because on all the other occasions when she had disturbed ducks, they had been quick away, with long necks outstretched into the wind. That morning they lingered.

A strange company of one teal drake, four mallards and three snow-white birds, they quietly paddled over the water so that they were beyond her reach. Gael could not understand why they did not fly from her. She stood in the thick screen of rushes to watch them, her nose thrust forward at the point, her black nostrils wrinkling for scent on the warm air.

A white butterfly twitched the top of her ear. A martin zipped over her head, its red mouth open to grasp the insects she disturbed. A brilliant blue damsel-fly was attracted to the sunlit gold of her coat, a flying jewel on fairy wings which hovered its inspection.

When Gael turned away to follow the faint scent of Ruso, the fox, who had earlier been stalking the ducks through the rush tangle, her movement did frighten the little teal to flight. Swimming apart from the small flock, the teal jumped straight into the air, but its flight was not the assured and normal flight of swerves and bends. It was unsure of its ability, it lacked the confidence of its wings, it swung back to alight on the water and rejoin the other ducks. The teal was loath to leave the safety of the reservoir water.

The ducks were in 'eclipse' and at their most vulnerable — they were changing feathers in the moult. Whilst they shed their old feathers and grew new ones, they were virtually flightless, though nature provided for their safety by replacing the usually bright feathers of the male birds in the first instance with dull browns to enable them to be less conspicuous in hiding.

Plumage of the drakes became so similar to that of the ducks that it was difficult to imagine that the teal drake normally had a lovely green band round the eye, running down to the nape of the neck, and that the male mallards were usually resplendent in glossy green head feathers with white collars.

Gael followed the scent of Ruso, the fox, away from the side of the reservoir. It was a faint taint, but she enjoyed the challenge of puzzling its line, for Ruso had been gone some two hours. The stillness of the warm air kept his smell around, and Gael slowly and laboriously unravelled his passage.

She paused to the call of curlews which trilled their music from their long, curved beaks. She watched seven birds lift their wings above their heads, run over the moorland rough, and climb high into the air. Two families, four adults and three youngsters, the curlews were ready to leave the hill and travel to the mud-flats of the Ribble estuary, 30 miles to the west.

There was no hurry in their departure, life was easy after the trials of family rearing, and the adult birds would rest to preen and cast feathers which had become frayed and broken, until their plumage took on the duller garb of winter.

It was the time of year when many of Gael's avian friends gathered into flocks to leave her company. The lapwings which harried and chivvied her with their mobbing tactics during the nesting period had left the high ground, joining others of their kind to make the journey to the lower valleys and the arable fields of the Fylde and South Lancashire. It was also the time of plenty. Food was readily available for a population of birds and animals at peak, and the weather was at its kindest with hot sunshine and warm rain giving no survival problems.

Whilst most creatures were able to relax through the long warm days of August, there were some whose lives were still very hectic. On her way from the high land towards the top of Rack Clough, Gael listened to the sing-song conversation of a pair of swallows, which of all the birds on the hill, were the most industrious, for they were still baby-sitting. Though there were hosts of insects around, and providing food for their family was never difficult, the swallows had a 'deadline' to meet. The babies had to be fed to maturity, learn to fly and look after themselves entirely before September when they would have to start their long migrational journey to their winter home in Africa.

The distant crack of a gunshot from off the adjoining hill pricked Gael's ears to the death of a grouse. The 'Glorious Twelfth' was past, and although the sheep-moors of the area carried but a small population of red-grouse, they were sought by a few guns.

The red-grouse is a hardy bird of the heather, feeding on the shoots, the flowers and the seed-heads of the plant. In its early days as a chick it is a tough, wonderfully quick catcher of insects. Grouse chicks love crane-flies for breakfast, and it was a host of crane-flies which scattered without purpose before Gael's boisterous entry to the top of Rack Clough.

The tang of rabbit had replaced the faintness of fox scent on her nostrils, and she bounded to the strength of the exciting smell. The gawky crane-flies fluttered

The urgency for the swallows was to get the youngsters fed, weaned, and fit to fly to Africa.

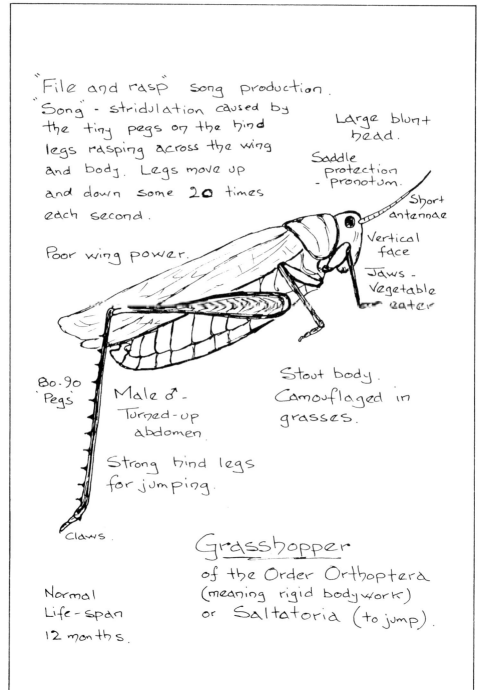

"File and rasp" song production.
"Song" - stridulation caused by
the tiny pegs on the hind
legs rasping across the wing
and body. Legs move up
and down some 20 times
each second.

Poor wing power.

Large blunt
head.

Saddle
protection
- Pronotum.

Short
antennae

Vertical
face

Jaws -
Vegetable
eater

80·90
Pegs

Male ♂.
Turned-up
abdomen.

Stout body.
Camouflaged in
grasses.

Strong hind legs
for jumping.

Claws.

Grasshopper
of the Order Orthoptera
(meaning rigid bodywork)
or Saltatoria (to jump).

Normal
Life-span
12 months.

away from the little collie's path, thin long wings ordered by the light breeze to pitch each body into the tracery of plant stems. Wings useless for determined direction, the tentacle-like legs of the insects were equally long and cumbersome, and so descriptive of the familiar name of 'daddy-long-legs'.

Insects abounded in the shelter of the rushes in Rack Clough, where the sun's rays were gathered and there was protection from the cooling counter of the breeze. Butterflies — whites, orange-tips, meadow-browns and small-heaths — danced their varied flight above the rushes; ladybird beetles sought aphid prey; and grasshoppers stridulated 'song' from their bodies in the meadow grasses.

Life is often very short for many insects, only a few hours in some species, but there is no danger of the countryside losing its population. Scientists tell us that there are around 230 million insects living in the nine inches of topsoil in an acre of meadowland.

Insects play various roles in the order of things, often very important ones as parasites, predators, scavengers and prey. The crane-flies which Gael unsettled in her hunting foray in the bogland had grown to flight from the well-known leatherjackets. As adult insects they were harmless, but their larvae, the leatherjackets, lived in the soil and caused much damage by eating the roots of garden and farm crops.

To stalk the grasshopper required the ultimate in stealth. First, Gael turned her ears to line-up the 'song' of the insect which was well hidden among the leaves of the long grasses under the shelter of the wall. Having fixed the general area of the grasshopper's perch by her keen hearing, she then pointed her nose to the precise direction of the insect's sound and, carefully placing her pads so as not to rustle the grass, she moved in. It was great fun to test her skill against the wary little insect that blended so cleverly into the grasses. She had virtually no scent to guide her to the stout insect body, although the quivering of the insect's legs, which rubbed against its body to produce the 'song', guided her sight.

Quietly Gael moved on to the grasshopper, and she had an audience. Sunning himself on the top of the stone wall, Kew, the little-owl, had not bothered to fly from Gael's approach. Kew lay on the top of the wall, his speckled wings spread out over the sun-warmed stone. Only when he saw Gael come to the point as she moved on to the grasshopper did Kew take an interest. What had the collie winded? It might be to his advantage to watch.

Kew drew in his wings tight to his body and, stretching his legs, stood alertly poised for whatever was to happen. The grasshopper sang on, the sound it made produced by stridulation — by the tiny 'pegs' which formed a file on its hind legs rasping across the poorly developed wing. This 'song-producing' action was a similar action to drawing a comb over the edge of a card, and resulted in rapid pulses of sound. The grasshopper's legs moved up and down to make the 'song', perhaps 20 times a second.

Gael's shadow across the grass, rather than her presence, warned the grasshopper that all was not as it should be. It rested its legs and, unsure of its safety, used them for their other prime purpose, stretching the strong muscles to take a mighty leap to change its perch.

Exploring among the vegetation, a relaxed rabbit was an inquisitive and playful individual.

It was a leap to death. Quick as the green and brown insect moved in its high jump, Kew moved quicker. As the grasshopper bounded from Gael's probing nose, Kew darted down to snatch it from above the tops of the tall grasses. He snatched it in his beak, crushed it to death, and winged away down the wallside with Gael surprised to a squat as the action eluded her. It was a premature death in the sun for the grasshopper whose natural life-span was short enough.

A frequenter of the grassland on the hillside, the grasshopper is of the insect order of *Orthoptera*, derived from the Greek for rigid bodywork, or the more descriptive family name of *Saltatoria*, from the Latin word *saltare* meaning to leap. Its normal life-span is but 12 months — from hatching in spring to being killed by the frosts of autumn.

Survival of the species is similar to that of many insects, the female adult leaving her fertilised eggs to survive the winter and produce the following year's insects. The eggs are laid, in clutches of around a dozen, under the surface of the ground, in protected crevices, or in plant tissue. They are covered with a frothy substance which hardens into a protective envelope to beat the frost.

The eggs hatch in spring, and although grasshoppers are not reckoned of a very high order, the young initially appear worm like for the precise purpose of wriggling their way to the open air. There, they discard their 'worminess' to become complete miniature grasshoppers, reaching adult size around June.

Kew and the grasshopper gone, Gael trotted down the wallside and followed the scent of a rabbit into the field adjoining the woodland. She nosed the carcase of a dead mole on which bluebottles were busily laying their eggs, and she drew back her twitching nostrils in distaste. She returned to the rabbit scent.

Unaware of Gael's approach, the rabbit was relaxed, for it had no hint of danger. Quite content, Cuni sat in the field and fed on the grass leaves. Her ears, held erect so that the sunlight passed through their skin, swivelled constantly to take every sound. Ever twitching, her nostrils read the messages of the light breeze. Every few seconds, still chewing contentedly, she lifted her head to look around, her big eyes wide open. Ever alert, for a rabbit's life rested on vigilance, she was quietly enjoying her food, yet ready to bolt to the shelter of her woodland burrow at the slightest hint of alarm.

Cuni listened to the gentle, lazy cooing of a wood-pigeon perched in the shade of the tall horse-chestnut tree at the edge of the woodland. She felt safe when the pigeon cooed, for none was quicker than the bird to proclaim possible danger. She swivelled an ear to the rustle of turning leaves when Chook, the blackbird, foraged on the ground beneath the trees. Again she read the signs of safety, for there was none so loud as Chook to give warning of intrusion.

Cuni, a young, sleek, well-grown doe, had learned to take notice of her woodland neighbours; she had learned that, whatever she was doing, she must always be ready for instant flight. Whether feeding, playing, or exploring beneath the bracken canopy on the woodland slopes, she must be prepared to react instantly to danger. She must ever be ready to bolt for the shelter of her burrow, and to disappear as noiselessly as possible from sight.

She cropped the green leaves in a semi-circle pattern before her, stretching forward to reach as far as she could before taking a step forward to graze another area. She crouched low as the shadow of a flying black-headed gull glided across the grass, then relaxed to the lazy buzzing of a bee, and nibbled at a dandelion leaf.

Suddenly, there was the crack and scutter of wings through branches as the wood-pigeon flighted, immediately followed by the scream of the alarmed blackbird. The birds had seen Gael.

Cuni remained still. She lifted her head and, ears fanning, eyes peering, nostrils quizzing, she sought the cause of fear. Although Gael pushed quietly through a thicket of tall, red-topped willow-herbs, whose white silk-borne seeds floated before the breeze, she was seen by the pigeon. The chain-alarm was triggered.

Cuni caught sight of Gael's golden body in the sunlight. Momentarily, she paused, her heart-beat quickened. Then she ran, bounding lightly into the taller fringe grasses of the field, and on into the woodland. Gael saw the movement, and instantly alert for the chase, raced after the fleeing rabbit.

The chase was short but gay, Cuni stretching her strong legs to dash and turn between the stems of bracken, Gael romping with increasing speed, though slower on the turns, until the rabbit reached the dark hole which gave her

Retreat to the safety of its underground home was the safest way to avoid being eaten by predators.

sanctuary below the roots of a sycamore tree. There, in the dimness of her burrow, her heart-beat steadied, and she calmed. Gael sucked her scent from the tunnel which was too small for the collie to enter.

Close by the entrance to the burrow were three pellets of indigestible fur and bones from the crop of Aluco, the tawny-owl, who peered down upon Gael from his roosting perch in the sycamore. Gael conceded to the rabbit, and seeking new fun, bit one of the pellets in a playful worry. The tiny bones of a field-vole which Aluco had eaten the previous night scattered over the ground. Gael nosed them, but the scent was dead, and she lifted her head to watch Ruddock, the robin, flit towards her through the lower branches of the rhododendron clump.

The atmosphere was heavy, and Gael panted the heat of her rabbit-chase from her lungs, her tongue lolling. Lazily, she yawned and stretched her body in the shade of the hawthorn hedge. Five minutes had passed when a group of five willow-warblers found her. Whispering to each other, they flitted through the twigs of the hedge to inspect her.

Tiny yellow-green feathered jewels, each no longer than a man's finger, the birds jumped from twig to twig, never still, to descend through the branches to view the collie. Gael twitched an ear to their insistent 'loo-ee' notes. She opened her eyes, and lifted her head, but the birds were difficult to see in the green darkness of the leaves.

Up and down the branches they flitted, from the dark interior of the foliage to the sunny exterior, barely weighing the spiky twigs in their lightness. Their plumage glinted as they passed through a probing shaft of sunlight, their freshness and brightness dimming the dark green tired leaves of the thorn tree.

Down to within two feet of Gael's twitching ears they descended, singly, and in turn, as they dared each other to the test. One made such a hasty retreat when Gael yawned with wide-open jaws that it darted into a spider's web and had to preen sticky threads from its trim feathering. The persistent calls of the warblers attracted attention. A great-tit flew across to see what all the excitement was about, its white cheek patches gleaming in the dim light among the branches. Ruddock joined it in the tree.

The warblers flew away down the hedgeside. They had seen enough of Gael, and they objected to the inquisitive approach of the other birds. Neither the great-tit nor Ruddock saw any cause for the fuss. The titmouse busied itself by picking insects from off the moss-covered trunk of the tree. Ruddock flew away to the top of a nearby post to preen his feathers in the sunshine.

Gael settled back on the grass and dozed in the heat, though her senses were alert to the happenings around. She heard the shrill voice of a spotted-flycatcher which alighted on the fence-wire close by Ruddock's post. The flycatcher darted above Gael's head to snatch an insect, then returned to its perch on the wire. Although their journeying was only casual as yet, flycatcher and willow-warblers were almost ready for the start of their return to Africa for the coming winter period. Gael had no such travel problems, and stretched at ease in the shade.

Chapter 15

Good friends

The strange affinity of collie-dog and badger leads to rugged play in a woodland; the birds gather for migration; and a less-friendly meeting for Gael on the hill before the ancient Sheep Fair.

Grunting quietly to herself, Jena, the young sow badger, walked up the tunnel of her sett. She poked her striped face out of the exit hole, and quivered her stubby black nostrils to the different scents on the damp air. It was still light, although the day was dying, and a greyness crept between the trees of Brockholes Wood.

Jena heard the 'tic-tic-tic' calls of Ruddock, the robin, from way down on the river bank when the bird saw Gael nosing into the hole of a water-vole. Rooks streamed across the grey sky above the woodland, coming to their roost in the tall trees. All seemed well and Jena ambled out of the sett, leaving her broad pad marks in the soft earth piled before the entrance hole.

The badgers — Jena, although eight months old, was still living with her brothers and parents in the same sett — had been excavating to enlarge the chambers and tunnels of their home, so that there was quite a pile of soft earth in front of the sett.

Jena was an early riser, and usually left the sett before her kin. She lifted her black and white striped face again and tasted the air, listened when Aluco, the tawny-owl, called 'ke-wick' as he started to hunt his supper.

Silence settled in the woodland, and Jena wandered down the path between tall bracken plants to start her own nightly prowl. She was a handsome well-grown badger with all the markings of maturity. She was almost two feet in length, ten inches high to the shoulder; her face was marked in distinctive stripes, and her squat body was covered with coarse grey hairs. She was strong and active; she had a good sense of smell and good hearing, although, like all her kind, her eyesight was not too good.

She ran along one of the bracken tunnels towards the riverside. She was thirsty, and dipped her mouth into the clear water to drink. Ever wary, she heard Gael's light-footed steps, and she lifted her snout from the water and tensed her body, waiting.

Gael left the cover of brown bracken, and on seeing her, Jena relaxed and lowered her head to drink again. For a moment Gael stood with one paw raised and stretched her neck, her nostrils questing for scent. Recognising the badger,

Badger
Jena.
Brockholes.
September.

Gael moved towards Jena who still lapped the water, unconcerned after having identified the interruption. Not until her thirst was slaked did Jena lift her head to acknowledge the collie.

Neither was unduly surprised for, since their first meeting in early April, when Jena was only an 11-week-old cub, there had been a strange affinity between the two animals, an understanding of tolerance and respect, for co-existence almost amounting to friendship.

But there were formalities to be followed, even with friends. The two animals touched noses, then each inspected the other's person, their nostrils sniffing over face, ears and neck to identify the other. All was correct. Gael flipped her tongue over Jena's snout and the badger purred a low, throaty bubbling sound of friendship. It was the normal greeting of badgers, and Gael was privileged.

Jena turned away from the river bank, disappearing into one of the bracken tunnels which she and her kind had made through the woodland. Gael romped after her and, when they emerged into a tree-fringed clearing, she nipped Jena lightly on her portly rump in an invitation to play. Jena swung round, and using her head and shoulders like a battering-ram, she sent Gael rolling across the clearing. Taking up the invitation for a game, Jena ran towards Gael, but the little collie, gathering her senses quickly, leaped over the charging badger.

Back came Jena, and the game developed into a boisterous and fast-moving game of tag, a rough and tumble with both animals mouthing and biting each other, rolling and somersaulting across the clearing in a frenzy of activity. All was in play and no bite or blow was delivered in anger, although Gael was quick to avoid the shattering impact of Jena's weight thundering into her, even in fun.

Jena charged, turning sideways to try to strike Gael's legs. Gael dodged, and nipped Jena on the side of the neck as she rushed past. Both animals enjoyed their game, Jena using her stocky weight and her head and body like a battering-ram; Gael, lighter and quicker, leaping away and bouncing back to tug the badger's fur. It was a barging and biting match where no harm was ever done, Jena careful to protect her sensitive nose, Gael careful not to catch the full weight charge on her supple legs. They frolicked in a circle, Gael mouthing the thick neck muscles of the badger, Jena butting the collie with her hard, tapering head. There was no rancour in the gambol, just fun.

Jena rolled on her back, purring her pleasure, and Gael bit at her short legs, deftly avoiding her flailing paws with their sharp claws. Snarling and yapping, yarling and yelping, they voiced their excitement and pleasure, calling an audience to their game.

Ruddock, the robin, flitted to a perch on a rhododendron twig beside the clearing to follow the action in his bright, round eyes. Pyat, the magpie, looked down on the jostling animals from a perch in a sycamore tree and, dancing from one foot to the other in his excitement, rattled his beak on the bough before scolding the rumpus. Aluco, the tawny-owl, floating between the tall trees like a large brown moth, alighted in a fringe oak and called 'ki-wick' four times. Merle, the blackbird, settling in the thick shelter of the bushes to roost the night away, tolerated the noise for only a minute before clattering to flight, her screams of alarm ringing through the woodland.

It was rugged play the birds watched, and suddenly Gael and Jena went rolling over and over down the slope towards the river. A bush of bramble halted their bumpy slide. Both were on their feet together. Gael shook her fur into place, tongue lolling from the energy expounded, eyes and ears alert to the next move. Jena purred her pleasure, and also shook her coat into a comfortable lie. But she had had enough. She musked the brambles, a process which Gael quickly dodged, though she took the scent on her twitching nostrils. Turning her black and white striped head in a final glance at Gael, Jena ran back up the slope towards the sett.

Gael watched her from sight, then pricked her ears to the twitter of swallows flying backwards and forwards across the patch of sky between the trees. On the thin, topmost twiggery of an oak tree, four baby swallows perched in the grey light, still awaiting the food supply from their parents. Fully-fledged, the youngsters would very shortly be starting their long journey to Africa.

Many birds had already left Gael's countryside, and many more would quickly follow them. These were birds which came to her land of East Lancashire just to rear their families, and having done so, they saw no reason to linger — especially when more exotic lands beckoned. Indeed, they could not afford to stay, for Gael's winter was too severe for them to survive.

Gael had watched these prospective travellers prepare for their long journeys.

She had watched them spend all their time in feeding, gorging and fattening their bodies to store the energy needed for a long flight over countless miles of land and water.

The woodlands of the area became busy air-terminals with birds passing through, resting on their way, feeding on abundant supplies. All flights were booked, for it was estimated that some 120 million land birds flew in and out of Britain each year.

Migration is a fascinating subject of which humans know very little. What is it that takes the swallow on a 12,000-mile round-trip each year with such accurate navigation?

The reasons for the bird journeys are simply breeding and food — survival in effect — and nature always takes care of the species, if not of the individual. Birds do not hibernate to escape the cold, so they must leave it behind, and generally it is the continent of Africa which attracts them.

In August, the swifts, sand-martins and adult cuckoos had left Gael. In September, the swallows and house-martins, the flycatchers, the wheatears, whinchats, redstarts and willow-warblers would be off, many to the savanna and scrub country where lions would be their neighbours.

Nature creates such wonderful provision for the great exodus of small birds, by making their departure coincide with harvest time so that there are plenty of berries on the trees, seeds on the plants, and insects on the wing on which to grow strong and prepare for their energy-sapping flights. Nature also fills the void which the migrants leave, for migration takes place both ways to and from Britain. During the autumn, the starlings come from Russia, the geese from the far north, and the redwings and fieldfares also arrive.

Internal migration also takes place. Some of the song-thrushes and blackbirds move southwards, while the skylarks which Gael was used to seeing on the hill would be off to lowland pastures, the curlews would return from the moor to the

Sheep-Fair. The curling horns of a Lonk ram.

coastal areas, and another of Gael's neighbours on the summer hill — the reed-buntings — would find a lower, more hospitable home. Small birds like the blue-tits would gather in family parties and shelter in the woodlands, and the finches, chaffinches, greenfinches and twites, would come together to spend their winter with their own kind.

A few days after her romp with Jena, Gael was on the hill to meet another, although less friendly, acquaintance — one of the many pedigree rams which ran on the farm. Bearing alert and manner aloof, the Lonk ram stood by the stone wall, the wind gently stirring the wool tips of his thick fleece. A big, strong-boned sheep with massive horns curling from a proud head, he was of aristocratic lineage.

He watched Gael come down the wall-side, standing his ground and never offering to move from her approach. It was Gael who swung away in a wide arc to pass the ram. She had no quarrel with the sheep, and past experience had taught her that the horns and skull of a disgruntled ram were very hard, and best avoided.

The ram was an impressive specimen of his breed. Of the biggest of the mountain classification of sheep, he had an arrogant Roman-nosed face coloured black and white. His strong legs, woolled to the knees and hocks, were speckled black and white. His shoulders were broad with the hint of power. His fleece was dense and weather-resistant, and his thick tail just brushed the ground.

For all his apparent weight and sluggishness, the ram was neatly proportioned, compact and even; his carriage was gay, and there was a suggestion of quick action in his general appearance. Only the single strand of plain wire which ran on posts above the top of the five-foot high field boundary wall turned him back if he leaped at the wall. He was as nimble and hardy as all his clan.

Lonks are the breed of horned sheep to be found on the Pennine hills of East Lancashire, and their origin is hazy, but they are of an old ancestry. At one time they were known as Improved Haslingden sheep; then the blue lonky stone quarried in that part of Lancashire may well have given them their name; or perhaps more likely, the dialect word 'Lanky' for Lancashire was the source.

Since the early days, and since farmers had become sufficiently interested to form a Flock Book in 1905 for recording purposes, the breed has improved gradually to the compact, well-woolled sheep of today. Much is demanded of an animal which can live throughout the year on the bleak Pennine moors, and turn such wilderness into an economical farming proposition.

Living on the poorest of grazings, bents, cotton-grass, mat-grass, sedges, heather and whinberry, by gritstone outcrops and peat bogs, the Lonk has become a great forager, ranging over the bleak land for its food. At between 1,000 and 2,000 feet above sea level, its home is lashed by rainstorm and snow blizzard, covered by cold, damp fog and cloud, and constantly ruled over by a wind whose voice is always on the verge of a scream.

To meet such exacting conditions, the Lonk grows a dense coat, impervious to the probing wet and cold. Breeding improvements in the coat of the Lonk have resulted in a better wool crop which, commercially, is used mainly for hand-

Sheep were penned to await judging—two Lonk rams at Holme Sheep Fair.

knitting and blankets, with the coarser grades going to make carpets, rugs and low quality tweeds. The wool clip for ewes is between six and seven pounds weight.

Lonk ewes are good mothers, and with most hill farmers content with one lamb per ewe, their motherly care rears a strong healthy lamb. September is the start and end of the sheep-farmer's year, the time when the older ewes, those which have reared three or four crops of lambs on the hill, are sold to lowland farmers. In the less rigorous climate of the valleys, they are then able to mother another two or three lambs. Those drafted ewes are replaced in the hill flock by gimmer hoggs, the best of the previous year's lambs. The current year's lambs are sent to lowland pasture for the winter, and rams are bought and sold, ready for the start of breeding in November.

Although the sale of pedigree Lonk sheep takes place under modern conditions in the auction-mart at Clitheroe, the gathering of the sheep for their annual breed show is a highlight of the village life at Holme, at the entrance to the Cliviger Gorge. Every September — usually the last Saturday in the month — the Lonk Sheep Breeders Association holds its championship show in the field at the rear of the Ram Inn. It is an historic occasion, for the village Sheep Fair is reputed to be one of the oldest in England, dating back to the days of the first Queen Elizabeth.

In days gone by, village fairs were very much a part of the country scene, and though many have failed to survive the march of progress, the Holme Sheep Fair which, in modern form, takes place in the village, is a link with the days of Merrie England. What it has lost in size, it has gained in stature, for although in the days of lazier traffic, sheep-pens lined the roadsides for hundreds of yards at Holme, the fair now attracts only the finest specimens of the Lonk breed to the show-ring.

Originally, its main purpose was the sorting of strayed animals, and the buying and selling of sheep, and many hundreds of ewes and rams were gathered together in the village to make the fair a red-letter day in the lives of the countryfolk. Although it has lost some of its glamour, perhaps the addition of sheepdog trials, and a fell race to the top of the Thieveley Pike has increased the interest and spectacle.

It is a day of meeting old friends, of examining and criticising the finest specimens of one of the oldest breeds of hill sheep in the country, and of testing the working prowess of sheepdogs in friendly competition. Farmers come to the fair from distances which were never dreamed of in the old days. They bring their dogs from the hills of the Lake District, the fells of Yorkshire, the Derbyshire dales and the mountains of Wales, for the Holme championship is one of the most coveted in the country. Many are international collies, dogs which have represented England and Wales in the highest competition.

When the first fair was held, the golden-eagle was reputed to have soared over the land, for Harrison Ainsworth, in *The Lancashire Witches* wrote that the Gorge of Cliviger was once the haunt of eagle and wolf.

The old country fairs of England were the supermarkets of their day. Country communities were virtually isolated settlements, for travel was exceedingly hard and difficult, so, once a year, tradesmen and merchants transported their wares to a central area where potential buyers gathered from the surrounding countryside. With the merchants came the entertainers, so that a good day was had by all. Similarly, the farmers of the area were able to bring in their stock and produce for sale, and city merchants were thus able to obtain their requirements in sufficient quantities from one central place.

Country fairs were consequently of great commercial importance to city, town and countryside. They were always held to fit into the country calendar, during the months of September and October when the farming year ended and another one began. Then there was surplus stock to sell, and crops to dispose of, and the cash they brought would be used to buy seeds and supplies before the winter set in. Another important aspect of the autumn fair was the hiring of farmworkers and domestic servants who were usually engaged on yearly contracts. (Stratford-on-Avon used to have two autumn fairs, the first when labour could be hired, and the second a few weeks later when the worker, after sampling his master's hospitality, could change his mind!)

When all the serious business had been attended to, there was time for pleasure, and that was provided by travelling showmen, so that the annual fair became quite an exciting event in the villages of rural England. With the coming of television and the fast motor-car, few fairs remain. Holme Sheep Fair is one of them — although a little imagination is required to recall the 'good old days'.

One famous fair of legend to survive is the Nottingham Goose Fair, which readers of the Robin Hood saga will know. It is held early in October, though

Sheep were lined up side by side for the judge's inspection.

Sheep were walked so that the judge could note their carriage and mobility.

Critical comment on the qualities of the sheep always came from the spectators.

now without geese! Another, which, like the Holme event runs sheepdog trials, is that at Widecombe in Devon in early September, recalling the legend of Uncle Tom Cobley and all.

It was Fair Day, and the folk of Holme were out for the day. 'It's much smaller these days,' one of the old men observed, somewhat ruefully. 'When I first came here as a boy, all the length of the village was filled with sheep-pens. Aye, they stretched way down yon road. The sheep fair then was the biggest event of the year.'

Diminished or not, the fair still attracts its crowd of people, mostly countryfolk, though many townspeople come from the nearby towns of Burnley and Todmorden. Autumn's tints touch the countryside of the Cliviger Gorge, marking the landscape with yellow and brown dashes of tree colour, the splashes of red berries, and the glint of hurrying water in the infant River Calder. On this particular day, a weak sun brightened the grey ruggedness of the hill tops above. Brown bents ran up to gritstone greys. Black and red beef cows patterned the lower greens of grazing grass.

A puckish breeze tugged playfully at Gael's silky coat. She lay on the flat top of the stone wall which bounded the main road above the paddock of sheep-pens. She was content to receive the pats of affection from the people who recognised her as they passed by. She had no committments on Fair Day.

She listened to the gabble of noise, the bleat of sheep, the buzz of talk from the humans, and the more interesting whistles of the shepherds who worked their collie-dogs in the sheepdog trials. She tasted familiar and new wind-borne scents, the scent of sheep and dogs, the smell of wet grass and churned mud, the reek of diesel-oil and petrol fumes, and the tart perfume of scrubbed cleanliness from the children who hugged her.

Sheep, encouraged by a pull on their horns by their handlers, were brought from the pens, and lined up, side by side before the white-coated judge. Sheep came out in classes of tups, ewes, shearlings, gimmers and lambs, denoting their ages and sex. All were closely weighed-up, criticised, and placed in order by the farmer-spectators, but the man in the white coat — his badge of office — had the final say.

He was not rushed in his opinions, making his way slowly down the line of sheep, looking at them from the rear, then walking in front to peer at their faces. He felt at the hard, close wool of each sheep, noted their rather arrogant-looking black and white heads, their bold eyes, sturdy legs, clean hooves and deep bodies. He opened their mouths to check their teeth. He ran them loose around the paddock to see their carriage.

With the rams, he asked the handlers to turn them up to note their functional potential. Slipping and sliding on the wet grass, and muttering a few oaths, a handler struggled to turn a strong tup, for a full-grown Lonk ram was no easy creature to throw on its back. 'That blighter's as strong as a lion,' muttered one onlooker.

The judge's minute inspection of each animal was to assess pointers to its conformation for hardiness and durability as a good hill sheep. 'That's too light in the bone,' as one tup was demoted; 'Jacket is a bit too open,' and another went back down the line.

Finally satisfied, the judge lined the sheep up in his order of preference. Prize-cards handed out, trophies won, hands shaken in congratulation, and the sheep were herded back into their transport wagons for the journey home. Show stewards dismantled the holding pens, and stacked the wooden hurdles for another day.

The onlookers drifted away, some for a pint of ale in the Ram Inn, others across to the adjoining field where a black and white sheepdog, its long hair rippling in the breeze, worked sheep to the whistled commands of its master.

The sheep show was over by late afternoon, but the sheepdog trials, the first event starting at 8 am in the morning, went on until the grey light of dusk was settling over the valley, and 80 collies had been tested on their ability to gather, fetch, drive and pen sheep. So vital to the management of sheep on high ground, the collies received a practical test of their prowess, for the trials tested the work that any dog would be expected to master in its daily duties of stock herding. There were no gimmicks or circus tricks involved in the trials, and judgement was given on a dog's capabilities to handle the sheep in a workmanlike manner, without putting them under undue stress and strain. This is the purpose of a proper sheepdog trial — to improve the collie by competition for its agricultural role of herding farmstock.

Chapter 16

New neighbours

Felfar comes to Rack Clough. His strong wings have brought him from Scandinavia, whilst lesser wings take puny butterflies to Europe. Energy of other kinds finds the woodpecker his food, and ensures the growth of fungi.

The gentle rustle and crackle of falling leaves was the only noise in the calm of Rack Clough as the shadows lengthened. Brown, brittle, lifeless leaves lost their hold on parent trees and spun to the ground, bouncing from bough to bough with a scurry, before swelling the thickening pile of ground carpet. The shadows dappled pattern over the earth cover, the sunbeams probed through the tree skeletons from a sun which rested low on the rocks of the Cliviger Gorge.

Gael played with the leaves, scattering the ground piles and rolling over and over on their brittle dryness, liking the noise of their rustling movement. She jumped to catch the falling leaves in her mouth, and worried them with mock ferocity. She played in many ways, with sticks, stones and withered plant stems, when her wild friends were unsociable, or had gone away, and the falling leaves were a seasonal addition to her games.

She played with the leaves until a harsh chakking voice startled the quietness of the woodland. It was an unfamiliar sound and Gael raised puzzled ears to trace it. Again she listened to the call. It had a faintly familiar tone, and it stirred her memory. It was the call of a fieldfare which she had not heard since April when the birds left her land to journey northwards to their breeding grounds. Now they were back, and their calls would once again be common to Gael's ears.

The fieldfare which disturbed Gael's play was a trim-feathered, handsome thrush named Felfar. Born in May in a wooded valley in Scandinavia, this was his first trip to England, and he had travelled hundreds of miles in the company of his kind, following that inbred urge to migrate to warmer lands before the cold and ice of his homeland made life impossible.

Gael was strange to Felfar, and her queer antics had provoked his call, a call to give himself confidence, and to ensure that his kin were still close at hand. He received the reply he sought from a bird which also had ceased its feasting on the red rowan berries to watch Gael's antics.

Felfar watched Gael with dark round eyes, his head tilted for a clear view, just like his cousin, the song-thrush, watched for worms when searching the grassland. He was not afraid, but wary, for the English countryside was as yet strange to his ways.

Throughout his migrational flight he had followed the path of his older companions though his own senses told him that the way was right. He had crossed snow-capped mountains, rising over the summits when conditions were good, using the shelter of valleys when the storms blew. He had been in Britain for a fortnight, reaching the coast of Northumberland after skimming only a few feet above the grey waters in the face of strong head-winds during the long crossing of the North Sea, and, still in the company of his kind, had travelled south and west wherever the feeding was good. A true nomad during that part of his life, a wanderer following food, he had arrived in Gael's woodland earlier in the day and, with plenty of rowan berries to eat, and open grassland to search for worms, he and his flock had lingered.

Felfar was young, strong and fit as the tightness and gloss of his plumage showed, and though strenuous, the long journey had taken little out of him. A few days' rest in the shelter of Northumbrian woodland and valley had replenished his energy.

Nature had provided for his wandering life with strong wings and a direct, moderate speed of flight. Bold in character, his attire was distinctive and more colourful than that of his British relations — the song-thrush, the mistle-thrush and the blackbird.

Most distinctive of all was the slate-grey rump colouring which, in some

'Tupping-time'—when the rams mated with the ewes—was in November on the hills of the Lancashire-Yorkshire Pennines. Here, rams of the Derbyshire Gritstone breed are molly-coddled—fed well to bring them to the peak of condition before going to the hill.

localities, gave him the name of Blueback. The soft French-grey colouring also marked his head and nape to contrast with the ruddy chestnut back, and the dark wings and tail. His thick bold spotting on the upper breast was also set off by the rich, buff ground colouring.

Satisfied that Gael could be of no possible threat, Felfar resumed his feeding on the rowan berries, pulling them from their stems with his strong beak. Evening was not far distant and he was anxious to fill his crop. Around him in the branches, and in the neighbouring rowans, his companions were of the same mind, and they made little noise, feeding quietly and flighting from tree to tree, and to the grassland adjoining the woodland for a change of diet.

The fieldfares, and their lesser cousins, the redwings, who came on the same long journey from the north, were back at the time of year when Gael often made strange new acquaintances. Wandering the high moor in a gleam of autumn sunshine on the previous day, she had walked along the shores of the reservoir and had met four Arctic terns. On passage to the Antarctic continent to spend the winter near the ice fringe, the terns were perhaps the greatest travellers of all, often journeying over 10,000 miles twice a year.

They come to Britain to nest, others of their kind even nesting further north in the Arctic, and they go south to the opposite end of the world to winter. Record travellers, the terns which nest in the Arctic land of the midnight sun also live the longest hours of daylight of any creature, for their winter is spent in the unending daylight of the Antarctic summer.

Gael puts the ducks to flight from Scholey pond in October.

They are small, up to 15 inches long, and are gull-like birds, but are readily distinguishable from the gulls which Gael knew by their size, their long thin beaks, pointed wings and deeply forked tails. Often called sea-swallows, the terns are at their best in the air, lightly graceful, agile and untiring. On land they waddle awkwardly on short legs. They swim well, and dive, dropping from the air into the top water to snatch fish and other marine food, often disappearing momentarily beneath the surface.

Although the terns faced an energetic journey from the reservoir on the moor, the countryside they would leave was settling quietly into restful winter. The rocks of Thieveley had no tops, their steep grey faces rising damply into the murk of early morning mist. Little stirred in a ghostly half-lit world.

A grazing ewe, its woolly coat blending into the greyness of the morning, nibbled the sparse grass on a narrow ledge, half way up the rock face. It scarcely bothered to lift its head when Gael passed by. Gracefully balancing her way from rock ledge to grassy shelf, the little collie came down the steep slope. Her sable coat was sequinned with the jewels of water drops which, stolen from the wet mist, glinted light in the murk of the morning.

She walked the narrow way of a sheep-trod, her pads silent on the compacted earth so that even Kee, the kestrel, perched on the rock outcrop by the track, did not hear her movement. He blinked his yellow-rimmed eyes when she passed by, but did not move, for Gael was no threat to him. He was not yet in need of food, and his world of open sky was a shrouded greyness of water vapour.

Scholey Pond was visited by many ducks in October whilst dairy cows grazed the late grass.

At the base of the rock-face, a hunting stoat darted for the safety of a crack in the stone when it saw Gael. Safely housed, it popped its head out of the crack, ready to spit abuse at the collie. Gael ignored it, and turned towards the trees of the clough, and a meadow-pipit flipped from under her feet, saved by her coming from the stoat's bloodthirsty fangs.

Watchfulness is ever the key to survival in the wild, though the time of year had come when other methods of staying alive were used by some creatures. Hibernation is one of nature's best known ways of survival, though few creatures actually use that method. Hedgehogs, bats and dormice are probably the only true hibernators, for they sleep so soundly that their breathing almost ceases, their body temperature drops almost to death, and the heart-beat can become as slow as one beat in ten seconds. That is really going to sleep!

Other creatures, like the badger and squirrel, sleep long and well, but wake up for a stroll during a spell of mild weather. Insects are the most vulnerable of creatures to face the growing cold, and for a time find some haven in the ground carpet of leaves which provides a warm and cosy home until the frost strengthens to kill so many of them. Before they die they lay the eggs which provide the following year's insects and which ensure the continuation of the species.

Some, like the caterpillars of the common white-cabbage butterfly, pupate to live out the winter, and the beautiful tortoiseshell butterfly hibernates in the shelter of hollow trees, behind the bark, or even in dwelling houses. The ladybird is another insect which sleeps away the winter.

Strange as it seems, the puny wings of some frail creatures, like the red-admiral butterfly which Gael frightened from the lingering flower of a dandelion, are capable of taking insects to follow the ways of the summer birds in order to migrate to warmer climes. The migrational feats of butterflies in no way compare with those of birds, but some butterflies have remarkable powers of flight, and often reach countries far distant from their original homes.

The restless clouded-yellow butterfly had flown across the English Channel to lay eggs on the clover plants on Scholey Hill, and the painted-lady had flown from North Africa to lay small green eggs on the thistles in Rack Clough. Though it had a strong, powerful flight for a butterfly, and could sustain its direction over long periods, the red-admiral from Calder Valley would fly south, but would probably never reach its ancestral home by the warm Mediterranean.

Success is very dependent on luck, the combination of fair winds and fine weather, and in autumnal Britain the odds are stacked against the butterfly. As a species, the red-admiral is really dependent on Continental stimulus in order to retain a presence in Gael's locality. Spring migration from Europe to Britain has a much greater chance of success than the reverse trip in bad weather. The butterflies which come in spring lay single eggs on nettle leaves to produce a generation of British-born children, but, when the time comes to face the colder days, most of them fight shy of attempting the autumn flight across the Channel to milder conditions. They make some attempt to hibernate, but, not being natural survivors, most of them perish in the cold.

As rain-showers scattered the mistiness of the morning, Gael heard the rattling

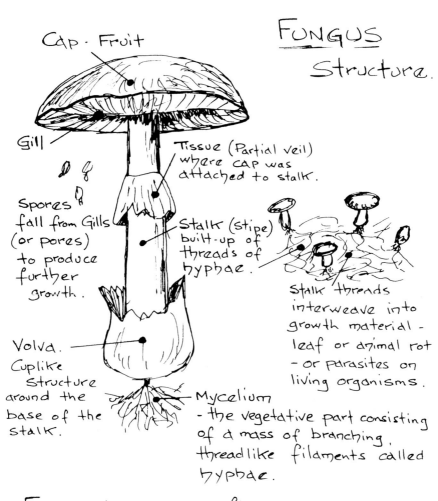

Cap - Fruit

FUNGUS

Structure.

Gill

Tissue (Partial veil) where CAP was attached to stalk.

Spores fall from Gills (or pores) to produce further growth.

Stalk (stipe) built-up of threads of hyphae.

Stalk threads interweave into growth material - leaf or animal rot - or parasites on living organisms.

Volva. Cuplike Structure around the base of the stalk.

Mycelium - the vegetative part consisting of a mass of branching, threadlike filaments called hyphae.

Fungus is a non-flowering plant which lacks chlorophyll (green matter) and relies on organic matter for its growth. Each cap - the fruit - produces millions of spores from which the next generation will grow. Fungi are usually seen in amount in autumn.

Little- owl.
Kew.
Scholey Hill.
October.

call of Dryob, the great-spotted woodpecker, whose rapid beak blows on a tree rang loudly in the air of Rack Clough. The bird, driving his sharp beak into the wood of a rotten sycamore tree, struck a sharp, vibrating noise, and Gael lifted her head to listen. She pricked her ears to the sound for, although she had heard it before, it often puzzled her since the actual noise of Dryob's insect search was so varied—dependent on the type and health of the tree he rattled.

She listened for a while and heard the woodpecker call his sharp pleasure on finding a cache of grubs in the old sycamore, but a sudden squall of wind-driven raindrops pricked at her eyes, and she sought shelter by the stone wall. By her crossed forepaws a cluster of mushrooms, greyish-capped fungi with brown gills, sprouted from the wet earth.

Typical of fungi growth and non-flowering plants which lack the green chlorophyll of other plants, mushrooms are one of many species to be found on wet hillsides at that time of the year. Left to its brief natural life, a mature mushroom is reputed to disperse over 15,000 million spores.

The spores are like the seeds of other plants, and fall from the gill, or underside of the mushroom's cap, which is really the fruiting body — and reproductive part, as with other plants — of a vast interwoven network of hair-like stalks which spread over or under the soil. The germination of the spores which fall from the mushroom's gill depends on the suitability of ground and weather, and many spores fail to produce.

Field mushrooms, the edible kind, are grey to creamy-white on the top of the cap, and a chocolate-brown colour on the gill (the underside), and their skins can be peeled quite easily. This is a reliable test, for there are 10,000 species of fungi in Britain, and many of them are poisonous, particularly the brightly coloured ones.

Lying by the wall, Gael swivelled her interest to a muffled mewing sound which suddenly came from a cavity between two of the stones. She jumped to her feet, and pushed her nose to the gap between the stones, and sucked for scent. A threatening spitting sound made her hastily step back, and Kew, the fluffed and ruffled little-owl, appeared in the opening. His round dark eyes threatening, his hooked bill open, Kew squeezed from the wall cavity, and took wing.

Kew had been searching the many cavities between the stones for beetles and spiders, a habit which he had grown accustomed to, for in the structure of the wall was food aplenty for his tastes. The walls criss-crossed the hillside and provided both refuge and safe passage for many creatures, most of which the tough little-owl could match. Although it was a strange environment for a bird, and his stature was not designed for scrambling along the narrow passages, Kew had caught mice and baby rabbits in the wall. The stoats and weasels which hunted in similar fashion through the wall were the only creatures Kew cared not to face.

Chapter 17

Timely intervention

The sudden, silent strike of a sparrow-hawk scatters the dainty titmice, and Gael is ignored by cheeky starlings, and tolerated by Pyat, the swaggering magpie.

Ever on the move, flitting from twig to twig through silver-birch trees stripped of their golden leaves by the beating of wind and rain, the mixed party of titmice searched for their insect food in the afternoon woodland of Brockholes. They were 20 in number, a motley, colourful crowd of restless movement and acrobatic grace, comprising nine green-washed blue-tits, six larger great-tits whose colouring was more distinct with their black bibs, one lonesome coal-tit with a large white nape spot on its black head, and a fairy family of four dainty white and pink long-tailed-tits.

Hanging upside down on a twig to see what insect was lurking there, examining with bright eyes the bark of a tree for spiders, and flitting to the crook of the branches to seize a grub, each bird was in constant scurry. Grey rain clouds in the sky cast a gloom over the woodland, but although the mirk shaded the ground-mat of vegetation, there was ample light among the skeleton twig tracery of the trees.

Rooks, black silhouettes against the cloud grey, streamed in flight over the tree tops. Krark, the heron, sensed some reason to leave his fishing place by the river and trailed his toes across the flood-water before his large wings lifted him into the air. Ruddock, the robin, perched in the deep cover of rhododendron bushes, called an anxious note. The sense of tension spread.

Most graceful of all the titmice, Rosac, senior of the long-tailed-tits, called 'zi-zi-zi' to his mate who took her name, Sisee, from the call-notes. In Rosac's voice was also a hint of anxiety, and, recognising the expresion of his call, Sisee joined him on a twig of the birch tree. With a flutter of her tiny wings, and a balancing turn of her long tail, she flitted to his side.

Rosac called his anxiety to the other two members of his family, the only survivors of a family of nine which he and Sisee had reared in the spring. One of the two youngsters was searching the bark of a birch trunk for grubs, but came to the call. The other was contesting, with a blue-tit, the winkling-out of a spider from a crack on the horizontal branch of an oak, and therefore ignored the call.

Only good fortune, and the size of the oak branch prevented either of the two squabbling birds from instant death. Accipita, the sparrow-hawk, having to swerve her flight suddenly to avoid the tree branch, mis-timed her strike. By barely an inch, the deadly snatch of her taloned feet missed the tits.

Immediately all was consternation. The sudden, silent dash of Accipita, a decisive trait so typical of her breed, spread panic among the flock of small birds. Wings whirring, they dropped into the green leaf shelter of the rhododendron bushes — all but the two birds on the oak bough. They flopped on to the bark of the oak bough, beaks gaping, hearts throbbing, totally incapable of immediate movement — and readily available for Accipita's second attempt at her prey.

The hawk, her white-barred breast catching the light, turned quickly for a return strike, just as Gael broke from the cover of the bushes on the ground. Chattering a defiant cry of anger at the collie's distracting appearance, Accipita was checked in her flight, momentarily, yet sufficiently for the two scared birds to lose their fear-paralysis and to tumble into the sanctuary of the covering bushes.

Accipita swung away from the oak tree, her chance of an easy prey foiled. Twisting a way between the trees, she speedily flew from sight. In the gloomy shelter of the shining rhododendron leaves, the titmice quietly passed the message that the hawk was going. Soon they flew back to the higher branches of the silver-birch trees to continue their feeding, as though nothing untoward had happened.

Gael had lifted her ears to the sparrow-hawk's threatening cry, and fast though Accipita was in retreat, she had seen the bird fly beyond her sight into the trees. She did not realise that she had upset the hawk's hunting, though she recognised the cry as one of anger and frustration. She watched the titmice when they returned to their feeding. Rosac saw her, and though he was unaware that she had saved the life of his daughter, he dropped down the branches of a birch tree to see her. His tiny nails grasped the twigs and his long slender tail balanced his perch as his round hazel eyes peered down at the dog.

Rain fell from the sky, spattering through the open branches. A spider scurried along a crack in the bark of Rosac's tree, and the titmouse snapped it in his beak. Food was paramount: Gael was forgotten. Whirring his wings, and with tail spread, Rosac flew to an adjoining beech tree, and, industrious and acrobatic, searched every bud knob and cranny for insects.

Deserted by the bird, Gael sought shelter in the gloom of the woodland undergrowth. Beneath the shelter of bracken plants which, in dying, had intertwined their sapless leaves to turn aside the direct fall of the raindrops, she knew a mild world where insects moved and brown-winged moths flew, where the wood-mice played in safe concealment from sky dangers, and where the rabbits gambolled in screened security.

The bracken patch, growing to a six-foot high summer jungle on the dry slope of the woodland, was threaded with badger tunnels and rabbit runs, the stems of the plants pushed aside by the animals so that their progress was unimpeded. The patch had settled with the decay of autumn, so that the leaf canopy was barely over Gael's head, and in places she walked with a slinking crouch. But she could move as easily as the badgers and there was always something of interest.

A tiny stump-tailed wren, a troglodyte of the gloom, flitted through the bracken stems before her, not worried by her coming. Gael wrinkled her black nostrils to the scent of rabbit. Sitting quietly on its haunches, grooming raindrops from its face with soft-furred forelegs, a rabbit became suddenly aware of the collie's approach and darted away.

Gael dashed after it. Along the clear tunnels, winding in and out of the bracken stems, up and down the slope, they chased. It was great sport, a game of hide-and-seek at its best. Up bobbed the rabbit through the golden canopy: up bobbed Gael in close pursuit. Perched in a tall sycamore tree, Pyat, the magpie, saw the appearances and disappearances of the two animals, and cackled his excitement. He followed the course of the chase by the top movements of the bracken leaves, and the fleeting glimpses of the contestants.

Skidding round the corner of a badger track, Gael momentarily nosed the white tail-scud of the rabbit as it finally darted into the sanctuary of a bolt-hole to the underground warren. The game was over, and Gael had to content herself with a nose-blowing, scent-sucking inspection of the hole which was too small for her entrance. She left the cover of the bracken, shook particles of soil and leaf from her bedraggled fur, and cocked her ears to the harsh and vulgar comments of Pyat

Afternoon rain fell from a grey sky on to the open woodland, soaking into the decaying leaf carpet, twitching the green shining leaves of rhododendron to a constant dance, streaming down the lichen-covered trunks of the tall trees.

Gael left Brockholes Wood and crossed the pasture to stretch herself on a dry couch by the stone wall. She licked water from her paws and was engrossed in her toilet when, falling like the wind-driven leaves of autumn, thousands of starlings whirled from the grey sky to settle on the grass. Thickly bunching together on the ground, they covered the green field with a seething black carpet. Undeterred by Gael's presence, they settled to leave a green vacant arc before her, the nearest bird some five yards distant.

Although her immediate reaction to any creature on the ground was to romp towards it in play, Gael was stilled by the deluge of birds, and she did not even rise to her feet. The chatter and squabble of noise to her ears was oppressive. Surprised she watched in wonderment, her ears cocked and swivelling to the hubbub, her nose tasting the warmth of the scent-lines drifting from the milling host. The starlings poked for grubs and worms in the soft, wet ground, jostling each other in their eagerness, squabbling for choice titbits, and some turning on their neighbours in anger, leaping up six inches off the ground, with long beaks clicking in vicious stabs.

Even in the vast throng, each was an individualist, each intent on its own interests, and jealous of its fellow's success. They screamed abuse at any rival to a juicy morsel. A restless crowd, the birds shook rainwater from varied colours of garb. Many wore the light-brown feathering of immaturity. The feathers of the adults ranged through the spotted buff-colouring of the moult to the more metallic hues of full plumage.

Many of the birds were visitors from northern Europe. Early roosters, the large

An opportunist, and smartly dressed, a starling took life at a cocky, swashbuckling pace.

flock of starlings feeding in front of Gael's couch had gathered before the dusk on their way to a roost in the Forest of Rossendale beyond the Cliviger Gorge. Liking company, they slept in a vast throng of as many as 100,000 birds.

More birds, in smaller flocks, fell with the raindrops to join the main gathering. Many birds alighted in the tall, leafless sycamore which grew by the boundary wall, perching on every available twig so that the tree took on the round silhouette of full leaf.

Gael had heard enough of the whistle and chatter which reached crescendo. She jumped to her feet to chase away the cheeky, strutting birds which disregarded her presence. When she ran towards them, the nearest birds ceased their chattering, and shouted the harsh rasping notes of alarm, then wave after wave of startled starlings rose into the air, the winnowing of their furiously beating wings loud in intensity.

Gael chased right across the feeding ground until every bird was airborne. They rose, a weaving, dancing multitude of individuals, so adept at flock membership that rarely did they collide with each other in flight, and so skilful that they performed the most complicated aerial evolutions. Still chattering, they climbed up the sky, closed up their formation, wheeled round, banked to turn sharply and, only two fields away, swept down to settle over the grass between five grazing black bullocks. The bullocks leaped in startled steps, the birds flighted back into the air, and trailing off in a drifting flock, crossed over the valley and pitched among grazing sheep on the far hillside.

The starlings gone, Gael saw Kee, the kestrel, slip from the close twiggery of a

Magpie.
Pyat.
Rack Clough.
November.

hawthorn bush. He had been watching the movement of the starling flock, for with such a large congregation of birds, his hunting was so much easier. Starlings were always of interest to Gael. She liked their cocky, swashbuckling attitude to life, although their gaggle of voices was sometimes irritating. She appreciated their sense of fun when she chased them around the hillside, although the birds were not so sympathetically inclined to her rompings.

Such uneasy tolerance also existed between Gael and another of her regular neighbours. Pyat, the magpie, regarded Gael as a necessary nuisance who usually disturbed his feeding, warned potential prey of his intentions, yet sometimes provided a pleasant distraction when he was in playful mood. He was always abusive when Gael caught him on the ground, and chased and harried him to flight. He regarded most of her antics with open hostility and voiced his disapproval of her with the loudest and unkindest language whenever they met.

Gael did not mind. She was aware of Pyat's bullying attitude to every small bird, and she felt no guilt in putting him to flight. He was a pompous, strutting rogue who felt affronted when he had to fly from her romping interference. Intelligent and cocksure, Pyat returned the insult by dropping twigs down on her whenever he saw her in the woodland, and he was always quick to shout her presence to the wildfolk, and spoil her stalking games with the rabbits.

Pyat and his clan were mainly ground feeders, scouring the land for worms, caterpillars, grubs, woodlice and insects, so that they were often within Gael's reach. They were adept at their feeding, picking food easily off the grassland, turning over the ground, and foraging into the tufts wih their strong, black beaks, and they would occasionally scratch at the surface with their feet like farmyard fowls.

Gale lived with them daily, for they roamed the same territory as she did, and, during the winter months, Pyat and his wife gathered their small family party of sons and daughters to spend the days together. Their presence on the upland fields, and in the leafless trees of Rack Clough and Brockholes Wood, brightened the drab winter months.

Pyat was a member of the crow family, but much more colourful than his cousins, the rooks, or Corbie, the carrion-crow. He had the swagger of his race, and the distinction of a dress of snow-white apron, plus epaulettes, to contrast the black of his head and back. His black colouring was made more glamorous with metallic tints of blue, purple and green.

And Pyat had that little extra to his relations in adornment—his long serrated tail which was his pride and joy. Always his tail received the most fastidious preening, and always it was held clear of the mud and dirt when he walked the ground. It was the threat to his tail, when he flew slowly from Gael's playfully snapping jaws, which made him so angry towards the collie.

In flight, the magpie was somewhat pedantic, but sure and direct, and his slim body, short rounded wings and long tail made him an unmistakable silhouette against the grey sky. Whatever his faulst — and they were many, for he had a liking for the eggs and nestlings of such song-birds as the blackbird and thrush — Pyat was an intelligent rogue. He was the local gossip, and he made it his business to know all that went on around him — so much that the Italians call him *gazza*, derived from the word gazette for a news-sheet of gossip and titbits. He dabbled in every other creature's business, he mobbed the tawny-owl in the woodland, chivvied the farm cats, and chattered a warning to the whole countryside whenever a fox was abroad.

The magpie's voice cannot be mistaken. It is harsh, chattering, squawking and loud, and in some localities earns its owner the name of chatter-pie. As with all distinctive characters, the magpie plays a part in folk-lore, and perhaps the best known rhyme goes: 'one for sorrow, two for mirth, three for a wedding, four for a birth, five for silver, six for gold, seven for a secret, never to be told'.

Whatever the number of his family party, Pyat and his colourfully-garbed clan always brightened Gael's wanderings in the countryside in the grey days of winter.

Chapter 18

Merry Christmas

Watching over the sheep flock on Christmas Eve; the festive bird which is a wolf in sheep's clothing; and simple provisions to bring the joy of birds to the garden.

The dusk of a cold, frosty night was closing down as I rested for a moment in the shelter of the stone wall. Gael came to push her damp nose into my hand, and I gave her a playful hug. Though her breath misted in the freezing air, she was warm and comforting as she settled by my side. Together we watched the sheep as they grazed quite placidly over the upland pasture. They were content, and bit at the short, frosted grass, scratching away the ice particles with their sharp hooves to reach their food. All seemed well with them.

Musing, I thought that it must have been a very similar scene for the shepherds on that first Christmas. My pastoral setting was different, but in the icy countyside of East Lancashire the shepherd still watched over his flock as did those shepherds of old. Today the shepherd is more technical and clinical, and his enemies are disease and sickness, but his watching is still as necessary as when his forbears guarded their sheep against wild predators.

The dusk deepened, and the furthermost sheep blended into the murk of greyness. Away in the distance the lights of Burnley twinkled and gained in brightness. 'Come Gael.' I rose and walked down the hill towards the valley. Passing through the bottom field-gate on to the lane, I echoed the sentiment as a passer-by called a cheery 'Merry Christmas.'

The signs of the festive season were all around. Christmas trees brightened the windows of the village houses, their branches sparkling with coloured lights. Holly and other greenery decorated the rooms, and colourful cards lined the shelves and window-ledges.

I wondered how many of those cards depicted the red-breasted robin, for Christmas and robins seemed to go together in people's minds. On countless greetings-cards this common, perky bird of the British countryside, pictured perched on snow-covered ground or on icy holly twigs, was coupled with seasonal rhymes and poems. The robin is consequently one of the few birds which everyone can identify, it is a bird which figures in our legends and nursery rhymes, and its bold, fearless nature makes it a favourite visitor to the garden.

Ruddock, the robin, who left his woodland home at that time of the year to spend some of the winter months in Gael's garden area, was a particular friend of the little collie. He left his summer territory where he mated and raised a family, and, but a minute's flight from the trees, established a fresh empire amid the sheltered garden lands of the village. There he found ample growth of shelter from the cold and the wind, and there were many bird-tables which contained readily-available food.

He usually welcomed Gael with a few notes of song when she came from the house into the garden, and bird and dog enjoyed each other's company on grey days when most other creatures skulked from the weather. He sang, from a perch on the top of the garden fence, flicking his wings, legs straight, red breast proudly presented, to call the little collie's attention to his presence.

Ruddock flew across to the bird-table, snatched a crumb, gave the blue-tit's bone a peck, and dropped down to the wet grass. Gael turned her eyes to the robin in acknowledgement of his joining her, but otherwise heeded him not. She continued her inspection among the low-growing conifers in the rockery. Ruddock followed her. She was sure to disturb some grub or other tasty morsel which would be appreciated by the robin.

The robin is probably the best known and the most popular bird in Britain. It is Britain's national bird, chosen by the International Council for Bird Preservation in 1961 as depicting British characteristics with its bold, chest-puffing individualism. Quite a personality, and certainly a bird of romantic legend, the robin in fact is far from being the ideal bird of Christmas when we are all led to think of peace and goodwill, and to forget the shortcomings of our neighbours.

Robin-redbreast is one of the most pugnacious and ill-tempered of birds, and its glorious red-feathered breast is, similar to the former scarlet uniform of the British soldier, simply war-paint to warn off any would-be aggressor. There is a code, however, which prevails throughout birdland — that the defender of a territory already claimed is the victor. Victory goes not always to the strongest,

Robin-redbreast, the bird of Christmas, is probably the best-known bird in Britain.

but to the righteous — the owner of the property. There, surely, is a message for Christmas!

Robins have learned that, when within their own territory, they must sing a challenge, display their war-paint, and, if necessary, fight in defence: if crossing or straying to another's territory, they must keep a low profile, move with caution, and if 'found-out', surrender and fly immediately to their own domain. Those which ignore the rules will, apart from feeding and sleeping, spend most of their lives in singing a challenge and fighting a territorial battle.

Thus, the Christmas cards which depict a single robin perched in the holly bush are naturally correct; the ones which show a group of robins perched together are incorrect and far removed from the season of peace and goodwill. A group of robins means an explosive situation from which furious conflict will arise. The robin is no angel. It can be a very belligerent character, though mainly when in defence of its territory, and when it resents competition on the bird-table.

Many wild creatures have a colouring of feathers or fur which blends with their habitat and helps them to camouflage their presence from potential enemies, but those which, like the robin, have some brilliance to spoil this camouflage use the colouring for some other vital role in their lives.

In the robin's case, the vivid breast colouring is used for display — not for a courtship display to attract a partner, but as a threatening sign to warn off an enemy, usually a trespasser of its own kind. Its red breast is the bird's most conspicuous feature and, in earlier years, gave the bird its name simply of 'redbreast'. This distinctive colouration is acquired by the robin at its first moult of feathers in July and August, for it leaves the nest in the dowdier plumage of speckled browns. Both male and female birds wear the red breast on reaching maturity.

Ruddock extended his territorial lordship to the bird-table, and it was here that he earned his unsavoury reputation among the other birds in the garden. He was the boss — and entitled to first choice of the titbits — in his opinion. In theirs, he was simply a bully with a bad-tempered nature, who always claimed priority.

Gael accepted Ruddock's nature for he always welcomed her company and showed her the respect and the courtesy due to the true owner of the territory — though he was never slow to profit from their understanding if the opportunity arose.

Should Gael disturb the spiders in the leaf-carpet under the birch tree in the corner of the garden, Ruddock would be close on hand to snap them up. When Gael rested on the lawn, Ruddock often hopped to within touching distance, and when he called to her, she pricked her ears to his voice, and she watched him with rapt attention. He was rarely silent, only ceasing to sing whilst he changed his clothing during the moulting of his feathers around August, so that he could always command her interest.

Gael had always liked to hear the robin's voice, ever since her puppyhood days in the garden, for it was one of the first wild voices she ever heard. It was this vocal communication at a period of the year when birds were generally silent, his trusting manner, coupled with the human trait to applaud any creature that could face adversity with such apparent cheerfulness, that made Ruddock and his kind so popular with people. The robin's friendly, trusting nature, its self-reliance and good humour, and its tameness earns it the affection it enjoys from humans. These traits are particularly appreciated at Christmas time — and this time, often a time of cold and severe weather when food is hard to find, is when the robin really exploits man's affections.

The robin's relationship with man is unique, for most other birds avoid humans like the plague, usually with good cause. Other birds will come to the bird-table for food but all retain their natural shyness, and to some extent, their fear of man. Not only does the robin visit, but also it often seeks human company, joining the gardener in anticipation of a nice juicy worm, or entering the kitchen for crumbs from the table.

This tameness, incidentally, is characteristic of the British robin only. Its continental cousin is not so trusting, for often the robin in France and Italy ends up as part of the Christmas dinner!

The robin has long been regarded as a symbol of Christmas, and, as already stated, it is a favourite of card and calendar designers. Some superstition, however, says that it is unlucky to receive a Christmas card bearing the picture of a robin. This belief undoubtedly stems from the superstition that for a robin to enter the home is a sign of death to one of the inhabitants, that a robin tapping on the window of a house where someone is ill means that that person will not recover, or that the person sitting on a chair on which a robin perches will not see the year out. Shades of the Lancashire witches!

Being so familiar, the robin has inevitably entered our folk-lore, and literature abounds with allusions to it. They range from 'Fat and merry, lean and sad: Pale and pettish, red and bad' to the eminently practical 'Robin-redbreast is esteemed a light and good meat' in a book of 1595.

Whilst many old-wives' tales carry some semblance of truth in the countryside, they often wrong the friendly robin. It is a useful bird in the eyes of the farmer, for it does great service in destroying large quantities of insect pests, and the legend that to kill or capture a robin will bring bad luck is more apt. The saying goes: 'He that hurts robin or wren will never prosper, boy or man'.

The robin was said to have covered, with leaves, the body of Our Lord, thereby staining its own breast with blood. There are other versions of how the robin came to have a red breast, one that the bird tried to draw a thorn from Christ's crown of thorns at the crucifixion and was stained by Christ's blood. Another religious version is that, whilst flying with water to the tortured souls in Purgatory, its breast was scorched by fire.

The balance is in favour of the cheery robin and, for those in doubt, its song should clinch the issue. Not only does it sing for most of the year, but its mellow, tender notes, compared on occasion with those of the nightingale, are particularly welcome in winter when other birds are silent. At the end of the 17th century, Nicholas Cox wrote that in 'the opinion of some' the robin 'for sweetness of note comes not much short of the nightingale', and the street entertainer and wayside

A blue-tit will readily come to take food to brighten up the drab winter days with its colourful feathering.

poet, William Henry Davies, wrote: 'Robin on a leafless bough, Lord in Heaven how he sings'. Whatever, the robin's cockiness, its bright eyes shining quizzically as it perches on the window ledge, and its apparent fearlessness and trust in humans makes it such a favourite around the house and garden, particularly during the festive period.

Ruddock was not the only bird that Gael welcomed to the garden in December days. Sparrows and starlings scattered from their feeding below the bird-table when she bounded across the grass, not finding her bustle and high spirits of simple playfulness at all humorous. They had to survive through the cold days, and life was a serious business. Though never becoming as involved as Ruddock in Gael's wanderings in the garden, they did, however, come to accept her boisterous nature as harmless, for there was always a regular supply of food to be obtained from the bird-table.

Gael found much pleasure from their various antics. She watched the dexterity of the blue-tits on the meat bones which were hung from the table; she lifted her nose, straining her neck to touch the tails of three pink chaffinches which balanced the seed-hopper; she was held intrigued by the to-and-fro swinging tempo of the wire basket caused by a pair of greenfinches prising out the peanuts. Squabbling over the nuts and flashing the yellow feathers of their wings to keep balance, the greenfinches were as clever as the titmice in clinging to the sides of the basket.

Gael could never understand the necessity for the noise and fighting of the starlings, so gluttonous and mannerless in their fear of being left hungry, when there was really enough for all. She was charmed by the dainty mouse-like movements of the dunnock which foraged the ground beneath the table, and she made no move to scare it. She chased, with malicious intent, to frighten away the big, bold, black and white magpie from her garden.

She was puzzled by the quiet, but distinctive, mew of welcome when a young tawny-owl perched in the silver-birch tree, and she cocked her ears to the unmistakable call of friendship. Although mobbed when discovered by some of the other birds, the young owl accepted the garden as a safe place, a haven where there was a degree of security. This was the attitude of most of the birds which visited and, accepting Gael's inevitable presence, they realised that the bird-table was a source of easy food.

When frost glued the carpet of leaves over the woodland floor into a solid mat into which it was impossible to prise a beak, when snow patterned the grassy slopes of the clough into a fairylike, but uninviting, food-forage, when ice sheathed the rushes and sealed the waters, when the cold had taken its toll on the insect population, the birds sought easier means of obtaining their food.

Providing birds with a free feed has, of course, a dual reward. Apart from keeping the birds alive, it provides endless enjoyment in watching their antics and habits from the cosy comfort of your own armchair. Providing food for birds in hard weather also has its obligations. The birds will, to some extent, become dependent on your food, and if you forget to provide it, they will suddenly be

The greenfinch—a doughty visitor to the Christmas bird-table—became quite a gymnast on the nut-basket.

Bird-table

Roofed version.

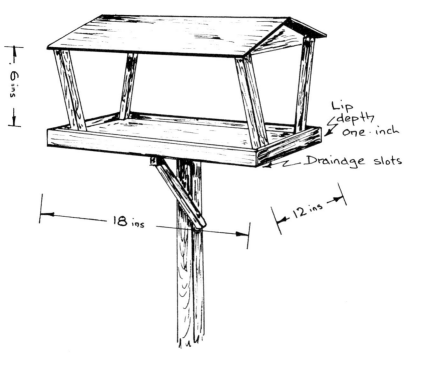

6 ins.

Lip
depth
one·inch

Draindge slots

18 ins

12 ins

Type as supplied
by
Royal Society for the
Protection of Birds

thrown back upon their own resources at a difficult time.

Hunger is more a killer than the cold. Even a healthy, small bird will die in a matter of hours if it is without food on a cold night. In cold weather — especially during the night — birds lose a lot of weight in keeping warm. This has to be made up during the short daylight hours.

Most kitchen scraps will be food for birds, and though the food is of paramount importance, the place where it is offered is also to be considered. It is asking for trouble, and a nuisance in the form of mice and rats, to scatter food over the ground, and the type of structure — and its siting — on which the food is placed must be acceptable to the birds.

Sited by a screening corner, or too close to garden bushes, a table will be an easy and concealed stalk for a cat. Birds are naturally and sensibly wary and suspicious of man-made structures, and until their fear of a trap is dispelled, the most replete table will have few visitors. Choose the correct site and there is no need for an architect-designed bird-table. If safe from predators, the top of the back-yard wall, a window-ledge, a flat board-platform fixed to the top of a garden post will be adequate. If the birds feel safe they will dine at your table.

Bird-tables come in various shapes and sizes, but basically need be little more than the flat platform erected in a safe position, and easily visible from within the house to obtain the pleasure of watching the birds. They range from the elaborate rustic type — usually the most expensive to buy and the most unsuitable for they are so easily climbed by cats — to the simple flat boards on tall posts which the birds prefer because they give full vision and enable possible intruders to be quickly spotted.

It is better if the board has a raised lip on each side to prevent your visitors from spilling too much food on to the ground — although such birds as the trim little dunnock, thrush and blackbird will prefer to feed on the ground. A roof can be a useful addition because it protects the food from the weather, but birds have to get used to this, for they are never keen to go under anything, fearing a trap.

Nowadays, one can purchase all manner of feeding gadgets, tit-bells, seed-hoppers, nut cylinders, scrap baskets and the like. All have their uses, and many are extremely good, but none are essential to enjoy the company of birds in your garden or yard, although some gadgets for holding peanuts — to attract the acrobatic titmice — will bring hours of pleasure. Half a coconut or a meat bone hung from the bird-table is equally good bait to attract the blue-tits. Blue-tits are the recognised acrobats of the bird-table, but Gael often saw just how adaptable birds could become when the threat of starvation hovered.

She watched a handsome greenfinch swing comfortably, head downwards, on the string basket, his feet grasping the wide mesh with ease, to work with his beak to free a nut from the container. In the past few days, the bird had mastered the art of clinging to the swaying basket to extract the peanut kernels with his strong, stubby beak. He had also found that, by severing a strand of the string, he could pull out a complete nut. Swinging backwards and forwards to the wind's will, the greenfinch deftly lifted the nut, and carrying it, dropped down to the grass to enjoy his meal.

Before he could really enjoy the nut, a house-sparrow flew in and boldly stole it from under his beak, and after such an effort to win the nut, the finch's lack of resistance to the theft was surprising. He just flew back up to the nut-basket, and started to prise out another nut with equal patience.

The greenfinch's greater size discouraged a blue-tit from landing on the basket. It flitted to the coconut kernel and, undisturbed, for no other bird could match its ability to cling upside down, picked a meal from the white nut. Master of balance and poise also on the string-threaded line of unshelled peanuts, the blue-tit rained hammer-like blows with its sharp beak to pierce the shell and expose the kernel. Its acrobatic actions, as it clung to the nut to counter the toss of the wind, were both skilfull and amusing. Confidently, the bird opened the shell just sufficiently to get at the rich brown kernel. The nut speared with its beak, it flew into the adjoining birch tree, there to hold the food with its foot and eat in comfort.

Comfort and sustenance can be provided in many ways to birds in winter for, unlike spring and summer when it can actually be dangerous to offer some scraps, in hard weather almost all kitchen scraps are acceptable. When the pressure of supplying the demands of ever-hungry babies is great, parent birds can take the easy way out, but then can harm their families of young chicks by feeding them the easily-come-by items from a bird-table. Brown wheaten bread is far better than white bread for birds; white bread has a tendancy to swell when wet. Other kitchen scraps which are most acceptable are bacon-rind, meat scraps and bones, bits of cheese and fruit, fat and dripping, stale cake and baked potato.

Birds will be attracted by any kind of scraps but, if you are setting out to offer them a wide variety, and are prepared to buy food for your visitors, then you can add oats, wheat, maize, peanuts, raisins, currants, suet, fruit and berries, and solid coconut — but not shredded coconut — to the seed mixtures obtainable from pet shops. Shredded, desiccated or dried coconut can be harmful for, like white bread, it swells when moist — inside the bird! Salt is also a killer, so that highly seasoned food scraps are best fed to the dog, if he'll take them, although birds will select only the things they like to eat and reject the rest. You need have little fear of poisoning the birds.

Do not forget a water supply in cold weather when natural ponds and other sources will be frozen over. It is far better to make regular changes to keep a fresh supply available, rather than to add such substances as glycerine to prevent freezing. Birds loathe a messy beak — and glycerine sticks.

Gael's garden was a valuable haven for birds and other wild creatures — as indeed are all gardens, with more and more land being used for industrial purposes. Bird gardens — where the plants and trees grown are the kind that produce food, shelter and 'home' for various kinds of birds — are becoming more and more necessary and interesting, for they, like the motorway embankments, provide a permanent, if straggling, nature-reserve.

Chapter 19

Colourful superstition

The brightness of holly and the frivolity of mistletoe are considered before the tups come in; and a low, purring sound welcomes Gael to the woodland.

The holly bushes in Rack Clough provided fine cover for the birds, their prickly leaves were perfect protection against the stoop of any predatory sparrow-hawk, and their dark recesses made relaxing haunts in which to skulk, and to build their homes.

When Gael nosed around the base of the holly which grew by the stand of young silver-birch trees on the bank of the rushing stream, her nosiness was chided by the sharp notes of jenny-wren. The little collie listened to the voice of the tiny, stump-tailed bird, and she cocked her ears with interest when the wren came flitting towards her through the twigs of the holly bush.

Trogo, the wren, was not afraid, and darted like a scuttling mouse with short, erratic jumps from perch through the twigs. Gael knew the bird well, and she pushed her nose towards its approach, her face pressing aside the spiny holly leaves without hurt. It was then that the wren resented the collie's interest, and flitted away.

Gael sank her pads deep into the mud of soft bog when she crossed the slope of the clough. There was the constant drip of water in her ears where the land drained to the stream. Griso, the grey-squirrel, clung to the bark of an oak tree to watch Gael pass below; and Pyat, the black and white magpie, for once showed little interest in her presence in the woodland. He and his tribe added some colour to the countryside throughout the winter months.

Colour is the hallmark of Christmas time, and one of the most popular of household decorations is the holly bough. Bright red berries and deep green, shiny leaves always add a touch of brightness to any room. The holly bushes in Gael's woodland were well-grown, and the female trees were bedecked in their clusters of red fruits. Though still attractive, they were past their best for, although we humans tend to regard the holly as a Christmas tree, the berries had ripened in October and November, and the birds had gorged their goodness by December.

The thrushes — song and mistle — and blackbirds, and the Scandinavian visitors, the fieldfares and redwings, had dined on the berries, although they preferred the softer, darker berries of the hawthorn. Bright red, holly berries

A coy
invitation
to play.

Grey-Squirrel.
Griso.
Rack Clough.
December.

Looking like the
tree-rat he is sometimes
accused of being
— stretching for Gael's scent.

contain four seeds which are so often distributed for propagation by the birds. The flowers which formed the berries were the pretty, small, white and waxy blooms of May.

The holly is one of Britain's few native evergreen trees, and is quite widespread, but usually grows as part of the lower strata, the gloomy underscrub, in our woodlands where the semi-darkness of the full-leaved summer canopy above it produces the dark green leaves which thrive, for as long as four years, on their parent tree. In December these leaves are store-rooms holding the tree's food. They are dark green above, paler green below, thick and tough, and covered with a smooth, waxy surface which retains water when the roots of the tree are frozen. When the thin, pliable leaves of oak, ash and beech, and other similar trees which withdraw the goodness from their leaves in order to store it in their trunks, are withered and shrivelled by the weather, the holly leaves can resist the ravages of frost.

Indeed, the holly is an adaptable tree, for its leaves have the additional protection of sharp spines to dissuade animals from browsing them, though deer are undaunted by the array of prickles, if no other food is available. The bark of the holly tree is usually smooth and grey, dependent on age, and holly trees can live up to 80 years; the wood is slow in growth, hard and white, close-grained and good for carving, and burns brightly on the fire. At one time, holly bark was used in the preparation of bird-lime, the vile substance which used to be manufactured for the trapping of song-birds before the sale of such birds became illegal.

The Pendle Witches used the holly in their mixtures of spells, and in herbal uses the berries and leaves possess entirely different properties. Berries for fevers, leaves for catarrh and as a tonic, are modern uses. The holly figures largely in legend at Christmas time, and is perhaps best known as the crown of thorns at Christ's crucifixion. Our forefathers believed that holly branches in the house protected it against bolts of lightening and the malice of the witches.

Perhaps more involved in legend at Christmas time is the mistletoe, an evergreen plant which Gael has never come across in her North Country haunts. It is a semi-parasitic plant which grows on broad-leaved trees, mainly in the south and west of the British countryside. Eaten safely by birds, the sticky berries are poisonous to humans.

In the old days people looked upon this parasite as a magic plant, for they could not understand how it came to be growing on the boughs of other trees. In fact the seed from the familiar white sticky berry is carried by a bird on to the host tree, where, in some crevice in the bark it takes root. It draws the sap, without causing any serious harm, from the host, but draws the carbon-dioxide necessary for plant growth from the air through its own leaves.

Mistletoe roots in the branches of apple, pear, poplar and oak trees were sacred to the Druids. The familiar custom of kissing under the mistletoe — 'a strange spirit of superstitious frivolity' — is linked either to an old fertility rite or to an agreeable custom of hospitality. A sprig of mistletoe placed in a baby's cradle wards off the fairies, and a sprig placed under your hat protects you against witches.

HOLLY (Ilex aquifolium)

Native evergreen.

Flowers. Male and
Female separate trees.
Small, white, waxy,
Close clusters.
Apl - May.

Leaves.
Smooth, waxy surface
Dark green on top, lighter beneath.
Thick and tough.
Sharp spines dissuade
    grazing animals.

Berries
Normally bright red.
Variable. 4 seeds.
Female trees.
October. Dec.

MISTLETOE (Viscum album)

Evergreen.

Flowers. Male and
Female separate
    trees.
Small. green.
Feb - Apl.

Leaves.
Thick. green.
Leathery.
    in pairs.

Berries.
White, Sticky.
Single seed.
Ripe. Nov - Feb.

Semi - parasitic - root draws sap from host tree.
on deciduous trees   leaves draw carbon-dioxide from air.
- apple, pear, oak,
poplar, hawthorn.

Christmas is a time of year when even the people of the towns and cities are made very much aware of the shepherd and his flock of sheep. In the countryside, sheep and those who tend them are never from the mind, and Christmas Day, in addition to its religious significance, means 'tups in before dinner, lads' on many hill farms. Before the family are allowed to sit down for their Christmas dinner, all the rams have to be gathered from the hill.

With the dogs at their heels as their essential helpmates, the 'lads' have to cover many miles of moor to find and herd home the rams before any Christmas fare is eaten. Christmas Day is thus reckoned to be the end of the mating season, as it is reckoned that all the ewes in the flock should have been mated by the rams which had been turned out a month previously.

With Gael at my side, I walked round the lambs which were wintering on the snow-spattered hillside pastures. All perfectly fit and well, they moved quietly from our approach. This basic shepherding work of watching over the flock could not have changed much since the first Christmas Day. The scene was different — my cold East Lancashire hillside, and modern skills to assist my watching — yet the shepherds who were present at the birth of Christ in that lowly manger in Bethlehem so very long ago were the founders of the craft of shepherding.

Sheep-farming, as with all aspects of modern agriculture in Britain, has progressed in efficiency down the years through the benefits of science and the growth of veterinary knowledge, but the skills of the shepherd, the man who actually tends the sheep, are still the most vital to the welfare of the flock. The regular inspections of the sheep are as essential as ever, though the advent of scientific knowledge has made the shepherd's craft one of the most highly professional jobs in the country.

So many of our town and city folk tend to regard the shepherd of the hills as something of a country yokel, or at best they look upon him as a 'little slow on the uptake', yet how many boffins from the city could be an efficient manager, a first-class stockman, a veterinary expert, a midwife, a naturalist, a butcher, know-ledgeable about clothing, a scientist, and an animal trainer all rolled into one? That is what a shepherd is.

He has to manage his flock of sheep to get the best from them and his land, he has to recognise and treat all their ills and sicknesses, decide when and what scientific concoctions will protect them against virus and disease, often he delivers their lambs, he learns the ways of the predatory fox at lambing time, decides when his lambs are ready for market, breeds to produce the best quality wool, and trains his collie dog to herd the flock. Few other jobs of work are so demanding, and although modern knowledge has made shepherding more efficient, if more complex and sophisticated, the basic craft has changed little over the millenia.

It was Christmas time when Gael met Griso, the grey-squirrel. She was simply meandering. She stalked under the twisted boughs of the bushes when the scent of rabbit came to her nostrils; she sniffed a great deal at the trunk of a rowan which Ruso, the fox, had soiled earlier in the morning; she lifted her head and drew back her lip in a silent snarl when Pyat, the magpie, spotted her and, from his safe perch high in a beech tree, chattered abuse at her.

Gael left the bird to his ill-temper and trotted away between the trees. She snatched at fallen leaves with her mouth, and for a short time played tag with them. Then she took the scent of Griso, the grey-squirrel, where he had scurried over the ground. Nose twitching to sift the smell of the squirrel over the conflicting aroma of decaying leaves, she slowly tracked the little animal.

Turning round the trunk of a sycamore, she came upon Griso. He sat on the top of a large stone which jutted up through the ground, squatting on his haunches, an acorn in his forepaws. His round, dark eyes watched Gael closely, and though her appearance, after he had heard her approach, had not frightened him, his muscles were tensed for instant flight.

The two animals were some four yards apart, their movements stilled, their eyes fixed upon each other. Griso was the first to react. He quietly spoke to the dog: 'Tuk-tuk-tuk.' It was a low, purring sound of welcome, rather than of annoyance or fear, and Gael received the greeting with pricked ears and twitching nostrils. The squirrel was for play.

Gael stepped quietly towards Griso, her head outstretched, her nose reaching. Griso went — and quickly. He dropped the acorn from his hands, swung round and, bushy tail streaming as a rudder, darted across the ground. But he invited the chase, for he did not take to the trees. Gael bounded after him, and for five minutes dog and squirrel played together. Both enjoyed the game, Griso often waiting until Gael was almost upon him before taking a 12-foot-long leap to show his marvellous athletic ability.

Griso chuckled his pleasure, and Gael yapped her excitement — and the rest of the woodland creatures scolded their exuberance. Trogo, the wren, churred his anger; Ruddock, the robin, tic-ticked his annoyance; Pyat, the magpie, fairly yattered his rage.

Up and down the sheep-trods between the trees, even along a badger tunnel through the bracken, Gael and Griso chased until they disturbed Ruso, the fox, from his sleep under a fallen birch tree. Griso immediately took to the nearest tree with a ten-foot vertical leap and ran up the trunk. Gael slid to a halt on the matted leaf-carpet, and Ruso, seeing her, bolted towards a safe rock-refuge beyond the woodland.

Gael let him go. She had enjoyed her romp with Griso, and she sought his company on the following day. But the squirrel was in a different mood. A flurry of snowflakes through the trees had upset him, their cold wet touch had put him in a temper and he tore at the bark of an oak tree with the claws of his forepaws whilst gripping with his hind claws, and hanging his head downwards against the trunk. When he saw Gael he barked a rapid 'Chuk-chuk-chuk-quaa' to attract her attention, and sent the scraps of bark flying over her back.

Gael simply sat on her haunches on the woodland floor and looked up at Griso. Surprised at the rumpus, there was puzzlement in her almond eyes and her nose twitched to reach for scent. Her pricked ears cupped the squirrel's voice. Quizzically, she angled her head on the left side, then on the right side. Griso was six feet up the trunk of the tree, hanging under one of the large lower branches of the oak, and she watched him closely. Why was Griso having a tantrum?

Gael sat quietly to wait for him to cool down, and hoped that then they could perhaps have a game. The squirrel's bark became less rapid, and he ceased to tear at the tree. He spun round with his sure movement, and ran out on to the low bough of the tree, and he changed his tune. His large, dark eyes looking at Gael in a fixed stare, Griso sat on his hind paws and gazed down at the collie. He fidgeted his front paws, scratched his white chest, flicked his hairy tail, and called 'Tuk-tuk-tuk'. Gael yapped a reply, and the two animals gazed at each other, watching each other closely for sign.

Perched on the bough of the oak, Griso was a handsome fellow. In his thick winter coat of fine, silvery grey, his white chest, and his half-inch long ear-tufts of white hairs, Griso was as striking as any red-squirrel — always classed the most beautiful of the two species.

Griso had a line of brown hairs down the middle of his back, and bands of bright russet hairs on each side of his body. Many of the hairs of his coat were banded black at the base, then yellow-brown, black again, and finally white, and in his bushy tail, which grew hairs to two inches long, were six different colour areas running from the base to the tip — so there was no drabness about Griso's appearance.

He was fully grown, over 18 inches from nose tip to tail tip, and was superbly fit, his muscles supple and strong to lead his acrobatic life in the tree tops.

Having sized-up each other with that instant animal instinct which discerned friend from foe on the previous day, Gael and Griso were tolerant of each other. His ill-temper gone, and simply for Gael's benefit, Griso flipped a backward somersault on the oak bough, landing expertly on his long hind toes. He purred a welcome, and Gael reared up on to her hind legs, balancing and stretching to show her own suppleness. Relaxed, Griso, like most of his tribe, was a playful creature and, trustful of Gael he dropped lightly from the branch, landing on the ground within two yards of the collie.

Gael jumped towards him, but natural caution outweighed complete trust and Griso darted away over the leaf-littered ground. Gael romped after him, and dog and squirrel delighted in a hectic game of follow-my-leader. Leaping over fallen boughs, twisting and turning round bramble clumps, racing across open clearings, Gael and Griso played together although never actually coming into contact. When Gael came too close, Griso side-flicked his supple body and raced up a tree trunk, dropped back to the ground away from the dog and chattered to her to continue the chase.

Chapter 20

Blood runs hot

With fire in his veins at the January calling-time, Ruso, the fox, seeks a mate, and chops at Gael; Kee the opportunist, stoops to snatch a meal from Hob, the stoat; and Gael meets Tofe, the tufted duck.

The taint of fox-soiling on the brown stems of the rushes by the hill-pond brought a questing twitch to Gael's nostrils. The soiling was fresh and the little collie had no problem in placing it. She leaned forward into the breeze which stirred the rushes, feeling with her nose for the scent-line. It was a characteristic smell, and one which Gael knew well. It was the scent of Ruso, the young dog-fox, whom she had often met in the winter gloaming.

Nose touching the ground, she turned away from the rushes and followed the fox scent over the mud patches along the fringe of the pond. Sucking the trace scents still lingering in the oval four-toed pad prints, Gael had no difficulty in walking the line taken by Ruso earlier in the day. The line took her away from the pond, was lost by the base of the stone wall, and was picked up again when Gael leaped to the top of the stones. Earlier, Ruso had sat on the wall top to listen to the sounds of the hillside. Gael did the same. The wind combed the fur of her

There was beauty and cunning in the features of the fox.

Dog-like in appearance, and feline in grace, Ruso was built for an active and interesting life.

back, and tossed the long silky feathering of her legs. She opened her mouth in a wide yawn, curling her pink tongue, whilst she watched the grazing sheep quietly move away from the wallside.

Ears pricked to the call of Corbie, the black crow, who circled on spread wings above her head, nostrils sifting the tell-tale scents of the air currents, Gael sat on the grey stones, so little different in appearance from Ruso, the fox.

Gael continued the trail of her wild acquaintance, leaping lightly to the ground and crossing the high pasture where Ruso's pads were clearly printed in the soaking close-cropped herbage. Squeezing under the bottom rail of the field-gate whose rusty roughness held hairs from Ruso's coat, she left a tuft of her own sable fur on the rail.

On the ground by the hedge of Rack Clough she savoured a tiny drop of blood which marked the killing of a field-vole by the fox. Under the gnarled roots of hawthorn, and between the trees where the taint of rabbit was strong, Gael's interest in Ruso faded. She romped along the badger trails, beneath the green screens of rhododendrons, and across the leaf carpet in a hectic game of tag until every rabbit was safely below ground. Then, panting the excitement from her lungs, she sprawled amid bracken cover to rest.

Fox

(Vulpes vulpes)

Male: Dog.
Female: Vixen.
Young: Cub.

Cunning. acute. intelligent.
Dog-like in appearance (Canidae)
Cat-like eyes. Feline acts.

Two feet long + 16" tail (brush)
14" high Shoulder. 12 lbs. av. weight.
Sexes similar - dog bigger than vixen.
Colour variation - sandy. russet. red-brown
Grey to white under. Sharp pointed muzzle.
Cheek ruffs. Pricked ears - black on back.

Dog-like
Pad-prints.

Legs - Sooty black down front.
Eyes react to light. Night hunter.

R.
Hind

Normally Solitary - mate January.
Single litter. 51-52 days gestation.
Cubs born late March - early April. Lambing-time.

L
Hind

Good parents - Suckle. conceal. provide. teach.
Cubs born blind. Av. 5. in earth.
Smoky-brown in colour. Eyes open 10 days.

R.
Hind

Out of earth at one month. Weaned 2 months.
Grow quickly - learn woodcraft in play.
Turned from home when schooled.
Adult at 6 months.

White-tipped
Tail - used for
balance.
A weapon in
a fight.
A muff over
nose in
sleep.
Grey-black
on the
front of
legs.

Branded a rogue for his
wanton urge to kill

Good hunter a lowly scavenger.
Smelly - scent glands under tail.

The likeliest and most
dangerous Carrier should
rabies reach Britain.

Her rest was short, and she left the woodland to the approach of an early dusk on a grey day, sending a flock of 20 fieldfares from their foraging when she left the shelter of the trees. At the corner of the field she met Ruso.

Although never over-friendly in her relationship with the fox, Gael had, on occasion, spent brief bouts of play with the animal, and both accepted their inevitable meetings with understanding. As ever, Gael turned to greet Ruso as a neighbour. She was surprised and startled when he turned on her with mouth open and teeth showing in open hostility. He had two yards to cover so that Gael was ready to counter his attack. She leaped aside in time for his teeth to miss their chopping bite on her cheek. She side-stepped to escape the swipe of Ruso's coarse tail, and before he could come at her again, she jumped right over him, swerved round a puddle, and ran from the squabble.

The fight was pointless in Gael's mind — so she left Ruso to his ill-temper. It was ill-temper—or intolerance—brought on by the time of the year, the time of the 'calling', the time when foxes mate. Intent on love, Ruso was intolerant of interference, even from one who was not his rival.

In the search for a vixen, the blood ran hot, and every dog-fox was another's enemy. Foxes become mortal enemies at that time of the year. Dog hated dog, and only a vixen was acceptable. Indeed, a vixen was the prize for the victor of the many skirmishes which took place in the countryside in January, and Ruso was inexperienced in such affairs of the heart.

He knew the reason for the fire in his veins, and indeed it was simply his inability to respond to the urge which had made him so bad-tempered towards

Awakened from a cat-nap, the fox was immediately alert—ears cupped to sound, nose in line for scent, and eyes watching. In sleep his brush would warmly cover his muzzle.

Fox
Ruso.
Rack Clough.
January.

Gael. On recent nights he had chased the weird banshee yowling of a vixen all round the Cliviger rocks with little success. He had been taught some very forceful lessons — mainly that he was young and inexperienced. He found that all vixens appeared to have many suitors, and that the most comely and desirable had a whole entourage of would-be husbands. That favours had to be won the hard way had really been impressed upon him only the previous night.

Delicately placing his pads in noiseless movement with a skill to be admired in a first-year fox, Ruso had approached a delightful vixen, a slim, trim, tightly furred creature who immediately roused his emotions. Admirably, he had restrained his impulses, for there was an immediate snag to his courtship. The vixen already had a consort — a big dog-fox, older and more powerful than Ruso. In fact, it was his own father, although he knew it not. A dispute was inevitable.

Ruso had used his woodcraft, he had used the wind right, his approach was in the gloom of rock shelter, and his father could have been proud under other circumstances. But, with the inexperience of youth, Ruso's final approach to the vixen was too open. The dog-fox saw Ruso instantly, and leaped to stop him reaching the vixen. He snarled, bared white teeth, and rushed to attack. Bristling with rage, tail flexed for swiping, the old fox charged at Ruso. He had no intention of giving his mate a choice of partners.

Ruso was no coward, but the ferocity with which the older fox closed on him, teeth chopping wickedly and brush swiping, had made him turn and flee in shocked amazement — a short, sharp lesson in courtship implanted on his mind.

His nastiness towards Gael had arisen simply from frustration.

Seven days and seven nights after Ruso's meeting with Gael, the young fox had travelled far in his search for a mate. He was leg-weary, cut and bruised, but more experienced from fights with older and wiser dog-foxes who happened to covet the same vixen.

A little disillusioned, Ruso lay in a hollow, protected from the falling rain by a grey overhanging boulder, and safely screened by tall bog-rushes. His handsome red fur was grimed with the mud of his travels, and his nose was painfully marked by the teeth of one of his older adversaries. But still the urge to find a mate was dominant, and he lay restless. The weather had not been good, and during the past nights of cold wind and rainstorm his fortunes had been similarly bad.

In contesting the favours of three vixens he had raced to safety once with a stronger dog-fox nipping at his heels, its yellowing teeth clicking close to his flanks; he had been sent sprawling by the lash of another's brush, and again had to retreat before the experience of a more mature adversary; and his cheek jowl had been raked and almost opened up by chopping teeth in a third clash.

Yet, if inexperienced, he was young and fit, and the questing fever still burned within his blood. Roaming many miles across the valleys of Sheddon and Cliviger, over the moorland above, he had ventured out on nights when normally the cold rain and high winds would have kept him in the shelter of his bed.

Passing like a silent shadow between the booming trees of the woodland clough in order to answer the yowling of a vixen on the far rocks of the valley, he cowered back in sudden terror when a heavy bough crashed across his path, riven from a tossing sycamore by the force of the gale.

On the high pastures he slipped into the blackness of the wall bottom, partly to conceal his passing but mainly to find some shelter from the stinging force of hailstones which struck his eyes, and from the relentless rainfall which matted his fur and soaked his coat.

Crossing the snow drifts on the moor top, he left a straight line of dog-like pad-marks; dashing across the main valley road, his eyes glowed green in the lights of a speeding car; jumping the white, foaming water which fell over rock ledges down the sides of Thieveley, he missed his footing on the slippery stones, and took a ducking. Ruso found little pleasure in wetness. Always there was the taint of vixen to drive him on.

Few creatures left their own shelter to see his wanderings. Even Aluco, the tawny-owl, normally familiar with the journeyings of Ruso and his like, flew only to hunt when food became necessary. Sheep, using the walls to break the force of the gale, moved quietly away when he passed, their shapes darkly indistinct in the murky night.

Constantly aware of the barking of his rivals and the wailing answer of vixens, food became of secondary interest to Ruso. He chopped and missed a rabbit when pushing through the thorn hedge into Rack Clough; on the breast of the hill he coursed Lepus, the brown hare, but was soon outpaced; he misjudged his final leap on to a vole in the bogland.

Ruso was hungry, for on the previous night his only hunting success had been the killing of a wood-mouse. Lying in the sheltered hollow by the bog whose rushes held snow drifts, he lifted his head to take scent on his black nostrils. Always before moving, he had learned to read the messages of the air. Strong on the wet wind was the smell of partridge. Ruso tensed his muscles; cautiously he lined the point of the scent; silently he moved towards the prey.

Entirely reliant on his twitching nose to guide him, he crawled noiselessly, body flat to the ground, invisible among the darkness of the rushes. Before him, four partridges, sleepily couched in hollows between the rushes, were unaware of his presence. His nose marking the exact position of one of the birds, Ruso flexed his hind legs into a crouch. His strike was accurate, silent and well-timed, and the partridge was chopped and held in his jaws before it could even attempt to fly. Ruso was tearing at the warm flesh to satisfy his hunger as the bird's three companions whirred on tremulous wings into the cold dark night.

Despite his hunting success, however, Ruso's quest for a mate remained unsuccessful until the following year. It is not uncommon for young dog foxes to remain bachelors at first, due to lack of experience and the fierce competition for vixens.

While Ruso was engaged in his search for a mate, the weather hardened, turning colder and frosty at night. Two days later Kee, the kestrel, opened his round eyes to the slight rustle of movement on the rocky ledge beneath his roost on the face of the Earl's Bower. Tilting his head for better vision, he saw Ruso carefully padding his way along the lofty sheep-track across the face of the crag. It was the brushing of the fox's pads against icy bents which caused the rustle of noise.

Six feet above the fox, Kee tightened his feathers, and was immediately alert to the possibility of his rest being disturbed, but Ruso did not see him. The kestrel was a blurred image, blending into the gloom of the rock face. Nor was Ruso interested. He was too concerned with the soreness in his cheek left from that painful bite of a more experienced fox with whom he had squabbled in an attempt to win the favours of a vixen.

He padded on and, following the track round an outjutting rock, passed from Kee's sight. The kestrel relaxed. It was yet too early to be abroad. The day was barely born and the gloom of night lingered among the rocks of the Cliviger Gorge. Only the lightening of the eastern sky heralded the coming of a new day. Kee closed his eyes, hunched his neck into his body, and fluffed his feathers to retain his body heat. He was warm and comfortable against the rock face, sheltered from probing wind fingers by the grey stone, and he was in no hurry to start the day.

It was a promising day, for the air was dry and not too cold with frost. The strengthening light to the east was clear of cloud murk, and it could develop into a good hunting day. Kee was not hungry, though his speedy digestion had cleared the vole he had taken before retiring for the night. He was content to slumber a while. He, unlike Ruso, had been careful that his hunting succeeded.

Only when the brimming light from the sky reached his niche in the rock, and the cry of a gull sounded above the crags, did Kee show interest in the day. He opened his great, yellow-rimmed eyes and looked out over his world. Every detail of his land was sharp in the clarity of his sight — the white frost-powdered bents where sheep grazed below his lofty perch, the intricate skeleton shapes of the leafless trees beyond the railway line, and the grey stone buildings of Bradget Hey Farm.

He was lord of all he surveyed, a noble hawk, a rider of the sky, majestic in appearance and an aristocrat in breeding. A blend of beauty and delicacy, of lightness and strength, Kee was lord of the crags.

His survey completed, Kee turned his attention to his plumage, the preening of his feathers being the first task of his day. He lay flat the streaked feathers of his breast, then, with neck twisted, the barred brown of his mantle. Separating the grey feathers of his tail with his beak, he smoothed the frayed edges until they closed like a fan. Wing feathers received particular care before he lazily and luxuriously stretched his wings. Lifting his taloned foot, he scratched the irritation from the tiny, soft feathers of his head and face. Finally, he shook to ruffle loose his whole plumage before settling each feather into place for action.

Spreading his wings, Kee sped from his roost in a gush of wind, breasting the upward flow of air from the valley and climbing swiftly to the sky. In his true environment, he soared on the wind, holding his wings to the air's strength, floating relaxed above the rocks of Thieveley.

For five minutes Kee spiralled against the sky, then, his morning exercise concluded, he banked, and side-slipping the wind, closed his wings in a dive. Not until he was some 40 feet above the rushes by the River Calder did he spread his tail and stretch his wings to brake his stoop. Hanging there in a static hover, he started the day's hunting.

His eye caught a movement close by the stone wall of a sheltered farm paddock. It was a restless movement, the weaving, darting movement of a hunting stoat. Sneaking along close to the wall bottom one moment, disappearing from sight into a hole between the stones the next, the stoat held Kee's attention. He saw it emerge from cover to stand on its haunches, its silky forelegs pawing the air rhythmically, its white face peering all round. Its sinuous, inconsistent motions held a curious fascination.

Holding his position on the wind, Kee watched the line of the stoat as the animal sneaked across open ground, its belly to the earth in a snake-like glide. The meandering pattern was typical of the hunter, and its strange performance of meaningless wandering had the desired effect.

A crowd of house-sparrows became an admiring audience, held by the strange hypnotic lure of the stoat. Kee watched, his presence above unnoticed even by so cautious a hunter as the stoat, whose hunger was great and whose mind was on the assembled sparrows. They also were too engrossed to notice the threatening hawk. They flittered around the stoat in a fascinated crowd. Never would Kee have a better chance.

Closing his flickering wings, he rocketed down in a controlled stoop, braked his speed as, with precise timing, he snatched a cock sparrow in his sickled talons and bore it away with a change of wing-thrust. The snatch was completed almost before the rest of the sparrows were aware of it. Then there was panic and they scattered each to find its own shelter in tree branches.

Hob, the stoat, was even more surprised than the birds. He stood, his muscles tightening for a final pounce on his prey, as if transfixed by the speed of Kee's initiative. Then he too ran for shelter, chakkering in frustration, but more in rage at the loss of a meal — and the audacity of the kestrel.

The lifeless sparrow clutched tightly in his talons, Kee flew to the top of a post which held a line of sheep-wire over the wall top. This was one of his plucking-posts, and there he stood on his victim whilst he tore the goodness from its puny form with his hooked beak.

Whilst Kee ravaged his bird, Gael met a strange bird to her land. She was far from the kestrel, some three miles away, and well beyond Kee's normal hunting area. Following the brown peaty waters of the stream from the moor of Hameldon, she came to the reservoir. Her coat was snow-blown, and she kept to the water-channel to avoid brushing between the icy grasses of the shoulder-high bents and hags of the open moor.

She approached the water's entrance to the reservoir with care, for always there was something of interest to be seen at that time of year. Her caution was rewarded, for she was in time to meet Tofe, the female tufted-duck, a visitor to her land. The bird was cautious, and with barely a ripple on the surface to mark her going, Tofe slipped from Gael's sight under the cold waters of the reservoir.

Ten feet below the surface, but a few yards out from the frost-rimed bank, Tofe pulled on the green weeds which grew from the bottom of the reservoir. Twenty seconds after her dive she popped up again to the surface, bobbing up like a dark brown cork to startle a black-headed gull which was swimming and lazily preening its feathers nearby.

Tofe was unaffected by, indeed almost indifferent to, the bitter cold, and swam on or under the water with the complete mastery of her natural habitat. She was alone on the wide expanse of water apart from the half dozen gulls which, whilst equally at ease, were a bit disgruntled at the coldness of the day — and they had taken note of Gael's arrival.

Gael sat by the water which quietly lapped the frozen pebbles of the reservoir bank. There was little life in the bleak high land of the Lancashire-Yorkshire border, only the fine whistle of a thin wind bearing the occasional bleat of a sheep to break the cold silence.

Tofe dived down again, cleanly leaving the surface and driving down over the weed bed with the kick of her webbed feet. She picked among a clump of starwort, and snapped up, in her flat, blue-grey beak, a water-beetle which broke from the cover of the weeds.

Up to the surface again, Tofe shook droplets of water from her nostrils, flipping her short head-crest in the act. Accepting Gael's presence as harmless, she rested on the water, idly paddling inshore near the floating gulls. Her composure and indifference annoyed a young black-headed gull, and the bird flew up from the water and swooped viciously at the little duck in a display of bad

From the top of the dry-stone wall Gael listened to the sounds of the hillside.

temper. Almost nonchalantly, Tofe slipped under water, and the gull was left floundering on the water surface, scattering spray into the air in frustration. The duck reappeared some 20 yards away, but the gull did not pursue its attack, and Tofe settled to preen her wing feathers.

It was Gael who eventually upset Tofe. Unable to make closer aquaintance with the bird, she rose to her feet and trotted away by the water's edge. Her movement startled Tofe. She crouched on the water, raised her head, stiffened her neck, and then, as the gulls around her took fright and flew up, she followed. She pattered across the surface of the water, flapping her wings until her momentum lifted her into the air. Airborne, she climbed high above the water, and flew away across the reservoir. Gael stood at the water's edge, head high, ears pricked, nose questing, her eyes straining, as she was left alone in the wildness of the moor.

Chapter 21

Miner activity

Adapting to a specialised way of life in a maze of underground tunnels, the mouldiwarp lives with the confidence of keen senses, but misplaced self-assurance leads to the crow's downfall.

Fast clear water escaped from the field-drain, sparkled in the cold light of freedom for two yards, then returned to its underground channel beneath the hill pasture. The water raced in the confines of its stone-lined course from the heights of the hill, bubbling and gurgling, escaping for a second whenever there was a break in the drain, or wherever the rabbits had burrowed from the surface to cause an obstruction. Such obstructions were temporary, for the force of the water eroded them away. The volume of the water which completely filled the old drain in its haste to leave the heights had sent the rabbits fleeing to find shelter in the cavities of the dry-stone field wall.

Rainfall had been constant for many days, and the land was soaking, soft and puddled with the marks of cows and sheep. Gael's print was left clearly marked when the little collie came through the sheep-hole in the wall. She went to where the water burst with a gurgle from the drain, and cast around for the scent of the rabbits which were usually active in the surrounding grassland. They had left no sign of their retreat from the drain to the wall, so Gael turned her interest to the freshly-turned pyramids of soil which an active mole had pushed up from its underground tunnels.

A restless creature, Talpa, the mole, felt the need to find a mate early in the year, and with mildness in the air, had been quick to take advantage of the softness of the earth, and the resultant ease with which he could tunnel it to expound his energy to clear and extend his system of tunnels. When he was ready, a straight tunnel, driven parallel to the field-wall for about 50 yards, would take him into the territory of Taupe, a neighbouring female.

Ten conically formed heaps of fine soil, each some six inches to the point, littered the surface of the grassland within an area of eight square yards. It was this activity of Talpa and his tribe, this method of ridding themselves of the soil they cleared from their tunnels, which caused annoyance to the farmer. Mole-hills, individually of little size and concern, did, in their entirety, cover large areas of grazing land.

The other charge which the farmer levelled at the mole was that it ate an awful lot of earthworms which were good for the land — but it also ate a considerable number of leatherjackets and wireworms which were bad for agriculture. Another contention was that its maze of underground tunnels could cause land-subsidence, and this could be dangerous when farm machinery was driven over these areas — but the tunnels also drained water from the land, and it was often difficult to do this by hand or machine.

Like so many other problems of confliction between man and animal, it would seem to be a case of numbers. A certain size of mole population was useful, even beneficial, to land: one mole too many and the balance was tipped to make the mole a nuisance. Whatever, there was a lot of nonsense talked about moles!

The little animal is often portrayed as a dozy, clumsy, blundering creature — mainly because the one thing everyone knows about the mole is that it is near-blind. In fact, the mole has eyes which are fully formed, perfectly constructed, and more than adequate to gauge the depth of its tunnels in the filtered daylight. The eyes are tiny, and like the ears, protected by fur to prevent irritation and damage from soil particles.

Talpa spent almost the whole of his life under the ground, and Gael followed his activities by scent rather than by sight, though she had met the mole. With deft swipes of her forepaws, she had swept away the half-inch of covering soil to catch Talpa when he ran shallow tunnels.

On one such occasion she had gently mouthed the mole in play, but dropped him in haste for the taste of his glands and the feel of his erect velvety fur were unpleasant. Ever afterwards, whilst she enjoyed a tracking and hunting game with Talpa, she never attempted to touch him with her mouth.

She had also caught the mole at his excavations, attracted to his presence by the shuddering, crumbling movement of soil growing up through the close sheep-bitten grassland to form a small pyramid. Her quiet and quick scattering of the soil usually produced a sight of Talpa's pink nose-tip before he fled along his tunnel.

This was the success of the little collie's instinct to hunt quietly, for she knew nothing of the mole's quickness to perceive danger. Talpa took warning at even the slightest hint of anything unusual. He had lived for two years under the upland pasture by always being awake to possible threat; he was extremely wary, and always used his particular talents to good effect. Nature had bestowed upon him extremely keen senses. He was able to identify the slight rustle of Gael's ever-light pads on the ground above his head, and the earth vibrations when she started to scrape away his excavation to reach his tunnel sounded like booming warning drums, and sent him scurrying from her interest.

Such quick notice of the happenings around him came from ultrasonic senses. Some of the hairs on his body, on his nose, and on his tail were finely tuned to the sense of touch, and they conveyed every ground impulse to a brain which was quick to interpret the cause.

Such tactile sense-organs warned Talpa of Gael's presence, and enabled him to diagnose any unusual happening which invaded his gloomy world of tunnels. They alerted Talpa to the placing of the farmer's trap in his route so that he approached it with caution and suspicion.

Gael also found the trap of interest, though her interest was of the man-scent it carried where it stuck up from the grassland. Similar to a metal pincer, the trap, with its lethal end set in the mole's tunnel, was designed to grasp the unwary animal to death. Ruthless in its precision, the trap was the farmer's way of keeping the mole population in check, although Talpa had evaded its death-dealing ways since he had been sent from his mother's territory to make his own way in life two years previously.

A wanderer for the first eight months of his life, Talpa had finally become dominant in the high pasture, and his strength and high degree of wariness had extended his territory to his chosen size of half an acre. Variable to his seasonal desires, it was an area comprised of good grassland soil, easily tunnelled, and drained into old, but effective stone-built drains which encouraged a good population of earthworms.

Talpa was a glutton and liked his easy supply of earthworm food. Indeed, food was the mole's great character weakness, and his whole pattern of life was governed by his appetite. He ate around 1¾ ounces (50 grams) of food in the day, and he never rested or slept for more than four hours at a time.

So that he would never go hungry, he kept a larder of fresh meat in a chamber in the ground under the dry-stone field wall, a store of live and captive worms, each one prevented from escaping its fate by the mutilation of its anterior segment. Gourmet that he was, he cleaned the earth from each worm by drawing it into his mouth through the nails of his forepaws.

Talpa lived his day in periods, dependent on the weather, but it was roughly split into shifts of four hours awake, four hours asleep. Around midnight he wandered along his tunnels, grabbed worms, cleared obstructions and extended his ways, going to sleep at about 3 am. His second shift was between 7 am and 11 am; his third in late afternoon, from around 3 pm to 7 pm.

It was usually during the dark hours of his midnight activity that Talpa chanced one of his few outings above ground, but he took a risk for, in the open air, out of his true environment, his senses were not so acute. Even so, he could always rely on his quickness to burrow to escape from any possible danger — Aluco, the tawny-owl, Hob, the stoat, and Ressel, the weasel, were prepared to taste his distinctively flavoured flesh. On the odd occasion when Gael had met Talpa on the surface, she had been astounded at his speed in burrowing. Rooting a hole in the grass with his snout, and tearing at the soil with his strong forefeet to get his head and shoulders into the opening, he squirmed his whole body below ground in a matter of ten seconds.

Talpa virtually swam through soft earth. Pointed snout pushing into the earth, he brought his forepaws up on each side to scrape aside the soil, straining forward with his hind feet against the sides of the tunnel. He needed immense strength for this operation, and his neck and arm muscles were powerfully grown. He could push 1½ pounds of soil to the surface to form mole-hills on his clearance operations. His forefeet were designed like the shovels of a mechanical-digger, large and broad with five strong, sharp claws.

Designed to tunnel, Talpa, the mole, bobbed up for a second to show hands like shovels, pointed snout to a cylindrical body, and tiny eyes.

Well-built, weighing four ounces, and six inches in length, Talpa had a muscular body which was pig-nosed, stocky and cylindrical, with no perceptible neck, and was covered in short erect and velvety black fur which never got really soiled.

Talpa was of an ancient tribe, his ancestors living in Britain for many centuries; and his old English name of mouldiwarp was derived from two words, *molde* meaning earth, and *werpen*, to throw.

The mole-hills which Gael inspected by the field-drain were Talpa's most recent excavations. They were his morning activity, marking his hunting in good worm country. Earthworms were also attracted to manure and, during a break in the soft weather, the pasture had been accessible to the farm spreader and the land had been covered.

Sought by Talpa, the earthworms were also relished by the crows, rooks, seagulls and starlings of the hillside, and the birds foraged for them across the land. Among the animal manure, straw and general farm waste, which was spread over the land, was food aplenty, worms, beetles and insects, as well as the odd carrion morsel.

Gael took the strong scent of the manure, the dominant scent which swamped the odour of sheep over her nostrils. She mouthed a white feather, preened by a gull, and when she dropped it the wind swirled it away. She nosed the brown mineral-block which the farmer had put down for sheep to lick.

Coming to Scholey Pond, she caused the noisy flight of three mallard ducks from the centre of the water. Head raised, ears up, Gael watched the ducks climb into the air with necks outstretched, and she listened to the thumping of their wings as they circled above her head. She slipped quietly between the rushes by the pond, poking her nose for scent into the cold tussocks.

An old weathered bone which had been carried to the pondside by Corbie, the crow, many weeks past, gave her some self-made pleasure as she tossed it into the air, caught it in her mouth, and rolled on it. Lying on her back, she saw Kee, the kestrel, stoop down to watch her antics. Thirty feet above her, the kestrel rode the wind, his wings dithering, his head down, his yellow-rimmed eyes wondering at her meaningless frolics.

Gael leapt up and, leaving the pondside to squeeze under the field-gate into the adjoining field, came face to face with Corbie. The black crow was on the ground and though he usually fled before Gael's approach, this day he stood to face her. Corbie had a prize which he did not intend to surrender. Among the manure on the ground he had found a smelly titbit of carrion food which he had no intention of losing.

He flattened his sleek black feathers and thrust forward his black ebony beak towards Gael. His round dark eyes flickered in a moment's doubt then steadied as he gazed at Gael in a truculent mood. Surprised at the crow's boldness, Gael stopped some two yards before him. She stretched her neck, and when her twitching nostrils took the scent of rotten flesh, she understood the reason for Corbie's boldness. Corbie was prepared to contest his food.

Although not desirous of Corbie's filthy titbit, Gael was always ready for a game, and often she had chased the crow from his foraging. Yet Corbie's attitude was a little disconcerting. Black from head to toe, his short beak feathers bristling, he stood resolutely in her path, his gaze challenging. Gael accepted Corbie's stand and turned aside to pass him.

Overcome by his sudden confidence, Corbie hopped bouncily after her, and nipped her tail as she passed. That action was his downfall. Gael swung round at him, her passive tolerance melting with a curl of her lip. Such indignity she would not tolerate. Baring her teeth in a snarl of anger, she ran at Corbie.

The crow panicked. He had been just a little too cocky. Springing from the ground, he scrambled to flight, one wing catching Gael's head in uncontrolled haste as he struggled to flee. He squawked in sudden fear and anger, his heart pounding, as he controlled his wings and climbed into the air. His food was forgotten, and his pride shattered.

The crow's sudden departure alarmed a group of rooks which were feeding 30 yards away, and they flew after Corbie. Cousins of the black crow, of the same family of *Corvidae*, the rooks were far more sociable creatures than Corbie. They preferred to spend their lives in flocks and communal gatherings for all their activities, rather than go the solitary ways of the crow.

The old country saying: 'If you see one rook, it's a crow; if you see a number of crows, they are rooks' was very apt, though the two birds differed in many other ways.

Baggy feather breeches tugged by the wind, their balance threatened by its force, the rooks foraged with little trouble among the newly-spread manure. Food was a necessity, and when such a banquet of insect and grub-ridden muck was laid before them, they did not spurn it. Like so many unsteady and drunken, though dignified, old gentlemen, the birds wandered across the manure-spread, their strong black beaks snapping juicy morsels quickly seen by bold, dark irises. Some 50 in number, they enjoyed their easily-gotten meal with sociable good humour, only squabbling when some particular morsel had to be won from a rival.

Even when Gael followed them to their let after Corbie's disturbance, they showed little concern, just spreading black wings to lift on the wind and plane up from the collie's route to settle back when she passed. With equal unconcern, a host of gulls lifted up on the wind gusts with wavering wings to avoid Gael's approach. The rainy gales which had deluged the west coast over the past days had brought the gulls inland.

Countryside happenings, the behaviour of birds and animals, the abundance or scarcity of berries and fruit, have long been pointed to as omens to the forecasting of the weather. Many such happenings hold some truth, and in the case of animal behaviour are often reliable, though obviously only in the short term.

The visit of the gulls to the hillside at that time of the year was a pointer to stormy conditions. 'Seagull, seagull, sit on the sand, It's never fine weather when you're on the land.'

Leaping the stone wall on the edge of the field, Gael surprised three lambs by her unexpected arrival. They ran with a little burst of energy, moved by a spurt of activity rather than by fear of the dog. Gael knew lambs well, and she knew their funny moods. She knew their quite irrational spasms which sent them chasing wind currents across the hillside. Maybe even at nine months old they still retained some of the frolicsome ways of their springtime gambols.

Gael knew that whilst the lambs — known technically at that time of January as hoggs — usually ignored her presence, and only moved slowly from her approach, they could just as easily 'gang-up' on her and stand their ground with inquisitive obstinacy. Just as easily, they would run a short distance as though the devil himself was after them, before again settling to graze the grass without the slightest care or worry. Sometimes the extreme actions of her regular hillside neighbours made Gael wonder at their state of mind!

As always, when faced with their tantrums, Gael ignored the sheep, and her sight followed the lazy, ponderous flapping of Krark's wings as the heron flew over the hillside towards the bogland at the top of Rack Clough. Gael saw the heron against grey sombre clouds which had built up over the hill. They leased a sudden squall of cold rain which spattered the ground and plastered Gael's long golden coat to her body.

Wind carried, the raindrops probed between the bogland rushes to dampen the soft, brown fur on the back of Lepus, the hare. Lepus was warm and content enough in his couch in the bogland. Rafted above the water level on matted reeds, the form was one of his favourite refuges for there was ample cover and protection from his enemies, and the very nature of the terrain made it easier for him to dodge them after hearing their splashing approach over the wet land. Agile and quick, Lepus could leap a speedy course across the solid grass tufts, should he have cause to flee.

Other creatures also found the bogland a haven of safety. For many generations, a family of water-voles had lived among the runnels and drains hidden from the keen eyes of Kee. Always during the dark hours, meadow-pipits hid their frailty in the dense tussocks from the icy night wind. Krark went to the bogland to seek the peace he could not always find in the lower valley by the Calder river.

Extended by the heavy rainfall, the bog covered up to six acres of the saucered depression on the moor. It was a place of open water, squelching wet earth with spongy sphagnum areas, brown rush clumps and gritstone boulders.

Towards its centre, in meandering channels, ran the waters to form a stream of movement, cutting into soft, peaty banks and dodging round barriers of great rush clumps until sufficiently strong in force to cut their own way in a more direct route for the lower valley and the final channel of the Calder.

Gael sits relaxed with the hillside in view.

It was a place where many creatures led their furtive, secret lives, a place beloved of the snipe which probed for food in the soft earth with their sensitive questing beaks, and a haven to which the curlews returned in spring to raise their families.

There, too, nested the black-capped reed-buntings and the twittering twites. It was a place which had a fascinating attraction for Gael who had learned so many of its secrets — the rock cranny where Ressel, the weasel, slept; the reed ridge behind which the partridges sheltered in winter; the many forms in which Lepus and his kin spent their rest; the hidden couches of snipe.

Splashing through the water-logged vegetation, chasing across the spongy carpet of peat, floundering to sink chest-deep in soft ooze, even swimming a dog-paddle across the flooded channels, Gael had learned most of the mysteries of the bogland.

When Gael reached the bogland it was Krark, settled to a grey shadow on stilt-legs among the rushes, who watched her approach. Unmoving, the heron stared through the black pupils of his yellow-rimmed eyes to see her enter the first growth of rushes on the edge of the bog:

Krark did not dally when Gael came closer. He stretched his great wings, lifted into the wind, and soared up from the ground. Legs stretched to trail, long neck tucked between his lean shoulders to couch his sharp bill, the heron called 'kraank' as he beat away slowly over the hill.

Couched in the cover of his ground form, Lepus heard the call and quietly ground his teeth, a habit which showed his displeasure, for the heron's voice told the hare of Gael's intrusion. His retreat from Gael's approach, though effective, was not as easy as Krark's. Hearing her approaching line through the tussocks of rushes, he slipped from the warm couch and, moving with the graceful rhythm of his kind, raced through the bog in a series of elegant bounds, leaping from island to island, big hind pads gripping the ground and thrusting him forward.

A handsome creature, Lepus was the athlete of the moor. His speed was the fastest of any; his easy ground leaps of over 15 feet, to change direction and break trail, were far greater than other animal's. And so, the five-foot high boundary wall he faced on leaving the bog was cleared without effort.

When Gael took the warm scent from the couch which Lepus had vacated and, casting around for the line of the hare's retreat, took up the chase, Lepus was already clear of the bogland and running easily across the adjoining field towards another of his established forms.

Chapter 22

Storm shelter

Gael finds respite from the snowstorm in the upland clough where the birds find food, shelter and sanctuary from gale and predators; whilst in the woodland she is puzzled by the antics of a tree-creeper.

Wind-whipped from the ground, and driven in a swirling white mass across the upland pasture, cold snowflakes streamed over the lip of the Scholey Hill into the basin of the clough. Sky-blown hailstones joined the swirling whiteness when grey clouds unleashed another shower. Tiny frozen balls of white ice under gale-force projection, they struck with stinging force.

Gael swept one from her eye with a swipe of her foreleg, and closing her eyes to mere sight-slits, the little collie raced towards the comparative shelter of Rack Clough. Sleeked with the force of the wind, her long, silky fur was plastered to her body, the feathering on her legs and ears streamed erratically, and she floundered for an instant in the grip of deep snow.

She found a respite from the storm in the shelter of the dry-stone field-wall. She shook, and the hailstones and snowflakes flew from between the hairs of her body in a shower of spray. She wiped the white flakes from her eyebrows with sweeps of her forepaws. She squatted on the snow couch to lick away the snow which had frozen between her toes. She bit off the snowballs from the long feather-hairs of her legs.

Wind-whipped from the ground, swirling white snowflakes swept across Scholey Hill.

Shielded from the raging force of the blizzard snow which whirled over the top of the field-wall, she lolled her pink tongue in a wide yawn of satisfaction. She was happy to be out on the hill, she was warm in body heat, and well protected by a dual coat of close-grown snugness and longer shedding hair.

Rising, she took the swipe of the snow-laden wind at a trot as she left the screen of the field-wall. She ran a noiseless path between snow-bent rushes, her pads leaving dainty prints in the ground snow until they were destroyed by the shifting snowflakes.

In the bottom of the clough where the snow showers pitched a patchwork of white around the unfrozen water pools, there was some shelter. The rushes grew in clumps strong enough to face the tempestuous wind, and though the bogland was a most inhospitable place of rush, moss, mud and water, it was a refuge for many of Gael's highland neighbours in bad weather.

There she could always find Capella, the snipe, for he was loath to leave the place of his birth where the food was always to his liking. Even so, with a healthy appetite to satisfy, he found that life became hard when storms swept the hill.

His haven was among rush clumps of pithy, dark stems which grew 18 inches to withered brown tips, damp rusty stalks of cotton grass and brown bents, and among shallow spreading water made cold with slushy snow, and snow-covered sphagnum moss. It had to be extremely cold for the ice to seal his larder totally among the root hags of this land. Only occasionally did the temperature drop to freezing in the base of rush clumps, and although life was tough, the instinct to survive was paramount.

Capella's food was obtained from the soft mud of the bog, and he was expert at snuggling deep into a couch of rushes to keep warm. On the occasions when cold dominated, Capella did retreat to the more sheltered land by the infant Calder in the valley.

Feathers tightly laid against the flurry of snow, Capella skulked deeper into the rush shelter. He walked beneath the reed canopy to where the muddy ooze was sheltered from the touch of cold by the thickness of growth. There, he pushed his long bill into the mud, seeking the worms and grubs which he so enjoyed. His food was sought by touch alone, and his extremely long bill — three inches in a bird which measured only ten inches in all — was very pliable and extremely sensitive. It carried a complex system of nerves which enabled Capella to trace the worms in the mud.

The bill's tip was bulbous, swollen and quite smooth, and was honeycombed with a multitude of tiny cells, each of which were nerve containers, and all were joined up with a great sensory nerve in his face. Used rather like a drinking-straw, the bill sucked up the food from the mud.

Capella moved easily across the snow-flecked black ooze on his thick, greenish-coloured legs, sheltered from the thickening snowfall by the dense rushy growth, and screened from even the keen eyes of Kee, who hovered low to escape the stormy buffeting of the wind.

Even with his beak fully submerged in mud, Capella was not defenceless against possible danger, for his eyes were so placed on the sides of his skull that he could still see all that was going on around him. Hearing, not sight, told him that Gael was close, and he tensed, ready for flight.

Splashing through the bog, the little collie frightened a shrew which slipped, panic-stricken, into the deep root cluster of a rush clump. She scattered a group of starlings which were foraging the mossland before flighting towards their mass roost in the nearby Forest of Rossendale, and she sent up a meadow-pipit with twittering protest.

Only when Gael was too close for comfort, less than six feet away, did Capella take wing. He sprang into the air, turned direction with a rapid tail twist close above the rushes, then climbing, disappeared from sight into the flurry of snowflakes.

Gael stopped to watch the snipe away, then, her nostrils twitching for trace, she found the couch where Capella had lain before rising to feed. It was a deeply-hollowed couch, screened and so well sheltered into the denseness of rush roots that the bird's smell still lingered warm. Amid the bleakness of the surrounding bog it was a haven of survival.

Survival was nature's concern, but it was survival of the species rather than of the individual, and always when the cold went, and the mildness of spring returned, there would be some members of every race to carry on the line. Only when man interfered did this rule break down.

Gael sucked warm scent from Capella's couch. She nosed into the rushes until a tiny voice lifted her ears to the most unexpected company. Prato, the little meadow-pipit, was calling to her. He skulked in the cover of a rush clump,

Meadow-pipit.
Prato.
Scholey Hill.
January.

crouched down below the force of the wind's bitterness, and sheltered by the tangle of vegetation from snow smother.

'Peep-peep-peep', Prato called again. His tone was conversational, and though Gael recognised it as the bird's usual note of communication, she was wrong in assuming the call was to her. Prato called to four of his kind who, like himself, were well hidden among the rushes.

When Gael responded to the call and ran among them they flew in sudden disarray, jerking on puny wings up into the full force of the gale. Undecided in direction, though the wind was really master of their course, they called to each other to keep in touch. When it seemed that the snow-laden wind must toss them across the sky to destruction, they all fell back to the ground, but little distant from their launch.

Gael watched them return to the refuge of the bogland's brown grasses whilst she lay in the lee of a rush clump. Quiet, and content to watch, she was no longer a threat to the little brown birds which, frightened no longer, ignored her presence.

Encouraged by their enforced activity, and screened from the relentless tug of the storm, the meadow-pipits searched among the thick vegetation for seeds or grubs. Jerkily bobbing head and tail, each bird sought the food which would maintain body heat and life in an environment which seemed hardly one for such small creatures. But meadow-pipits were birds of the moors and, only some three inches tall, found shelter between low-growing hags which baulked the brute force of the wind, and only lightly held the fallen snowflakes.

Prato had lived on Scholey Hill for all his two years of life and knew its differing moods. He had faced snow blizzard before, and had survived it. Unlike most of his clan, he had not moved southwards at the coming of the cold weather, but had joined up with a party of his kind which had come down from more northern climes. Now he led them in their nomadic wanderings over the immediate moorland and cloughs.

Prato was a smart little bird, the trim brown plumage of his body neatly pencilled on the feather-edging, and his white outer tail feathers bright and clean. He ran between the bent grasses, eyes alert for morsels of food, bobbing and jerking his head and tail in constant movement. The backward-pointing toes of his pale brown feet were long and adapted for his life on the ground.

He had been born in a nest woven between the grasses and, as much of his life was spent on the ground, his powers of flight were not good and very indecisive. He would spend the whole of his life in those austere surroundings.

Suddenly, the meadow-pipits ceased their foraging and crouched low into grass and snowflakes. Instinctively, Gael read their message and crouched her body to the ground in like manner. It was unlikely that whatever had caused the birds to take alarm would be a threat to Gael, but able to read the signs of the wild, she responded to the warning. Until the cause of the birds' disquiet became apparent, she was prepared to act with caution, and respect the message.

Out of the whirling snowflakes came a bird which called 'Ik-ik-ik' to the wind. The call was strange to Gael and she listened with head angled. The cry was one of anger at the rawness of the weather, the bird was the size of a fieldfare, and its flight was sure into the bustle of the wind. It was Keir, the male merlin, the smallest of the falcons and no longer common to the area.

Killer of meadow-pipits, Keir was gone as speedily as he had arrived. Gael relaxed her tension, dropped her muzzle on to her crossed forepaws, and listened to the screaming voice of the snowstorm through the clough. Prato and his friends were not quick to relax. Keir was the enemy of their kind. The merlin classed them as food.

Known as the stone-falcon on the Northern moors, Keir hunted the pipits, skylarks, twites and wheatears by outflying them with swift strokes of his long narrow wings, harrying them at every twist and turn until able to strike them down with his taloned feet. A bundle of feathered fury when roused, the merlin was known as the lady's falcon in the days when falconry was common.

Keir, the male, was mantled with dark slate-grey feathers, his breast was rufous streaked with brown, and his tail was barred in black. He had the typically hooked beak of the falcons.

Gael lay amid the rushes until the mood of the pipits eased, until they again picked at the grasses for food. With every flurry of snow which settled over her back, Gael blended into the bogland as a white hump between the rushes. It was camouflage which fooled a small party of snow-buntings which came to join the pipits in their search for insect larvae and vegetable seeds among the rushes.

Gael did not move, her almond eyes watching the rare visit of the pretty snow-finches to her high-land domain. They were winter-garbed in brown-tipped black and white feathers, snow-white breast feathers and chestnut tinged caps, and they scattered between the rough hags, sheltering from the wind and seeking their food. Used to wild remote places in their Northern homeland, with little company other than sheep, they were not timid, and when Gael jumped to her feet to shake the snow-wrap from her body, they were loath to leave their feeding.

Gael listened to their piping, wing-borne notes of contact whilst she explored the tasteless scents of the thin air which blew across her twitching nostrils. There were no messages on the white plumes which flew from the wind-carved snow cornices at the top of Rack Clough, and Gael turned towards the lower woodland where the turbulence of the snowstorm would be calmed between the trees.

By the frozen skeletons of thistle plants, past the stands of brittle rushes, and across lichened, snow and ice-spattered rocks where her nails spread to grip, Gael ran for the simple pleasure of the exercise. She pawed the snow, and bit at it with her mouth. She romped in it and rolled. She bounded through deep drifts. Snowflakes settled on her coat, and she sent the wet, clinging wrap flying in a mist of spray when she shook herself.

Kee, the kestrel, saw her as the only living thing in the white wilderness below when he flew over the hill. He watched her run across to the deep snow drifts in the lee of the wall, before slanting his wings to the wind and drifting away down towards the valley fields.

Gael was digging and playing in a four-foot deep drift against the wall when a trumpeting came from the sky. She lifted her head to listen. For a while she did not move, standing up to her shoulders in the snow. She was puzzled, and she turned her ears to the line of sound. Over her head, too high in the sky for her to mark them, 35 whooper-swans flew in vee-formation towards the north-east. Large white wings slicing the snowy air, long slim necks outstretched, they passed over the hill, and they called to each other as they flew.

Gael did not move until their voices were out of her hearing. Then she raced away across the white carpet on the hill to see if there was some activity to interest her among the wild creatures of the woodland. Between the trees there was some shelter. A tiny wren scolded the little collie as it darted like a brown-feathered mouse under the snow canopy which covered the dead bracken stems.

A party of blue-tits and great-tits, flitting among the tree branches in their search for grubs, took Gael's attention with their conversations. She sat on a snowy ledge of the steep bankside and listened to their calls to each other. Her head cocked on one side, her ears pricked to the cheerful, rippling tinkle of the blue-tits and to the squeaky rasp of the great-tits. Feathered jewels of yellow, blue, white and black, the tiny birds were industrious in their search of the trees' bark, hurriedly examining the crannies in birch and rowan trunks.

Probing with chisel-like beaks, they reached every crack, hanging at all angles with gymnastic expertise, swinging, head downwards, clinging upright, balancing with fluttering wings. It was vital that they found sufficient food to warm them through the cold of the coming night.

By the trunk of a rowan tree, Gael crossed the print of a rabbit in the carpet of snow. She followed, tracking by sight until the prints disappeared into a burrow in the ground. Hearing a chuckle of movement, she pricked her ears to the flow of the narrow stream in the bottom of the clough. Spraying icicles on to the overhanging grasses, the water ran fast in its channel from cold heights towards the Calder. Swallowing a swirl of errant snowflakes in its leap over rock, it lingered momentarily in a pool, before pouring again towards the lower valley.

Gael followed the waterside path which was covered hard with packed snow from the weight of sheep's hooves. She turned round a grey rock and frightened Zit, the dipper, to flight. Plump and white-breasted, Zit lifted his short wings and flew away, skimming low along the water's course. As he went, wings whirring, he called his name to the collie in a voice which was as much greeting as annoyance, for Gael had relieved the monotony of the snow-blown hour.

At the bottom of Rack Clough, Gael entered the gentler world of Brockholes Wood. Less successful in penetrating the thicker woodland, the snowflakes mottled the more permanent carpet of scrub, bracken and leaf-mould. She passed under the branches of an alder tree whose catkins were red, and into whose tracery had been woven the cradle of a crow's nest.

Among the branches of the alder a small flock of canary-like finches was restlessly and busily foraging, the while constantly twittering and chattering in continuous discussion. Gael settled on the soft snow by the water's edge and listened to their chatter.

Acrobatic almost to the same degree of skill as the titmice she had watched earlier, the finches hung and perched in whatever positions would enable them to attack the rounded alder cones, their strong bills enabling them to pick out and feed on the flat red seeds.

Restless, the birds flitted from cone to cone, often dropping on fluttering wings to the waterside to drink, and then back again to the trees. The birds were siskins — in a winter bachelor party journeying through the woodland. They were mainly olive-green coloured on their backs and upper parts, with distinctive yellow rumps, and yellow, black-fringed tails. A yellow streak marked each head behind the eye, and every beak was of a grey colour.

They were attractive little finches, seen in their winter plumage, but when they journeyed northwards to their breeding haunts in spring, they would be even more resplendent. Then, their colouring would be more vivid, their bills brighter, and the black patch each wore on its throat more distinct.

The siskens sent the alder cones flying asunder to the deft strokes of their beaks as they robbed the seeds, and the waste seed-cases fell in tiny pieces to litter the snowy grass, many falling over Gael. The birds were too busy to mind her presence, and she listened to their calls with ears pricked, her head angled to the line of constant chatter.

A mouse-like creature ran upside down along the underside of the bough of an oak tree, its jerky movement catching Gael's interest. Apparently defying the pull of gravity with more skill than any other bird she had seen, it was Certho, the tree-creeper, the large-footed crawler of tree bark.

Unaware of Gael's puzzlement, indeed unaware of her presence, for she was so still and quiet, and he was too intent on his business of seeking food-grubs, Certho probed into every crack and cranny in the rough bark with his curved, needle-thin beak.

Grasping the roughness with his sharply-pointed toes, and maintaining his balance by pressing his stoutly-feathered tail against the bark, he had not the slightest difficulty in moving in an upside-down position. Nature and evolution had formed him to his way of life, strange though it appeared to an earth-bound dog.

Slim and supple in build, and smaller than a sparrow, Certho's adaptability enabled him to reach every insect's hiding place in the bark of the tree — even those which the acrobatic blue-tits could not reach. Coming to the end of the oak bough, Certho opened his wings and flew across to an adjoining sycamore tree, breaking the spell which held Gael to his mousy movement, but leaving her greatly puzzled and wondering. Certho was a new experience for her.

Chapter 23

Glad companion

A moorhen escapes the fangs of Tigrid by Gael's timely intervention, but the pipits are not so fortunate in the stoat's dance of death. Brave and greedy when food is the prize, Tigrid cares little about providing food for his family.

Running along the bank of the ditch by the wall, Kittic, the moorhen, made his way towards Scholey Pond on the hill. He had been away from the hill-pond for some time, spending his days among the rushes around the infant River Calder in the lower valley where the air was warmer. Now he was on his way home, for although the wind was still cold, Kittic preferred the stretch of water on the hill as his permanent residence. It was so easy on the rush-fringed depth of water to submerge in order to dodge his enemies.

Kittic ran with a lightness in his stride, a moorhen jauntiness which kept his

Stoat.
Tigrid.
Scholey Hill.
March.

Stoat.

(Mustela erminea)

Male: Dog
Female: Bitch
Young: Kitten

Great exponent of woodcraft
Stalks prey - hunts by scent - sinuous
Relentless - bloodthirsty killer - induces
terror in prey - "charms" hypnotises.

Fearless. Alert. Agile. Energetic.
Active day and night.
Swims well. Climbs well.
Curious by nature.
Scent acute : Hearing acute.

Called ermine in winter when
its colour changes to white,
except for black-tipped tail.

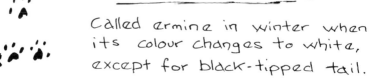

Tigrid
-
his
mark

Slender body.
Long neck.
Short limbs.
Reddish -
brown
Black
tip

White
tinged
yellow

clan so capable at surviving the dangers of life in sparse places. With his long green toes quickly, yet carefully, placed as he dodged between the clumps of rushes beneath the wall, he had the perky, yet stealthy, manner of knowing his vulnerability away from water.

Fly he could, but his wings were not strong until taken up by the wind, and his efforts were more of a scuttering, half-running movement. His legs were bouncy and were his most reliable means of hurried retreat, for they could spring him to the top of the stone wall, should he meet danger on his way to the pond. So he hugged the wall, high-stepping his toes over the wet grass and rush clumps, bobbing his head low in a furtive choice of route.

He heard the bubbling notes of a curlew, and the more clamorous cry of Teuk, the redshank, from higher up the hill. He shied away when, on rounding a clump of rushes, he met a grazing ewe, for his fear of detection and inbred wariness was acute. Had Kittic been aware of a much more dangerous follower on his trail, he would have ignored the harmless sheep, and speeded his journey.

Tigrid, the stoat, his sense of smell so keen and strong, had taken the scent of the moorhen, and followed the line with an awesome determination. A hunter born and bred, sharp-toothed and bloodthirsty, Tigrid lived for the chase, and any small creature was fair game. He sucked the scent of the moorhen. Its weakness delayed his stalk, but he had a relentless purpose to hunt, and he unravelled the trace though Kittic was some 30 yards past.

Flicking his black-tipped tail, silently sniffing the taint of the moorhens passing, Tigrid tracked Kittic. By a sheep-grazed rush tuft, round a bunch of sprouting nettle plants, over a scentless water-run, Tigrid followed with sinuous authority. The gap between hunter and hunted closed as Kittic hesitated on sight of the grazing sheep, and the danger to his life grew. It was saved by interruption from an unexpected source.

Gael, the little collie, came running across the hill pasture towards the wall. Kittic immediately jumped on springing legs, spreading his short wings to reach the top of the wall. He called a harsh 'kaak' of fear. With an angry chakker, Tigrid darted to the safety of a gap between two lichened stones in the wall. Safe into the opening, he turned round to gibber in fury at Gael, the cause of his sudden frustration. She ignored his glaring threat, and ran off down the wall-side.

Not all Gael's meetings with Tigrid ended so easily. Tigrid was by nature a killer, born to live on red meat and gifted with the skill to obtain it. Since his birth in a leafy nest in a hole on the side of Rack Clough three years ago, he had learned to hunt with a dedication which was frightening in its single-minded purpose.

He performed his dance of death to an unsuspecting group of meadow-pipits. With excited peeping notes, the brown birds pranced in the air above the stoat, rising and falling on vibrant wings, attracted and puzzled by his seemingly crazy actions. They found a curiously fascinating interest in Tigrid's inconsistent movements. His sinuous, snaking actions held an almost hypnotic spell over them.

Six feet out from the bottom of the stone wall on the close-cropped upland pasture, Tigrid wandered like a creature lost, circling with belly to earth, pawing the air with his forelegs, darting from side to side. The pipits, continuously squeaking their approval, flipped lower and lower over the dancer. One dropped to within two feet of the stoat's back, then hastily climbed back into the air when Tigrid reared up, gibbering with fangs bared, white whiskers twitching, and face grimacing.

Quick to realise his mistake as the birds flighted higher, Tigrid recommenced his gliding, mazy actions, careering round and round in a circle. Lured back, the pipits came again to watch. Utterly fascinated, one made the fatal mistake and came down too low. Tigrid made no mistake this time. Leaping lightly from the grass, he grabbed the bird by the wing, pinning it under his claws as he fell back to the ground. The pipit died as its companions scattered in confusion.

The spell was broken, but Tigrid had achieved his aim. He licked the blood from the death wound on the bird's neck and, picking it up in his mouth, carried it into a cavity in the bottom of the stone wall.

It was three minutes later when Gael picked Tigrid's strong musk scent from the ground by the wall. All that told her of the dance of death was a forlorn brown feather lying on the grass. She wrinkled her nose to the hated taint of musk and, following it to the wall, disturbed Tigrid at his feast. He was safe in the wall cavity, and spat defiance at her intrusion, chakkering his anger at her nosiness into his affairs.

Gael drew back and left the stoat to his meal. She had no respect for his ferocious ways, and preferred to avoid his company. Running down into the valley of the bogland clough, she played a game of tag with the flock of meadow-pipits which had settled to their normal foraging after the excitement of the stoat's dance. They ran and flitted among the brown grasses, seeking insects, and as Gael chased one and then another, they fluttered into the air, their white outer-tail feathers distinctive in the weak sunshine.

They were far more mobile than the little collie, though their wing fluterings seemed weak and inadequate, for whilst she sank and squelched in the soft mud of the bog, they barely disturbed the mud with their light weight, appearing to walk on the water. They danced around her, quickly forgetting the disaster of the stoat's dance, twittering and trilling their voices, jerking above her head in aimless flight before pitching back to the ground.

Some 50 in number, they had returned to their upland breeding grounds and Gael welcomed their return, for although Prato, the pipit who had remained on the hill throughout the winter, had been her companion in the cold 'and lonely months, the return of the flock marked the return of warmer days.

Constant neighbours throughout the summer months, their voices welcomed Gael at every visit, but scolded her when their ground nests were built and eggs laid. Their mouse-like movements between the grasses gave her the fun of stalking them.

Gael tended to take them into her protection from the ravages of the moorland predators whenever possible, for they appeared so ill-equipped, with their puny stature, weak indecisive flight and twittering calls, for life in high places. In fact they were beautiful birds and their plumage was so well designed to give them perfect camouflage against the brown moorland that they often went unnoticed.

Safe from detection in the shelter of the wall cavity, Tigrid enjoyed his meal of warm-blooded pipit, selfishly eating his fill and ignoring the needs of five kits that he had fathered. They were in the care of his mate, Hermelin, couched in her nest in the bottom of the stone wall across the upland pasture from where Tigrid gorged his food.

The kits were well-grown and, though still suckled by their mother, were quite able to have feasted on the flesh of the meadow-pipit. Tigrid was too independent to care. It was some time — the previous July — since he had mated with Hermelin, and he was too selfish to think too much of her needs, though he paid token responsibility by sleeping near the nest, and occasionally taking food to her for the family.

Stoats are subject to delayed implantation — they mate in summer, but the development of the baby stoats within the mother's body is delayed until the following spring when, after a gestation of 21 to 28 days, the kits are born.

Tigrid always satisfied his own needs before the needs of others, ruthless in claiming and keeping his own, just like some of his other less-agreeable neighbours on the hillside.

It was the following day when two of the most notorious of the hill's residents proved their selfish natures, and tested their strengths — when Tigrid, along with Corbie, the black crow, disputed a rare prize of succulent meat.

Planing easily, with primaries spread on the cold wind which swept over the hill, Corbie turned his head from side to side to scan the ground. By the base of the stone wall he spotted the crumbled bundle of brown fur. Ever cautious, he glided lower for a closer look, slipping the air currents from his wings to sweep above the furry bundle again.

There was no movement on the ground, other than the dancing of the wind-bent rushes, so Corbie braked on the air and, thrusting out his black legs, settled gently on to the wall top. Head angled, his bright eyes gleamed with pleasure when he saw that the heap of fur was the body of a dead hare — carrion food to be prized. Calling 'Kaaah — Kaaah — Kaaah' to Crahen, his mate, who was riding the wind 50 yards away, Corbie dropped to the ground. Still with some caution, he walked to the dead hare. Deft blows of his cruel bill tore open the carcase, its soft, warm, brown fur scattering on the wind.

The meat was cold, the hare had been dead for some hours, but the rich red flesh, eight pounds in weight, was a banquet for the carrion eater. Death had been painful for the hare; a festering wound in its side had been caused by a pellet of lead from a mis-aimed shotgun. Its final role was to provide food for its contemporaries on the high land.

Stabbing viciously with his sharp black bill, Corbie gorged the meat. Tearing at the carcase, almost choking on the pieces of meat he gulped down, he enjoyed his gluttony. Crahen was quick to join him, but was driven off as he turned his stabbing beak on her. Only when his crop was tight did he let her join him, but he still claimed the choicest morsels.

Soft fluff from the hare's coat was tossed by the wind, and the carcase taint was carried with it. The crows enjoyed their food. It was particularly welcome, for the day was cold.

All was well until the faint taint of carrion meat reached the keen nostrils of Tigrid. He was lying in a cavity in the base of the stone wall, a popular couch which shielded him from prying eyes. Lifting his head into the wind-borne scent, he sniffed, his dark eyes lighting up with interest and anticipation. He moved to investigate. His sinuous, lithe body of reddish-brown fur slipped silently from the wall cavity.

Keeping close to the base of the wall so that refuge was always available, Tigrid ran into the wind. His progress was stealthy and cautious, a few yards gallop of his quick body, then a halt whilst, with small head raised high, he peered around, shining eyes watching, nose sniffing for whatever presence.

Within three yards of the two crows he glided into the cover of a hole in the wall. Unseen by the birds, Tigrid watched, assessed the position, and decided that he was ready to take his share of the food. When food was the prize he was a bold contender.

His eyes glinted, his black-tipped tail twitched, he prepared to attack. Without fear, he recognised the strength of the sharp-billed crows, but weighed his own chances with favour. Yakkering with lust, Tigrid ran at the crows. His sudden spitting aggression scattered them in flight. Corbie and Crahen flew up in squawking alarm, surprised by the attack.

Tigrid took his stand by the hare's carcase, ready for a counter-attack. Gaining composure as they controlled their hurried wing beats, the two crows circled over the wall top. Corbie swooped back to the fray, skilfully balancing the air in his wings, and stabbing with his vicious bill at Tigrid's head. Crahen joined her mate, and spitting and snarling and twisting his lithe body to avoid the striking beaks, Tigrid was forced back towards the refuge of the wall. Successfully aimed, any one blow of the crows' beaks would have split open his skull, and he realised the danger.

It was Gael again who interfered in Tigrid's affairs and brought an end to the contest. The scent of the hare's carcase, opened by the crows, drew her down the wallside, and she nosed the carrion to the harsh departing screams of abuse from Corbie and Crahen, and to the yakkering rage of Tigrid as he disappeared into the sanctuary of the wall.

When Gael had gone, Tigrid slipped from his hideaway and fed on the hare's body without further interference, for Corbie and Crahen had flown across the hillside. Finally satisfied, he returned to the shelter of the wall to sleep away the effects of over-indulgence.

And so Tigrid's mate Hermelin had to hunt the food to satisfy his family. She stalked a young rabbit on the edge of the woodland and, with a single bite to the side of the neck, killed it. Grasping the warm carcase in her mouth, she lifted it and ran slowly towards her nursery in the cave-like gap between the stones at the base of the wall across the field.

Although the baby rabbit was bulky and awkward for her to carry, she had little difficulty with the weight. Unable to adopt her usual caution with such a prominent burden, Hermelin forsook her normal and carefully chosen route through cover, and crossed the open field. It was unusual for her to risk such an open journey, but little stirred on the sweeping wind, and the brown grasses blended with her colouring to hide her partially. They did not hide her from Gael, for the little collie, playing with a truss of wind-blown hay from the sheep-rack, was attracted by the movement of the stoat and was intrigued by the unnatural outline of its burden.

Gael ran at Hermelin, for she had little liking for the stoat. Hermelin loosened her grip on the rabbit to threaten the unexpected attacker, standing her ground to glare at Gael, and flicking her black-tipped tail in anger. She faced Gael with an angry chakker, hatred in her eyes, her maternal mood ready to contest the food for her family. But Gael was too big and strong to fight, and brave as she was, Hermelin suddenly accepted that she was too small to win. Turning, she dropped the rabbit and dashed for the sanctuary of the wall.

Gael followed, but kept her distance. Whilst she loathed the stoat, she respected her bravery, and was mindful of Hermelin's sharp-toothed nip if pushed to fight. Gael accepted surrender in the stoat's flight, and, to prove her superiority, she tossed the baby rabbit in her mouth whilst Hermelin chattered her frustration from the safety of the wall.

For a few moments Gael played with the dead rabbit. She nosed it, savouring the delicious scent of fresh meat, flicking her tongue over the thin fur, and then she left it. She was not hungry — and she had put Hermelin to flight. Her ego was high.

Five minutes after Gael had leaped over the wall and gone from the field, and before any other creature could claim the rabbit, Hermelin slipped from her sanctuary to repossess her kill. Continuing her journey without further inter-

Simon, who also loved Gael, with her on the battlements of Berwick-upon-Tweed.

ruption, Hermelin delivered the food to her family whose gluttony and savagery tore the carcase to pieces. She watched them with pride and pleasure — by that savagery alone would they grow to maturity and survive.

Like any other mother of the wild, Hermelin was proud of her family, and she cared well for them. They were a month old and were dressed in fur which was lighter in colour than their mother's. Each had the distinctive black tip at the end of its tail, the hall-mark of every stoat. They were well-grown, comfortable, warm and dry in a nest of hay and leaves which filled the gap in the centre of the stone wall.

Hermelin was content to tend to their wants herself, and prepared to defend them against any possible danger, and, because she refused even to trust her mate, she never allowed Tigrid into their presence. On the rare occasions he brought food, she took it from him outside the nest, though it gave her a feeling of security to know that he was on hand in case of an emergency she could not meet.

Hermelin was eight ounces of the most fearless and vicious of creatures in the countryside, a clever and skilful exponent of the art of woodcraft and a mother who would protect her kits at any cost.

λ   λ   λ

And so I close the notebooks. They now record 13 years of happy times which Gael and I have spent together in the often bleak, yet bonny, countryside of East Lancashire in which we live. Gael lies under the desk at my feet as I write. Her body is sprawled lazily on her side. Seemingly, she is sound asleep, though I know her eyes flicker open and her ears lift to my movements. But her eyes are dimming with age, and the ears are not as keen in perception as they were. I glance at her, bend down, and run my fingers through her silky soft coat. Her tail twitches in response.

She has been — still is — a glad companion. Utterly faithful and devoted, she is gay and humorous, happy in her ways, gentle in her nature, wise and quick to learn, and she has shown me many of the wonderful things around. We shall have other adventures together, for although her senses are getting old, her spirit is willing. Half an hour ago she was following the fresh scent of a hunting weasel down the wallside. But age cannot be denied. Although mentally and physically alert, she is now sleeping her time away — after the rabbits have been chased and the moorhens visited on the pond of course!

She may never see another generation of lambs grow to maturity but, could they do so, the sheep would record her loyalty and devotion to their welfare. The birds and animals on the hill will miss her, for although she is known to very many people through word and picture, she is only truly happy among the wild creatures of the countryside and away from the limelight. She has actually come to dislike the sight of a camera, television or otherwise. So be it. Gael will never be forgotten, and should the more intimate details of her adventures become dimmed with the passing years, these notes will bring them back to me in fond and vivid clarity.